W9-BFW-163

PRACTICE
MAKES
PERFECT

Beginning
Spanish
with CD-ROM

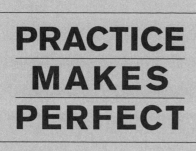

**PRACTICE
MAKES
PERFECT**

Beginning Spanish
with CD-ROM

**Ronni L. Gordon, Ph.D., and
David M. Stillman, Ph.D.**

New York Chicago San Francisco Lisbon London Madrid Mexico City
Milan New Delhi San Juan Seoul Singapore Sydney Toronto

The McGraw-Hill Companies

Copyright © 2011 by The McGraw-Hill Companies, Inc. All rights reserved. Printed in the United States of America. Except as permitted under the United States Copyright Act of 1976, no part of this publication may be reproduced or distributed in any form or by any means, or stored in a database or retrieval system, without the prior written permission of the publisher.

1 2 3 4 5 6 7 8 9 10 11 12 13 14 15   QDB/QDB   1 9 8 7 6 5 4 3 2 1 0

ISBN   978-0-07-163865-4 (book and CD-ROM set)
MHID   0-07-163865-2 (book and CD-ROM set)

ISBN   978-0-07-163863-0 (book for set)
MHID   0-07-163863-6 (book for set)

Library of Congress Control Number: 2010924602

Trademarks: McGraw-Hill, the McGraw-Hill Publishing logo, Practice Makes Perfect, and related trade dress are trademarks or registered trademarks of The McGraw-Hill Companies and/or its affiliates in the United States and other countries and may not be used without written permission. All other trademarks are the property of their respective owners. The McGraw-Hill Companies is not associated with any product or vendor mentioned in this book.

Interior design by Village Typographers, Inc.

CD-ROM for Windows
To install: Insert the CD-ROM into your CD-ROM drive. The CD-ROM will start automatically. If it does not, double-click on MY COMPUTER; find and open your CD-ROM disk drive, then double-click on the install.exe icon. The CD-ROM includes audio instructions to guide you in using this program effectively.

CD-ROM for Mac
To install: Insert the CD-ROM into your CD-ROM drive. A window will open with the contents of the CD. Drag the program icon to your Applications folder. For easy access, create an alias of the program on your desktop or your dock.

Minimum System Requirements
Computer: Windows 2000, XP, Vista / Mac OX X 10.3.x, 10.4.x, 10.5.x
Pentium II, AMD K6-2, or better / Power PC (G3 recommended) or better; any
Intel processor
256 MB RAM
14" color monitor
8x or better CD-ROM
Sound Card
Installation: Necessary free hard-drive space: 500 MB
Settings: 800 x 600 screen resolution
256 (8-bit) colors (minimum)
Thousands (24- or 32-bit) of colors (preferred)

MP3 Downloads
MP3 files can be downloaded from the CD-ROM. Select Download All, save and then expand the compressed zip folder.
    To load onto your iPod or similar device, drag and drop the expanded folder into your LIBRARY in iTunes.
    Once synced with your iPod, locate the files in Music/Artists under: "Spanish: PMP Beginning Spanish."

Call 800-722-4726 if the CD-ROM is missing from this book. For technical support go to http://www.mhpsoftwareassist.com

McGraw-Hill books are available at special quantity discounts to use as premiums and sales promotions or for use in corporate training programs. To contact a representative, please e-mail us at bulksales@mcgraw-hill.com.

This book is printed on acid-free paper.

Para Alex, Mimi, Kathleen, Juliana y Moriah,
los soles de nuestro universo

Contents

Preface

Practice Makes Perfect: Beginning Spanish with CD-ROM is a comprehensive, user-friendly program that provides extensive audio practice to introduce and reinforce the basic structures of Spanish. The program corresponds to one to two semesters of class-based instruction. It is designed for beginning learners of Spanish who want to master the basic structural patterns of the language and acquire a broad vocabulary that will be useful in communicating with native speakers of Spanish on a wide variety of topics. Dialogues and exercises reflect authentic, current language usage and touch on all areas of modern life including business and technology.

Practice Makes Perfect: Beginning Spanish with CD-ROM is different in its design and conception from other language courses. It takes full advantage of the pedagogical potential of electronic media to deliver the content of the course both orally and in writing. It allows you instant access to all the material of the course, such as grammar explanations and vocabulary, so that you can customize your learning as you see fit.

The interactive features will motivate you and facilitate your mastery of the material. The program is outstanding for its accessibility and portability, which means you can practice Spanish at your convenience and go at your own pace. MP3 files can be downloaded from the CD-ROM and loaded onto your iPod or other device.

Structure and components

Practice Makes Perfect: Beginning Spanish with CD-ROM is comprised of sixteen lessons, all structured in the same way. Each chapter opens with a list of the grammar points to be presented and practiced followed by "Communication goals," which present the chapter's objectives for desired learner achievement.

Diálogos

Introductory *diálogos* present new vocabulary and grammatical structures targeted in the chapter. Each *diálogo* contains two to four exchanges. There are between four and nineteen *diálogos* in each chapter. Learners have instant access to both the written text of each *diálogo* and a recording of it done by native speakers with pauses for repetition. The *diálogos* offer delightful snatches of conversation in authentic settings. You meet real-life people at work and school, traveling, talking about their family and relationships, shopping, restaurants, entertainment, their daily routine, health, holidays, business and the cost of living, and their life goals. These meaningful conversational exchanges help you develop both competence and confidence in speaking and understanding Spanish.

Análisis

Linked to each *diálogo*, the *análisis* provides a linguistic breakdown of the new material in each of the sentences of the *diálogo* and is accessible via links (Grammar notes) for your reference as you practice the *diálogos*.

Variantes

This section expands the grammatical structures presented in the *diálogos* and presents new structures based on the material presented in the *diálogos*. The structures and new vocabulary related to the theme of each *diálogo* are presented in patterned sentences in a meaningful context. Like the *diálogos*, this material is also available to learners in both written and recorded form.

Grammar file (grammar notes)

The Grammar file contains the explanations of all the grammar topics presented in the course. All the grammatical information is accessible through links strategically placed in the *análisis* and *variantes* so that learners can reference linguistic explanations as they need them.

Práctica

A hallmark of this program is the vast amount of systematic oral practice provided for learners so that they can master the structures of Spanish and use them with confidence.

Vocabulary

Learners have instant access to an electronic Spanish–English word list containing all the words introduced in the course. Each word has a reference number to the chapter in which it first appears.

Listening for key contrasts

These drills target some of the most important sound contrasts in the Spanish verb system. They will help you distinguish verb endings that may sound similar to English-speakers but are very different in meaning. Mastery of these sound distinctions will facilitate your comprehension of Spanish and your ability to make yourself understood in the language.

Workbook

This volume gives learners additional written practice in the grammatical structures and vocabulary of each chapter. It includes an answer key to facilitate self-study and verb charts for reference. It also contains the complete text of the Grammar Notes so that you can study when away from your computer.

You will be delighted to see how much you understand and can say in Spanish after you have worked through the *Practice Makes Perfect: Beginning Spanish with CD-ROM* program. For more practice, reinforcement, and progress we recommend that you use our acclaimed *The Ultimate Spanish Review and Practice: Mastering Spanish Grammar for Confident Communication*, now in its second edition.

Ronni L. Gordon, Ph.D.
David M. Stillman, Ph.D.

Finding your way around • *Hay*

The following exercises provide written practice to reinforce your understanding of the corresponding chapter on the CD-ROM.

⊙ CD-ROM

Diálogos, análisis, variantes

- ☐ 1.1 ¿Qué hay en la caja?
- ☐ 1.2 Hay dos farmacias
- ☐ 1.3 ¿Hay un cibercafé por aquí?
- ☐ 1.4 El centro comercial

Contents

- ◆ **hay** *there is, there are*
- ◆ nouns and articles
- ◆ compound nouns
- ◆ **ser** *to be*: third-person singular
- ◆ negative sentences
- ◆ question formation: information questions, yes/no questions
- ◆ numbers 1–20

Communication goals

- ◆ Asking for directions in a Spanish-speaking city
- ◆ Finding stores in the city
- ◆ Giving gifts
- ◆ Vocabulary: *stores, everyday items, numbers*

Nouns and articles. *Write the correct definite and indefinite article for each noun.*

MODELO   libro → _el_ libro   _un_ libro

DEFINITE ARTICLE   INDEFINITE ARTICLE

1. _____ maleta   _____ maleta

2. _____ cine   _____ cine

3. _____ reloj   _____ reloj

4. _____ librería   _____ librería

5. _____ hotel   _____ hotel

6. _____ oficina   _____ oficina

7. _____ teatro   _____ teatro

8. _____ restaurante   _____ restaurante

9. _____ cámara   _____ cámara

10. _____ paquete   _____ paquete

11. _____ teléfono   _____ teléfono

12. _____ bar   _____ bar

13. _____ cibercafé   _____ cibercafé

14. _____ farmacia   _____ farmacia

15. _____ maletín   _____ maletín

Write the plural form of each noun with its corresponding definite and indefinite article.

MODELO   libro → _los_ libros   _unos_ libros

DEFINITE ARTICLE   INDEFINITE ARTICLE

1. maleta   _____   _____

2. cine   _____   _____

3. reloj   _____   _____

4. librería   _____   _____

5. hotel   _____   _____

6. oficina   _____   _____

7. teatro   _____   _____

8. restaurante   _____   _____

9. cámara   _____   _____

10. paquete   _____   _____

11. teléfono   _____   _____

12. bar   _____   _____

13. cibercafé   _____   _____

14. farmacia   _____   _____

15. maletín   _____   _____

EJERCICIO 1·3

Translation: **Las tiendas.** *Write the name of each store or office in Spanish. Then write the plural form of each one.*

1. the clothing store   _____   _____

2. the computer store   _____   _____

3. the tourist office   _____   _____

4. the appliance store   _____   _____

5. the sports store   _____   _____

6. the department store   _____   _____

EJERCICIO 1·4

Preguntas (*Questions*). *Write questions using the strings of elements.*

1. hay/en el armario/qué

_____

2. regalo/es/un

_____

3. una/por aquí/heladería/hay

_____

4. tiendas/hay/qué

_____

5. un/cibercafé/es

_____

6. en la esquina/dos/zapaterías/hay

_____

7. hay/el estante/qué/en/libros

_____

8. el centro/tienda de cómputo/en/una/hay

_____

No. *Answer each of these questions negatively.*

MODELO   ¿Hay una farmacia por aquí?
          No, no hay una farmacia por aquí.

1. ¿Es una agenda electrónica?

_____

2. ¿Hay quince libros en el estante?

_____

3. ¿El reloj es para Carlos?

_____

4. ¿Hay una tienda de deportes en el centro comercial?

_____

5. ¿Es un regalo para Rosario?

_____

6. ¿Hay ropa en la maleta?

_____

7. ¿Hay un cartapacio en la oficina?

_____

8. ¿La computadora es para Mario?

_____

¿Qué hay en la caja? *Tell what gift is in each box using **es** and the noun with its corresponding indefinite article.*

MODELO   libro → *Es un libro.*

1. billetero   _____

2. cartera   _____

3. reloj   _____

4. agenda electrónica   _____

5. bolso   _____

6. cámara   _____

7. iPod   _____

8. cartapacio   _____

El regalo no es para Eduardo. *Write sentences stating that the gifts mentioned here are not for the person named in the first cue but rather for the person named in the second cue.*

MODELO   libro/Benito/Tomás

      El libro no es para Benito. Es para Tomás.

1. billetero/José/Juan

_____

2. cartera/Matilde/Julia

_____

3. reloj/Jorge/Alberto

_____

4. agenda electrónica/Lorenzo/Nora

_____

5. bolso/Rosa/Margarita

_____

6. cámara/Luz/Daniel

_____

7. iPod/Susana/Guillermo

_____

8. cartapacio/Carlos/Roberto

_____

Los números 1–20 _Express the noun phrases in Spanish. Write out the numbers._

1. 1 computer _____

2. 2 shoe stores _____

3. 3 watches _____

4. 4 suitcases _____

5. 5 movie theaters _____

6. 6 tourist offices _____

7. 7 hotels _____

8. 8 gifts _____

9. 9 cameras _____

10. 10 ice cream stores _____

11. 11 boxes _____

12. 12 Internet cafés _____

13. 13 backpacks _____

14. 14 telephones _____

15. 15 shelves _____

16. 16 supermarkets _____

17. 17 beauty parlors _____

18. 18 department stores _____

19. 19 packages _____

20. 20 sports _____

Describing places and things • Adjectives

The following exercises provide written practice to reinforce your understanding of the corresponding chapter on the CD-ROM.

CD-ROM

Diálogos, análisis, variantes

- [ ] 2.1 ¿Cómo es el hotel?
- [ ] 2.2 Las calles del centro
- [ ] 2.3 ¿De qué color es tu carro?
- [ ] 2.4 ¿Qué hay en el maletín?
- [ ] 2.5 Mis libros

Contents

- ◆ adjectives: agreement, position
- ◆ possessive adjectives
- ◆ contraction **del**
- ◆ **ser** *to be*: third-person plural
- ◆ question formation: yes/no questions

Communication goals

- ◆ Describing places and things
- ◆ Asking about hotel accommodations
- ◆ Indicating possession
- ◆ Vocabulary: *colors, academic subjects, houses and hotels, qualities and attributes of things*

También (*gender of nouns*). *Write sentences in which the noun asked about has the same quality as the noun in the original sentence.*

MODELO   El teléfono es viejo. ¿Y la cámara?
La cámara es vieja también.

1. La zona es comercial. ¿Y el barrio?

_____

2. El condominio es nuevo. ¿Y la empresa?

_____

3. El café es animado. ¿Y la heladería?

_____

4. El supermercado es grande. ¿Y la tienda por departamentos?

_____

5. La mochila es pequeña. ¿Y el cartapacio?

_____

6. La agenda electrónica es importante. ¿Y el BlackBerry?

_____

7. El paseo es peatonal. ¿Y la calle?

_____

8. La computación es útil. ¿Y el inglés?

_____

También. *Write sentences in which the plural noun asked about has the same quality as the singular noun in the original sentence.*

MODELO   El teléfono es viejo. ¿Y las cámaras?
Las cámaras son viejas también.

1. La pulsera es hermosa. ¿Y los relojes?

_____

2. El teatro es animado. ¿Y los cines?

_____

3. El maletín es negro. ¿Y las maletas?

_____

4. La tienda de ropa es grande. ¿Y las zapaterías?

_____

5. El contrato es fácil. ¿Y los documentos?

_____

6. La revista es aburrida. ¿Y los periódicos?

_____

7. El libro es corto. ¿Y los folletos?

_____

8. El paquete es chiquito. ¿Y las cajas?

_____

***Two nouns joined by* de.** *Join each pair of nouns with* **de.** *Write the corresponding form of the definite article for each noun and the contraction* **del** *where needed.*

MODELO   artículos/periódico
los artículos del periódico

1. restaurantes/centro

_____

2. farmacia/esquina

_____

3. interior/carro

_____

4. armario/cuarto

_____

5. juguetes/juguetería

_____

6. mesas/oficinas

_____

7. peluquería/hotel

_____

8. color/billetero

_____

EJERCICIO
2·4

Descripción. _Describe things by forming sentences with_ **es** _or_ **son** _and the elements given. Change the form of the adjectives to agree with the nouns they refer to and link them with_ **y**.

MODELO   el paseo/comercial/muy animado
            El paseo es comercial y muy animado.

1. la avenida/largo/muy bonito

_____

2. las habitaciones/muy grande/muy claro

_____

3. la música/hermoso/muy interesante

_____

4. el bar/chiquito/feo

_____

5. los hoteles/moderno/muy cómodo

_____

6. las calles/ruidoso/muy transitado

_____

7. el informe/muy pesado/malo

_____

8. el garaje/muy pequeño/oscuro

_____

Translation. *Express the following dialogues in Spanish.*

1. What is the mall like?

   It's big and lively.

   _____

   _____

2. What are the books like?

   They're difficult, but very interesting.

   _____

   _____

3. What is the car like?

   It's small and quite comfortable.

   _____

   _____

4. What color is the car?

   It's red, and the inside is blue.

   _____

   _____

Adivinar (*Guessing*). *Try to guess what is in the box your friend is holding by asking yes/ no questions in Spanish.*

1. Is there a gift in the box?

   _____

2. Is it for Susana?

   _____

3. Is it big?

   _____

4. Is it blue?

   _____

5. Is it quite useful?

_____

6. Is it very pretty?

_____

7. Is it from a department store?

_____

8. Is it from a bookstore?

_____

9. Is it clothing?

_____

10. Is it an iPod?

_____

Translation. *Express the following dialogues in Spanish, paying particular attention to the possessive adjectives.*

1. Is your (**tú**) neighborhood lively?

_____

No, my neighborhood is quite quiet.

_____

2. Are your (**Uds.**) chemistry books interesting?

_____

No, our chemistry books are boring.

_____

3. Is their company new?

_____

Yes, their company is new and very important.

_____

4. Are her suitcases black?

_____

No, her suitcases are brown.

_____

5. Are his articles difficult?

_____

No, his articles are easy.

_____

Oraciones (Sentences). *Write sentences using the strings of elements.*

MODELO   es/muy/avenida/la/bonita
           La avenida es muy bonita.

1. grandes/los/muy/son/armarios

_____

2. ruidosas/son/calles/bastante/las

_____

3. es/el/muy/centro/animado

_____

4. las/son/bastante/cómodas/habitaciones

_____

5. muy/la/es/hermosa/música

_____

6. de/muy/los/interesantes/economía/son/libros

_____

7. útiles/los/portátiles/son/teléfonos/muy

_____

8. bastante/empresa/la/es/importante

_____

Talking about nationalities and professions, food, and films • *Ser*

The following exercises provide written practice to reinforce your understanding of the corresponding chapter on the CD-ROM.

⊙ CD-ROM

Diálogos, análisis, variantes

- ☐ 3.1 ¿De dónde son?
- ☐ 3.2 ¿De qué origen son?
- ☐ 3.3 Somos de Madrid
- ☐ 3.4 Los estudiantes chilenos
- ☐ 3.5 Unos restaurantes mexicanos
- ☐ 3.6 Una película mexicana
- ☐ 3.7 Un restaurante auténtico
- ☐ 3.8 ¿De dónde son los profesores?

Contents

- ◆ **ser** *to be*
- ◆ subject pronouns
- ◆ demonstrative adjectives
- ◆ adjectives of nationality
- ◆ adjectives: position
- ◆ questions

Communication goals

- ◆ Asking and telling about nationalities and origins
- ◆ Learning about the Spanish-speaking world
- ◆ Talking about restaurants and films
- ◆ Vocabulary: *countries, foreign languages, food, professions*

La comida y la bebida. *Write the relative position of each of the following foods and beverages you're referring to by using the correct form of* **este**, **ese**, *and* **aquel**.

MODELO _____*este/ese/aquel*_ pavo

1. _____/_____/_____ pollo

2. _____/_____/_____ hamburguesas

3. _____/_____/_____ ensalada

4. _____/_____/_____ arroz

5. _____/_____/_____ huevos

6. _____/_____/_____ quesadillas

7. _____/_____/_____ fruta

8. _____/_____/_____ sándwiches

9. _____/_____/_____ té

10. _____/_____/_____ legumbres

11. _____/_____/_____ cerveza

12. _____/_____/_____ jugos

Las cosas. *Fill in the correct forms of the demonstrative adjective for each noun.*

MODELO _____*este/ese/aquel*_ maletín

1. _____/_____/_____ región

2. _____/_____/_____ cine

3. _____/_____/_____ países

4. _____/_____/_____ ciudades

5. _____/_____/_____ coche

6. _____/_____/_____ cámara

7. _____/_____/_____ relojes

8. _____/_____/_____ cajas

EJERCICIO
3·3

La descripción. *Form phrases from the strings of elements, paying particular attention to the position of adjectives.*

MODELO mexicana/comida/la
la comida mexicana

1. mexicanos/esos/restaurantes

_____

2. caras/tiendas /unas

_____

3. auténticos/los/platos/todos

_____

4. hermosos/muchos/jardines

_____

5. estudiantes/franceses/dieciséis

_____

6. carros/varios/azules

_____

7. la/comercial/toda/zona

_____

8. películas/diferentes/varias

_____

EJERCICIO
3·4

De muchos países. *Rephrase each sentence using the adjective of nationality that corresponds to the country.*

MODELO Osvaldo es de México.
Osvaldo es mexicano.

1. Lucie es de Francia.

_____

2. Marcos es de Perú.

_____

3. Lidia y Greta son de Alemania.

_____

4. Javier y Pedro son de España.

_____

5. María es de Grecia.

_____

6. Margarita y Antonio son de Polonia.

_____

7. Graciela es de China.

_____

8. Alberto y Nora son de Japón.

_____

9. Raúl es de Puerto Rico.

_____

10. Silvia y Daniel son de la República Dominicana.

_____

EJERCICIO
3·5

Preguntas. *Write the information question that elicited each response. For some responses there might be more than one possible question.*

MODELO   Ramón es de Guatemala.
             ¿De dónde es Ramón?
             ¿De qué país es Ramón?

1. Patricia es de origen irlandés.

_____

2. La película es bastante divertida.

_____

3. Soy estadounidense. (**tú**)

_____

4. Hay una pizza en la caja.

5. Su carro es azul.

_____

6. Somos de Bogotá.

_____

7. Mario es contador.

_____

8. Los actores son muy buenos.

_____

¿De qué país son? *Write sentences with the correct form of the verb* **ser** *to tell what country these people are from.*

MODELO   ellos/Panamá
           Ellos son de Panamá.

1. Ud./Chile

_____

2. nosotros/Argentina

_____

3. ella/Japón

_____

4. yo/Italia

_____

5. Uds./Francia

_____

6. ellas/Canadá

_____

7. tú/ Israel

_____

8. él/Escocia

_____

¿De qué origen son? *Write sentences telling the origin of these people.*

MODELO   Uds./ruso

Uds. son de origen ruso.

1. yo/italiano

_____

2. Eduardo/iraní

_____

3. Juanita y su hermana/español

_____

4. tú/japonés

_____

5. nosotros/polaco

_____

6. Ud./portugués

_____

7. Gabriela/griego

_____

8. Ud. y yo/inglés

_____

Translation. *Express the following dialogues in Spanish.*

1. What country are you (**tú**) from?

_____

2. I'm from Mexico.

_____

3. From the capital?

_____

4. No, I'm not from Ciudad de México. I'm from Guadalajara.

_____

5. Where are you (**Uds.**) from?

_____

6. Mi husband and I are Chilean.

_____

7. What is your (**Uds.**) background?

_____

8. I'm of Scottish origin and Rafael is of German descent.

_____

9. Is Juan Miguel an accountant?

_____

10. No, he's a consultant.

_____

11. And his wife is a lawyer?

_____

12. No, Isabel is an engineer.

_____

13. How's the food in this Italian restaurant?

_____

14. All the dishes are good.

_____

15. Are the pizza and pasta tasty?

_____

16. Oh yes. And the sauce is very authentic.

_____

Describing people, emotions, and health • *Ser* and *estar*

·4·

The following exercises provide written practice to reinforce your understanding of the corresponding chapter on the CD-ROM.

CD-ROM

Diálogos, análisis, variantes

- ☐ 4.1 ¿Cómo estás?
- ☐ 4.2 Estoy inquieto
- ☐ 4.3 Estamos preocupados
- ☐ 4.4 Estamos muy atrasados
- ☐ 4.5 ¿Dónde está el museo de arte?
- ☐ 4.6 Los gerentes están reunidos
- ☐ 4.7 ¿A qué hora es la reunión?
- ☐ 4.8 El museo no está abierto
- ☐ 4.9 Nuestro carro está descompuesto

- ☐ 4.10 La comida está rica
- ☐ 4.11 ¡Yo estoy frito!
- ☐ 4.12 Pablo y su computadora
- ☐ 4.13 Los señores Ortega están de vacaciones
- ☐ 4.14 ¿Cómo es el novio de Laura?
- ☐ 4.15 ¿Cómo es Isabel?
- ☐ 4.16 ¿De quién es?
- ☐ 4.17 ¿De qué son los suéteres?
- ☐ 4.18 Mi trabajo es aburrido
- ☐ 4.19 Regalos para mi familia

Contents

- ◆ **ser** *to be*
- ◆ **estar** *to be*
- ◆ **estar** contrasted with **ser**
- ◆ adverbs of place with prepositions
- ◆ yes/no questions with **ser** or **estar** + adjective
- ◆ tag questions

Communication goals

- ◆ Talking about feelings, emotions, and health
- ◆ Describing people
- ◆ Locating people and places
- ◆ Telling time and days of the week
- ◆ Vocabulary: *the family, articles of clothing, emotions, health*

¿Cómo están? *Write sentences using the verb **estar** to tell how the members of your family are today. Make all agreements as necessary.*

MODELO   mi primo/contento
                Mi primo está contento.

1. yo/bien

_____

2. mi mamá/entusiasmado

_____

3. tú/regular

_____

4. mi cuñada/molesto

_____

5. mis hermanos y yo/emocionado

_____

6. mis sobrinas/estresado

_____

7. nuestros tíos/cansado

_____

8. el abuelo/preocupado

_____

9. la tía/enfermo

_____

10. las hijas/resfriado

_____

11. mi papá/nervioso

_____

12. los nietos/acatarrado

_____

¿Dónde están? *Write sentences telling where these places are located using the verb* **estar**. *Add* **a** *and* **de** *as needed and make all necessary changes.*

MODELO   la biblioteca/una milla/la escuela
La biblioteca está a una milla de la escuela.

1. el restaurante mexicano/cerca/el teatro

   _____

2. el museo de arte/en frente/el hotel

   _____

3. la tienda de cómputo/al lado/la librería

   _____

4. el taller mecánico/detrás/la gasolinera

   _____

5. el cine/a la izquierda/el club de jazz

   _____

6. el colegio/cinco cuadras/el parque

   _____

7. el estacionamiento/delante/la tienda por departamentos

   _____

8. la autopista/lejos/el centro

   _____

¿Ser o estar? *Write the correct form of* **ser** *or* **estar** *to complete each sentence.*

1. Hoy _____ sábado.

2. Los técnicos _____ de viaje.

3. Estas camisetas _____ de algodón.

4. Tú _____ mujer de negocios, ¿no?

5. ¿Por qué _____ Uds. inquietos hoy?

6. La boda _____ en un hotel hermoso.

7. Nosotros _____ reunidos en mi oficina.

8. _____ la una ya.

9. Los juguetes _____ de Luisito.

10. La tienda de cómputo _____ cerrada.

11. Tú _____ de muy buen humor.

12. Yo _____ de origen ruso.

13. El director y yo no _____ de acuerdo.

14. Yo _____ muy ocupado todo el día.

15. María Elena y yo _____ amigos.

Translation. *Express the following sentences in Spanish.*

1. Pedro is boring.

_____

Pedro is bored.

_____

2. Where are the reports?

_____

Where is the meeting?

_____

3. Her aunt and uncle are annoying.

_____

Her aunt and uncle are annoyed.

_____

4. Whose camera is it?

_____

Who is the camera for?

_____

5. What are Eva and Vicente like?

_____

How are Eva and Vicente?

_____

6. Her sister is cheerful (by nature).

_____

But she's not cheerful today.

_____

7. What time is it?

_____

At what time is it?

_____

Preguntas. _Write the information questions that elicited the following responses._

1. Estamos un poco acatarrados.

_____

2. Son las nueve y cuarto.

_____

3. El museo está a la derecha.

_____

4. La fiesta es en el hotel.

_____

5. El examen es a la una.

_____

6. Rosario está contenta porque está de vacaciones.

_____

7. Los hermanos Reyes son muy trabajadores.

_____

8. El abrigo es de lana.

_____

9. Hoy es sábado.

_____

10. Somos estadounidenses.

_____

11. Los regalos son para mis hijos.

_____

12. El pollo está muy rico.

_____

Statements and yes/no questions with ser or estar + adjective. *Create sentences using the correct form of* **ser** *or* **estar** *and the elements shown. Then create yes/no questions that ask for the information given in the sentence. Make adjectives agree with their subjects.*

MODELO   los niños/acostado

Los niños están acostados.

¿Están acostados los niños?

1. el director/inteligente

_____

_____

2. la impresora/descompuesto

_____

_____

3. los espectáculos /aburrido

_____

_____

4. el museo de arte/moderno

_____

_____

5. estas regiones/hermoso

_____

_____

6. la carne/muy hecho

_____

_____

7. los dentistas/deprimido

_____

_____

8. el actor/rubio

_____

_____

9. las tiendas/abierto

_____

_____

10. la sala de conferencias/grande

_____

_____

Talking about work and travel • *Ir* and *hacer*

The following exercises provide written practice to reinforce your understanding of the corresponding chapter on the CD-ROM.

CD-ROM

Diálogos, análisis, variantes

- ☐ 5.1 Hacen ejercicio
- ☐ 5.2 Vamos al club
- ☐ 5.3 ¿Esperas a alguien?
- ☐ 5.4 Una fiesta de cumpleaños
- ☐ 5.5 Vamos a ir de vacaciones
- ☐ 5.6 Encargamos una pizza
- ☐ 5.7 En tus horas libres

Contents

- ◆ the present tense of regular verbs: -**ar** verbs
- ◆ **ir** *to go*
- ◆ **ir a** + infinitive *to be going to do something*
- ◆ **hacer** *to do, make*
- ◆ contraction **al**
- ◆ personal **a**
- ◆ relative pronoun **que** *that, who*
- ◆ negative words
- ◆ adverbs of time

Communication goals

- ◆ Talking about work, vacation and travel, and leisure activities
- ◆ Telling how you celebrate your birthday
- ◆ Telling when things happen
- ◆ Vocabulary: *sports, the computer, meals, music, the seasons and months*

EJERCICIO 5·1

Los deportes. *Write sentences using **-ar** verbs to tell what sports and exercises people do.*

MODELO   Paco/levantar pesas
          Paco levanta pesas.

1. yo/montar a caballo

   _____

2. Ud./trotar

   _____

3. Daniela y su hermana/nadar

   _____

4. nosotros/patinar

   _____

5. Roberto/montar en bicicleta

   _____

6. tú/caminar

   _____

7. Uds./levantar pesas

   _____

EJERCICIO 5·2

¿Adónde van? *Write sentences using the verb **ir** to tell where these people are going.*

MODELO   ellos/la playa
          Ellos van a la playa.

1. Pablo y yo/la piscina

   _____

2. la familia Soto/el campo

   _____

3. Beatriz/el mar

   _____

4. yo/la cancha de tenis

   _____

5. tú/el estadio

_____

6. Ud./la pista

_____

7. Victoria y Samuel/el bosque nacional

_____

EJERCICIO
5·3

Hacer. *Write the correct form of the verb **hacer** to complete each sentence.*

1. Tú _____ yoga.

2. Él _____ las maletas.

3. Nosotros _____ ejercicio.

4. Yo _____ un viaje.

5. Uds. _____ camping.

6. Ellos _____ programación.

7. Ud. _____ turismo.

EJERCICIO
5·4

¿Qué van a hacer? *Expand each sentence using the **ir a** + infinitive construction.*

MODELO   Ella toma fotos.
          Ella va a tomar fotos.

1. Yo llevo mi cartapacio.

_____

2. Ellas diseñan un sitio web.

_____

3. Tú sacas a pasear al perro.

_____

4. Nosotros vamos de compras.

_____

5. Ud. mira la televisión.

_____

6. Él alquila una película.

_____

7. Yo hago la comida.

_____

8. Ud. visita a sus abuelos.

_____

9. Uds. preparan unos platos muy ricos.

_____

10. Ella va de vacaciones.

_____

EJERCICIO
5·5

La _a_ personal. *Complete each sentence, writing the personal **a** where necessary. If it is not needed, write an X in the space. Don't forget to use the contraction **al** as needed.*

1. José busca _____ su teléfono celular.

2. Llevo _____ mi esposo a la exposición de arte.

3. ¿Llamas _____ alguien?

4. Vamos a esperar _____ el tren.

5. El analista ayuda _____ el contador.

6. No miran _____ nada.

7. Van a invitar _____ el ingeniero a la reunión.

8. ¿Por qué no visita Ud. _____ los señores Cela?

9. Tocas _____ el piano, ¿verdad?

10. Paseo _____ mi perro.

11. Buscamos _____ el doctor Madariaga.

12. No esperan _____ nadie.

A y al. *Complete each sentence writing* **a** *or the contraction* **al** *where necessary.*

1. ¿Vas _____ viajar _____ México?

2. El abogado llega _____ el bufete.

3. Caminan _____ la piscina.

4. La cancha de tenis queda _____ unas cuadras de aquí.

5. Vamos _____ el cine pasado mañana.

6. Llevo _____ los músicos _____ el club.

7. El concierto es _____ las siete.

8. Llaman _____ el médico.

Mis amigos. *Write sentences using a relative clause and the relative pronoun* **que** *to tell about your friends.*

MODELO   Ana es mi amiga. (Mi amiga habla italiano.)
            Ana es mi amiga que habla italiano.

1. Pedro es mi amigo. (Mi amigo toca la guitarra.)

   _____

2. Lorenzo es mi amigo. (Mi amigo cocina muy bien.)

   _____

3. Rebeca y Nora son mis amigas. (Mis amigas pintan cuadros.)

   _____

4. María Teresa es mi amiga. (Mi amiga desarrolla software.)

   _____

5. Manuel y Matilde son mis amigos. (Mis amigos trabajan en mi oficina.)

   _____

6. Ricardo es mi amigo. (Mi amigo canta en una banda.)

   _____

EJERCICIO

5·8

¿Qué es exactamente? *Write a relative clause to tell which person or object is being referred to.*

MODELO   ¿Qué libro? (El libro está en el estante.)
            El libro que está en el estante.

1. ¿Qué museo? (El museo está abierto los lunes.)

   _____

2. ¿Qué directores? (Los directores ganan mucho dinero.)

   _____

3. ¿Qué hombre de negocios? (El hombre de negocios viaja mucho.)

   _____

4. ¿Qué coche? (El coche está descompuesto.)

   _____

5. ¿Qué cancha de tenis? (La cancha de tenis queda al lado de la piscina.)

   _____

6. ¿Qué blusas? (Las blusas son de algodón.)

   _____

7. ¿Qué estudiantes? (Los estudiantes hacen deportes.)

   _____

EJERCICIO

5·9

Translation. *Express the following sentences in Spanish.*

1. Whom are you (**tú**) looking for?

   _____

2. I'm not looking for anyone.

   _____

3. Are they waiting for someone?

   _____

4. No, they're not waiting for anyone.

   _____

5. Are you (**Uds.**) going to take a trip in the winter?

   _____

6. No, we're going to go on vacation in June.

   _____

7. Javier and Raquel are going to the seashore the day after tomorrow.

   _____

8. Isabel is my friend who designs web sites in her spare time.

   _____

9. What are we going to have for dinner?

   _____

10. Let's order (in) Chinese food.

   _____

Talking about what you need and what you know; shopping and cooking • *Tener, saber,* and *conocer*

The following exercises provide written practice to reinforce your understanding of the corresponding chapter on the CD-ROM.

CD-ROM

Diálogos, análisis, variantes

- ☐ 6.1 Estudiamos español
- ☐ 6.2 ¿Tú sabes francés?
- ☐ 6.3 Hace mal tiempo
- ☐ 6.4 Quiero aprender a cocinar
- ☐ 6.5 No conozco al nuevo gerente
- ☐ 6.6 ¡Yo no puedo comer nada más!
- ☐ 6.7 No puedo imprimir el informe
- ☐ 6.8 Tenemos planes para el fin de semana
- ☐ 6.9 Las gangas - ¡No puedo resistir a la tentación!
- ☐ 6.10 No sé dónde queda su casa
- ☐ 6.11 Pablo juega al tenis

Contents

- ◆ the present tense of regular verbs: **-er** and **-ir** verbs
- ◆ stem-changing verbs
- ◆ **hace** + expression of time + **que** + verb in present tense *have/has been doing something*
- ◆ **tener** *to have*
- ◆ irregular verbs: **saber** and **conocer** *to know*
- ◆ verb + infinitive construction
- ◆ verb + connector + infinitive construction
- ◆ connectors/prepositions: **a, de, en, con, que**; **por** and **para**
- ◆ numbers

Communication goals

- ◆ Talking about shopping, learning a foreign language, learning how to cook
- ◆ Telling what you want, need, prefer, are able, intend, and know how to do
- ◆ Telling how long you have been doing something
- ◆ Vocabulary: *weather expressions, foreign languages, business, tennis*

Regular -er and -ir verbs. *Complete each sentence with the correct present tense form of the regular -er or -ir verb in parentheses.*

1. (creer) Yo _____ que va a llover.

2. (subir) Uds. _____ al avión.

3. (romper) Ella _____ con su novio.

4. (vivir) Nosotros _____ en una ciudad grande.

5. (compartir) Él _____ su apartamento con dos amigos.

6. (leer) Tú _____ el plano.

7. (resistir) Ellos no _____ a la tentación.

8. (meter) Ud. _____ la tarjeta en el parquímetro.

¿Qué hace la gente? *Write sentences using -er and -ir verbs to tell what these people are doing.*

MODELO   ella/aprender/ruso
          Ella aprende ruso.

1. Jaime/escribir/un informe

   _____

2. tú/comer/huevos revueltos

   _____

3. Anita/abrir/unos regalos de cumpleaños

   _____

4. Pablo y Miguel/discutir/el problema

   _____

5. María y yo/aprender/a cocinar

   _____

6. yo/beber/vino

   _____

7. Uds./imprimir/sus documentos

_____

8. Ud./comprender/el problema

_____

Stem-changing verbs. *Complete each sentence with the correct present tense form of the stem-changing verb in parentheses.*

1. (querer) Yo _____ comprar una raqueta de tenis.

2. (comenzar) La película _____ a las ocho y media.

3. (dormir) Los niños no _____ todavía.

4. (probar) ¿Por qué no _____ Uds. este plato?

5. (pensar) ¿En qué _____ tú?

6. (volver) Yo _____ del viaje de negocios el jueves.

7. (poder) Nosotros no _____ encontrar la calle en el plano.

8. (entender) Ud. no _____ nuestra idea.

9. (jugar) ¿Quiénes _____ al béisbol hoy?

10. (empezar) Nosotros _____ a leer la novela.

Estudian idiomas. *Write sentences using stem-changing verbs to tell about the foreign language learning experiences of these people.*

MODELO   Marta/empezar a hablar español
            Marta empieza a hablar español.

1. Ud./seguir con su clase a distancia

_____

2. Juan Diego y Pilar/pensar estudiar inglés

_____

3. tú/querer dominar el ruso

_____

4. esos estudiantes/preferir aprender japonés

_____

5. Felipe y yo/no poder hablar chino muy bien

_____

6. yo/comenzar a practicar el alemán

_____

7. Uds./entender bien el francés hablado

_____

EJERCICIO

6·5

Saber y conocer. *Write the correct forms of* **saber** *and* **conocer** *to complete these sentences.*

1. Pienso que él no _____ nada.

2. Yo no _____ a nadie en esta ciudad.

3. Tú _____ hacer programación, ¿verdad?

4. Yo creo que tú me _____ muy bien.

5. Nosotros no _____ por dónde empezar.

6. ¿Uds. _____ que Lidia es una compradora compulsiva?

7. Yo _____ que Uds. _____ el país muy bien.

8. ¿Quién _____ la dirección electrónica de Federico?

9. ¿Ud. _____ aquella tienda por departamentos?

10. Ellos no _____ al ingeniero pero sí _____ quién es.

Complete each sentence with the correct connector: choose **a**, **de**, or **que**, or write an X if no connector is required.

1. Aprendemos _____ jugar al tenis.

2. Quiero _____ asistir al concierto contigo.

3. No tienen _____ ir a ninguna parte hoy.

4. ¿Ud. trata _____ descargar el documento?

5. Sara piensa _____ tomar una clase a distancia.

6. Comienza _____ nevar.

7. Acabamos _____ servir el postre.

8. Hay _____ resolver el problema.

9. ¿Prefieres _____ ir al mar o al campo?

10. Yo no puedo _____ comprender su punto de vista.

11. Debe _____ usar el español en su trabajo.

12. Van _____ volver la semana entrante.

Expand each sentence using the verb in parentheses. Add the correct connector where necessary.

MODELO   (necesitar) Usamos esta receta de cocina.

Necesitamos usar esta receta de cocina.

1. (esperar) Domino el español.

_____

2. (empezar) Juega al baloncesto.

_____

3. (preferir) Viven en la costa.

_____

4. (poder) ¿No encuentras el plano?

_____

5. (acabar) Volvemos de la cancha de tenis.

_____

6. (lograr) Tiene éxito.

_____

7. (saber) Leo el alemán muy bien.

_____

8. (querer) Asisten a la reunión.

_____

9. (deber) Cuentas con nosotros.

_____

10. (tener) ¿No discute su idea?

_____

EJERCICIO
6·8

¿Qué tiempo hace? _Tell what the weather is like and will be like by expanding each sentence with the verb in parentheses. Add the correct connector as necessary._

MODELO   (ir) Hace frío.
                Va a hacer frío.

1. (comenzar) Hace sol.

_____

2. (ir) Nieva.

_____

3. (acabar) Despeja.

_____

4. (empezar) Llueve.

_____

5. (ir) Hace setenta grados.

_____

6. (comenzar) Truena.

_____

7. (ir) Hiela.

_____

¿Cuánto tiempo hace que…? *Write sentences using the strings of elements to tell how long things have been going on.*

MODELO   un año/Pedro/estudiar/inglés
           Hace un año que Pedro estudia inglés.

1. seis meses/yo/tomar/una clase de español

_____

2. siete años/nosotros/vivir/en esta casa

_____

3. dos horas/Carmen y Alfredo/jugar/al golf

_____

4. poco tiempo/Ud./escribir/su informe

_____

5. una semana/tú/estar/acatarrado

_____

6. media hora/Beatriz/servir/la cena

_____

7. mucho tiempo/llover

_____

8. dos días/nevar

_____

Translation. *Express the following dialogues in Spanish.*

1. Do you (**Ud.**) know how to cook?

   _____

2. No, but I want to learn to cook.

   _____

3. The weather is nasty. It's cold and windy.

   _____

4. And it's beginning to rain.

   _____

5. I feel like going to the shore. Do you (**tú**) want to go with me?

   _____

6. I've just come back from the shore. I prefer to go to the country.

   _____

7. Luis has been working in this field for fifteen years.

   _____

8. He knows the market very well.

   _____

9. They intend to take an online Spanish course.

   _____

10. They know they have to practice a lot to master the spoken language.

    _____

11. This café serves the best desserts in the city.

    _____

12. That's why I'm ordering two. I can't resist the temptation!

    _____

¿Cuántos? *Express the following numbers in Spanish.*

1. 36 _____ días

2. 71 _____ idiomas

3. 100 _____ ciudades

4. 531 _____ raquetas de tenis

5. 948 _____ compañías

6. 1,000 _____ ingenieras

7. 1,495 _____ tiendas

8. 1,761 _____ países

9. 10,826 _____ impresoras

10. 235,000 _____ hoteles

11. 1,000,000 _____ personas

12. 76,000,000 _____ dólares

Entertaining at home • *Tener*

The following exercises provide written practice to reinforce your understanding of the corresponding chapter on the CD-ROM.

💿 CD-ROM

Diálogos, análisis, variantes

- ☐ 7.1 Los invitados vienen a cenar
- ☐ 7.2 Vemos televisión
- ☐ 7.3 Dan una película
- ☐ 7.4 ¿Oímos música?
- ☐ 7.5 ¿Cómo se dice?
- ☐ 7.6 Cae la nieve
- ☐ 7.7 Los libros no caben
- ☐ 7.8 Una chica pesada
- ☐ 7.9 ¿A qué hora vienes?
- ☐ 7.10 No los puedo llevar
- ☐ 7.11 Yo lo llamo a Ud.
- ☐ 7.12 Yo la ayudo
- ☐ 7.13 No lo conozco
- ☐ 7.14 Tienes prisa
- ☐ 7.15 ¿Quién trae el vino?

Contents

- ◆ irregular verbs
- ◆ direct object: nouns, pronouns
- ◆ word order
- ◆ **tener** + noun = English *to be* + adjective

Communication goals

- ◆ Talking about being hungry, thirsty, warm, cold, sleepy
- ◆ Telling how you prepare for a dinner party
- ◆ Talking about television and movies
- ◆ Vocabulary: *home appliances, entertainment*

Irregular verbs. *Complete the dialogues with the correct present tense form of each irregular verb in parentheses.*

1. (oír) ¿Uds. no _____ el timbre?

   (oír) No, no _____ nada.

2. (venir) Teresa y Pedro _____ a vernos mañana, ¿no?

   (venir) Teresa sí _____, Pedro no.

3. (tener) Yo _____ frío. ¿Y tú?

   (poner) Sí, mucho. Yo _____ la calefacción.

4. (traer) ¿Qué regalo _____ Ud.?

   (traer) Yo _____ una cámara digital.

5. (hacer) _____ mal tiempo. Va a nevar.

   (caer) Mira. La nieve ya _____.

6. (decir) ¿Cómo se _____ *car* en español?

   (decir) Bueno, en México, nosotros _____ **carro**.

7. (caber) ¿Todos nosotros _____ en el taxi?

   (caber) No todos. Yo no _____.

8. (hacer) Yo _____ el almuerzo pronto.

   (poner) Y luego nosotras _____ la mesa.

9. (ver) ¿Uds. _____ las noticias ahora?

   (ver) No, _____ una telenovela.

10. (poner) ¿Qué película _____ en el cine Metro?

    (decir) Es un nuevo film italiano. Todo el mundo _____ que es fabuloso.

Yo también. *Write sentences using irregular verbs to tell that you are also doing what other people are doing.*

MODELO   Martín/hacer cola

              Martín hace cola. Yo hago cola también.

1. Paula/dar consejos

_____

2. tú/conocer al gerente

_____

3. ellos/tener paciencia

_____

4. Ud./oír la música

_____

5. Uds./caer en la nieve

_____

6. Bernardo y Leo/traer noticias

_____

7. Felipe/traducir el documento

_____

8. tú/decir que sí

_____

9. todos Uds./ir

_____

10. Marta/salir a las siete

_____

11. Ud./saber su dirección

_____

EJERCICIO

7·3

¿Qué tienen? *Translate the sentences into Spanish using the correct forms of* **tener** *to describe what these people are experiencing.*

1. Mis hermanos _____. *(are very hungry)*

2. Tú y yo _____. *(are right)*

3. Las niñas _____. *(are sleepy)*

4. José Luis _____. *(is very jealous)*

5. Uds. _____. *(are afraid)*

6. Tú _____. *(are very warm)*

7. Yo _____. *(am very thirsty)*

8. Ud. _____. *(are very lucky)*

Direct object nouns to pronouns. *Answer the following questions in the affirmative, changing the direct object nouns to pronouns in your responses.*

MODELO   ¿Lees el periódico?

Sí, lo leo.

1. ¿Haces las maletas? _____

2. ¿Sara pone el lavaplatos? _____

3. ¿Uds. oyen el anuncio? _____

4. ¿Ellos meten la tarjeta en el parquímetro? _____

5. ¿Ud. ve los documentales? _____

6. ¿Gabriel conoce a esos asesores? _____

7. ¿Terminas la base de datos? _____

8. ¿Ellos esperan a las ingenieras? _____

9. ¿Entienden Uds. su punto de vista? _____

10. ¿Ud. sirve esta torta? _____

11. ¿Escribes los correos electrónicos? _____

12. ¿Eduardo diseña las páginas web? _____

Direct object pronouns. *Expand each sentence, using the verb (or verb + connector) that appears in parentheses to make a verb + infinitive or verb + connector + infinitive construction, and change the direct object noun to a pronoun. Write each expanded sentence in two ways, according to the model.*

MODELO   (necesitar) Daniel imprime el informe.

Daniel necesita imprimirlo.

Daniel lo necesita imprimir.

1. (pensar) Graban la telenovela.

_____

_____

2. (acabar de) Oímos las voces.

_____

_____

3. (querer) Raquel ve a sus hermanos.

_____

_____

4. (ir a) ¿Haces el viaje?

_____

_____

5. (deber) Pongo la radio.

_____

_____

6. (lograr) Uds. devuelven la pelota.

_____

_____

7. (comenzar a) ¿A qué hora sirves el almuerzo?

_____

_____

8. (preferir) Pruebo el arroz con pollo.

_____

_____

9. (tratar de) Ud. no entiende su punto de vista.

_____

_____

10. (empezar a) Abrimos los regalos.

_____

_____

11. (poder) Los jugadores usan estas raquetas de tenis.

_____

_____

12. (esperar) ¿Compras ese microondas?

_____

_____

EJERCICIO
7·6

Direct object pronouns. *Complete the answers to the questions, using the direct object pronouns that replace* **Ud.** *and* **Uds.**

MODELO   ¿Me conoce Ud.?

No, señor, *no lo conozco*.

1. ¿Me lleva Ud.?

   No, señora, _____.

2. ¿Nos busca Ud.?

   No, señores, _____.

3. ¿Nos llama Ud.?

   No, señoras, _____.

4. ¿Me comprende Ud.?

   No, señorita, _____.

5. ¿Me ayuda Ud.?

   No, señor, _____.

6. ¿Nos conoce Ud.?

   No, señoritas, _____.

7. ¿Me quiere Ud. visitar?

   No, señor, _____.

8. ¿Nos piensa Ud. esperar?

   No, señoras, _____.

EJERCICIO
7·7

¿Dónde vas a comprarlo? *Write sentences using the* **ir a** *+ infinitive construction to tell where people are going to buy certain items. Change direct object nouns to pronouns in your responses.*

MODELO   ellos/el jugo/el supermercado

Van a comprarlo en el supermercado.

1. nosotros/la lavadora y la secadora/la tienda de electrodomésticos

   _____

2. yo/los juguetes/la juguetería

   _____

3. tú/el iPod/la tienda de cómputo

_____

4. ellas/los zapatos/la zapatería

_____

5. él/la raqueta de tenis/la tienda de deportes

_____

6. Uds./la torta de cumpleaños/la pastelería

_____

7. ella/el regalo de bodas/la tienda por departamentos

_____

8. Ud./las revistas/la librería

_____

EJERCICIO
7·8

Word order. Tell who is bringing each item to the party by correcting your friend's incorrect information.

MODELO   Alberto trae los refrescos, ¿no? (Rafael)
            No, los trae Rafael.

1. Patricia trae los sándwiches, ¿no? (María)

_____

2. Paco y Lidia traen el vino, ¿no? (yo)

_____

3. Tú traes los postres, ¿no? (Uds.)

_____

4. Nosotros traemos la pizza, ¿no? (Guillermo y Sofía)

_____

5. Tú y Franco traen las tapas, ¿no? (tú)

_____

6. Juan trae la cerveza, ¿no? (nosotros)

_____

Translation. *Express the following dialogues in Spanish.*

1. Do you (**tú**) know those businessmen?

   _____

   No, I don't know them but I hope to meet them.

   _____

2. Miss, can you help me with the database?

   _____

   Yes, ma'am, I'll help you right now.

   _____

3. I think Sergio and Eva are coming now.

   _____

   Yes, I see them.

   _____

4. Do you (**tú**) want to listen to this compact disc?

   _____

   I've just listened to it.

   _____

5. Our friends say the film is excellent.

   _____

   They're right. I've just seen it.

   _____

6. Are you (**Uds.**) hungry?

   _____

   No, we're not hungry but we are very thirsty.

   _____

7. There will be a lot of people at the theater.

   _____

   It's true. We're going to have to stand in line.

   _____

8. Antonio is taking the photos today, isn't he?

_____

No, Vicente intends to take them.

_____

9. It's cold today. I'm very cold. What about you (**tú**)?

_____

The snow is falling but I'm not cold.

_____

10. I'm putting the TV on. I want to see the soap opera.

_____

I want to see it too.

_____

Your daily routine • Reflexive verbs

The following exercises provide written practice to reinforce your understanding of the corresponding chapter on the CD-ROM.

CD-ROM

Diálogos, análisis, variantes

- ☐ 8.1 Carlos el aguafiestas
- ☐ 8.2 Comprometerse y casarse
- ☐ 8.3 Los novios se quieren
- ☐ 8.4 Nos damos prisa
- ☐ 8.5 Cómo cuidarte mejor
- ☐ 8.6 La rutina diaria
- ☐ 8.7 No se llevan bien
- ☐ 8.8 Matricularse o graduarse
- ☐ 8.9 ¿Cuál es su nombre?

Contents

- ◆ reflexive verbs
- ◆ reflexive verbs with reciprocal meaning (*each other*)
- ◆ adverbs
- ◆ **al** + infinitive
- ◆ ordinal numbers

Communication goals

- ◆ Talking about your daily routine
- ◆ Telling how you take care of yourself by eating well and exercising
- ◆ Talking about feelings and relationships
- ◆ Vocabulary: *everyday activities such as getting up, brushing your teeth, getting dressed; being happy, excited, angry; falling in love and getting married*

Reflexive verbs used as transitive verbs (with a direct object). *Write sentences using reflexive verbs as transitive verbs. Use the personal* **a** *as necessary.*

MODELO   Carlos/cortar/el pan
            Carlos corta el pan.

1. yo/despertar/mis hijos

   _____

2. Arturo y Sofía/lavar/su carro

   _____

3. Isabel y yo/cuidar/el niño

   _____

4. el jefe/reunir/los asesores

   _____

5. tú/acercar/la computadora

   _____

6. Uds./tranquilizar/estas personas nerviosas

   _____

7. Matilde/vestir/su hermanita

   _____

8. Ud./alegrar/sus invitados

   _____

9. los chicos/bañar/su perro

   _____

10. yo/probar/unos platos picantes

   _____

Reflexive verbs. *Now write sentences using the verbs shown (the same ones used in the exercise above) as reflexive verbs.*

MODELO   Carlos/cortar/con el cuchillo
                Carlos se corta con el cuchillo.

1. yo/despertar/a las siete

   _____

2. Arturo y Sofía/lavar/la cara

   _____

3. Isabel y yo/cuidar/bien

   _____

4. el jefe/reunir/con los asesores

   _____

5. tú/acercar/a la computadora

   _____

6. Uds./tranquilizar/fácilmente

   _____

7. Matilde/vestir/antes de desayunar

   _____

8. Ud./alegrar/al ver a sus invitados

   _____

9. los chicos/bañar/al llegar de la cancha

   _____

10. yo/probar/unos trajes

   _____

Reflexive or transitive verb? *Complete each sentence by selecting the reflexive or transitive form of the verb in parentheses and writing its correct form.*

1. (aburrir/aburrirse) Nos _____ esta obra de teatro.

2. (maquillar/maquillarse) Olivia _____ la cara.

3. (enfadar/enfadarse) Parece que Uds. lo _____ por algo.

4. (preocupar/preocuparse) ¿Por qué _____ tú por ellos?

5. (acostar/acostarse) Yo _____ a los niños a las ocho.

6. (colocar/colocarse) Paco _____ en una buena compañía.

7. (divertir/divertirse) María y Raúl _____ en el club.

8. (entusiasmar/entusiasmarse) Pablo y yo _____ en el partido.

9. (asustar/asustarse) Esas películas de terror nos _____.

10. (pintar/pintarse) ¿De qué color _____ (tú) las uñas?

11. (llamar/llamarse) Yo _____ a Virginia lo antes posible.

12. (exasperar/exasperarse) Últimamente Alberto nos _____ mucho.

Reflexive verbs: expansion. *Expand each sentence using the verb + infinitive or verb + connector + infinitive construction that appears in parentheses. Write each sentence following the word order in the example.*

MODELO   (desear) Se acuestan ahora.

Desean acostarse ahora.

1. (pensar) Julia se casa con Manuel en marzo.

_____

2. (deber) Nos damos prisa.

_____

3. (necesitar) ¿Te despiertas temprano?

_____

4. (poder) Se mantienen en contacto.

_____

5. (esperar) Yo me reúno con los técnicos.

_____

6. (querer) ¿Ud. no se viste todavía?

_____

7. (preferir) Se sientan más cerca.

_____

8. (tener que) Te acuerdas de la fecha.

_____

9. (ir a) Nos cortamos el pelo el viernes.

_____

10. (empezar a) Los invitados se divierten.

_____

11. (comenzar a) La niñita se ríe.

_____

12. (lograr) ¿Calmas a tus amigos?

_____

13. (dejar de) Se quejan por cualquier cosa.

_____

14. (acabar de) Me despido de ellas.

_____

15. (tratar de) Nos cuidamos mucho.

_____

EJERCICIO
8·5

Reflexive verbs: expansion. *Expand each sentence using the verb + infinitive or verb + connector + infinitive construction that appears in parentheses. Write each sentence following the word order in the example.*

MODELO   (ir a) Se levantan.
          Se van a levantar en seguida.

1. (querer) Me paseo por el jardín.

_____

2. (deber) Alfredo se afeita.

_____

3. (poder) Se matriculan esta semana.

_____

4. (ir a) Se gradúan en mayo.

_____

5. (acabar de) Te resfrías, ¿no?

_____

6. (ir a) Nos arreglamos ahora mismo.

_____

7. (acabar de) Alicia se pinta la cara.

_____

8. (poder) Nos instalamos en el condominio.

_____

9. (querer) ¿No te relajas?

_____

10. (deber) Uds. no se enojan.

_____

_____

EJERCICIO
8·6

Reflexive verbs with a reciprocal meaning. *Write sentences that express a reciprocal meaning (equivalent to English* each other).

MODELO   Lorenzo y Fernanda/ayudar

Lorenzo y Fernanda se ayudan.

1. Inés y Roberto/ver todos los días

_____

2. Felipe y yo/hablar por teléfono celular

_____

3. Carmen y Miguel/querer mucho

_____

4. tú y yo/mandar muchos correos electrónicos

_____

5. los abogados y los asesores/conocer muy bien

_____

6. Ester y yo/dar regalos

_____

7. Juan Diego y su prometida/besar

_____

8. Uds. y yo/comprender perfectamente

_____

EJERCICIO

8·7

Adverbios. *Write the adverbs that derive from the following adjectives that you have learned in chapters 1-8.*

1. hermoso _____

2. estupendo _____

3. inteligente _____

4. honrado _____

5. regular _____

6. alegre _____

7. nervioso _____

8. compulsivo _____

9. comercial _____

10. triste _____

11. cómodo _____

12. fácil _____

13. atento _____

14. arrogante _____

15. asustado _____

Adverbios. *Write the base form (masculine singular) of the original adjective from which each adverb derives.*

1. perfectamente _____

2. generalmente _____

3. cuidadosamente _____

4. recientemente _____

5. últimamente _____

6. difícilmente _____

7. frecuentemente _____

8. rotundamente _____

9. pesadamente _____

10. fríamente _____

11. normalmente _____

12. ruidosamente _____

13. pobremente _____

14. amablemente _____

15. tranquilamente _____

Translation. *Express the following passages in Spanish.*

1. La rutina diaria

My name is Gabriela Franco. When I wake up (Upon waking up), I brush my teeth, take a shower, and wash my hair. After I get dressed I put on makeup and comb my hair. My husband Gerardo showers, shaves, and gets dressed. Gerardo and I dress our children and then we all have breakfast. Gerardo and I take the children to school and then we go to our offices.

_____

_____

_____

_____

_____

2. Hago planes

My name is Antonio Lapesa. I've just graduated from the university and I'm looking for a job. I'm an accountant. I hope to get a position with an important firm. I've also just gotten engaged. My fiancée Pilar, who is a web designer, wants to get married this year but I think we shouldn't hurry. We have to work a few years in order to be able to buy a house. We don't worry because we love each other, we understand each other, and we always help each other.

_____

_____

_____

_____

_____

3. Necesito cuidarme

My name is Mateo Vargas. I catch colds very frequently. I've been feeling sick for six weeks. The doctor tells me that I'm fine, but that I should take better care of myself. That's why I'm going to start exercising. I want to get into shape. I'm going to jog and lift weights. I also intend to eat better. I'm going to stop eating junk food. And I have to relax more, go to bed earlier, and live more calmly. How boring!

_____

_____

_____

_____

_____

EJERCICIO
8·10

Ordinal numbers. *Replace the cardinal number with the ordinal number in each sentence.*

MODELO   Es la reunión número dos.
           Es la segunda reunión.

1. Su nieto número cuatro se llama Juan Miguel.

_____

2. Leemos el libro número nueve.

_____

3. Escribo el correo electrónico número seis.

_____

4. Siguen el plan número tres.

   _____

5. Tomas la clase a distancia número cinco.

   _____

6. Es la semana número ocho del semestre.

   _____

7. Se reúnen el miércoles número uno del mes.

   _____

8. Es la conferencia número uno del año.

   _____

9. Es la vez número tres.

   _____

10. Hacen el ejercicio número dos.

    _____

11. Es la semana número siete del viaje.

    _____

12. Es el año número diez de la empresa.

    _____

Talking about trips; your likes and dislikes • The preterit

·9·

The following exercises provide written practice to reinforce your understanding of the corresponding chapter on the CD-ROM.

CD-ROM

Diálogos, análisis, variantes

- ☐ 9.1 Un vuelo directo
- ☐ 9.2 En el aeropuerto
- ☐ 9.3 A bordo del avión
- ☐ 9.4 El vuelo
- ☐ 9.5 Recuerdos: viaje de vuelta a Estados Unidos
- ☐ 9.6 Nuestro viaje al sudoeste
- ☐ 9.7 Los viajes de negocios
- ☐ 9.8 ¡Qué tráfico!
- ☐ 9.9 Una excursión a Toledo

Contents

- ◆ the preterit tense
- ◆ indirect objects
- ◆ reverse construction verbs

Communication goals

- ◆ Talking about past events
- ◆ Describing airplane, train, and car trips
- ◆ Telling about a trip from Madrid to Toledo, Spain
- ◆ Talking about likes and dislikes
- ◆ Vocabulary: *travel, the airport, cardinal points, traffic*

Write the corresponding preterit form of the verb for each present tense verb form.

1. lleva _____

2. compartimos _____

3. trabajan _____

4. toco _____

5. siguen _____

6. corres _____

7. miramos _____

8. caes _____

9. empiezo _____

10. imprimen _____

11. esperas _____

12. vuelve _____

13. comprendemos _____

14. hay _____

15. juego _____

16. saben _____

17. vienes _____

18. vamos _____

19. estoy _____

20. hace _____

De presente a pretérito. *Rewrite each sentence, changing the verb from the present to the preterit.*

MODELO   Sube al avión.

                Subió al avión.

1. ¿Regresas a Madrid?

   _____

2. Leen unas revistas.

   _____

3. Va al aeropuerto.

   _____

4. Vengo en tren.

   _____

5. Estamos agotados.

   _____

6. ¿Uds. hacen los trámites?

   _____

7. Ud. escribe un correo electrónico.

   _____

8. Llego a la puerta de embarque.

   _____

9. ¿No puedes encontrar tu equipaje?

   _____

10. Nadie lo cree.

    _____

11. No quieren quedarse.

    _____

12. Eres auxiliar de vuelo.

    _____

13. Saco los billetes en línea.

    _____

14. Preferimos tomar un vuelo directo.

_____

15. No le digo nada.

_____

16. Tienen que irse.

_____

17. Recorremos el nordeste.

_____

18. Le muestra su pasaporte.

_____

19. Me pongo de pie.

_____

20. Te diviertes mucho.

_____

EJERCICIO
9·3

Preguntas. *Answer each of the following questions with a verb in the preterit, saying that the things being asked about have already happened. In questions that include direct object nouns, change the direct object nouns to pronouns in your responses.*

MODELO   ¿Él va a comer las enchiladas?

           Ya las comió.

1. ¿Ellos van a pedir el vino?

_____

2. ¿Ud. va a almorzar?

_____

3. ¿Gerardo va a traer los disquetes?

_____

4. ¿Vas a hacer las maletas?

_____

5. ¿Los directores van a ponerse de acuerdo?

_____

6. ¿Ud. y sus amigos van a oír esta música?

   _____

7. ¿Julia va a ver a sus primos?

   _____

8. ¿Ellos van a construir la casa?

   _____

9. ¿Uds. van a ir al zoológico?

   _____

10. ¿Tú y los asesores van a analizar los datos?

    _____

11. ¿Ud. va a navegar en la Red?

    _____

12. ¿Marta va a servir el postre?

    _____

13. ¿Ellas van a vestirse?

    _____

14. ¿Vas a despertar a las niñas?

    _____

15. ¿Vas a comenzar el informe?

    _____

EJERCICIO
9·4

¿Qué hicieron? *Tell what you and other people did by writing the correct preterit forms of the verbs in parentheses.*

1. Esta mañana yo _____ (despertarse) a las siete. Al levantarme, yo

   _____ (cepillarse) los dientes, _____ (ducharse) y

   _____ (vestirse). Luego yo _____ (desayunar),

   _____ (ponerse) el abrigo y _____ (irse). Yo

   _____ (llegar) a mi oficina a las nueve.

2. Hoy Teodoro _____ (levantarse), _____ (ducharse), _____ (afeitarse) y _____ (ponerse) el traje, la camisa y la corbata. Él _____ (ir) a la estación de tren en coche. _____ (Aparcar) su coche y _____ (tomar) el tren al centro. _____ (Llegar) a su oficina donde _____ (tener) una reunión con su equipo. Él _____ (pasar) todo el día en su oficina y _____ (volver) a su casa a las nueve de la noche.

3. El año pasado, mis padres, mis dos hermanos y yo _____ (hacer) un viaje a Europa. Nosotros _____ (conocer) Inglaterra, Francia y España. Primero nosotros _____ (viajar) a Inglaterra donde _____ (pasar) una semana en Londres y otras ciudades. Luego _____ (tomar) el tren del Chunnel a Francia y _____ (quedarse) en París una semana. Finalmente, nosotros _____ (llegar) a España. Nosotros _____ (tener) que quedarnos más tiempo en España porque mis papás tienen muchos familiares por todo el país. Nosotros _____ (poder) conocer Madrid, Barcelona y muchas otras ciudades.

4. Mi amiga Consuelo _____ (cumplir) veintisiete años ayer. Anoche yo _____ (asistir) a su fiesta de cumpleaños. Todos nosotros los invitados _____ (comer) muy bien y _____ (beber) mucho vino. Consuelo _____ (alegrarse) al abrir sus regalos. Yo le _____ (traer) flores y unos discos compactos. A la una de la mañana, Javier _____ (tener) la idea de ir a un club de jazz. Todo el mundo _____ (entusiasmarse) mucho. Nosotros _____ (ir) a un club donde _____ (oír) música hasta las cuatro de la mañana.

5. Isabel y Franco _____ (estudiar) administración de empresas en la universidad. Ellos _____ (graduarse) hace cinco años. Isabel _____ (colocarse) en una empresa de mercadeo. Franco _____ (comenzar) a trabajar en una compañía de software. Isabel y Franco _____ (comprometerse) y al año siguiente _____ (casarse). Ellos _____ (comprar) una casa y luego _____ (tener) un hijo. Isabel y Franco _____ (estar) muy contentos.

Indirect object pronouns. *Using the following strings of elements, write sentences that have a verb in the preterit and an indirect object pronoun.*

MODELO   ella/dar/un regalo (a ellos)
Ella les dio un regalo.

1. yo/explicar/mi idea (a él)

   _____

2. ella/escribir/un correo electrónico (a nosotros)

   _____

3. Uds./hacer/una comida muy rica (a ellas)

   _____

4. tú/decir/lo que pasó (a mí)

   _____

5. nosotros/regalar/libros (a nuestros hijos)

   _____

6. él/mostrar/su pasaporte (al aduanero)

   _____

7. ellas/leer/los documentos (a Uds.)

   _____

8. Ud./devolver/el dinero (a nosotras)

   _____

9. ellos/traer/el periódico (a ti)

   _____

10. ella/pedir/un favor (a Ud.)

   _____

Indirect object pronouns. *Using the following strings of elements, write sentences that have a verb in the preterit, an indirect object noun, and the noun's corresponding indirect object pronoun.*

MODELO   él/mandar/un regalo/a su novia

Él le mandó un regalo a su novia.

1. ellos/regalar/una raqueta de tenis/a su hermana

    _____

2. Daniela/servir/unas tapas/a sus invitados

    _____

3. Ud./ vender/sus libros/a otros estudiantes

    _____

4. yo/hacer/unas preguntas/al asesor financiero

    _____

5. tú/entregar/el informe/a los directores

    _____

6. Uds./dar/el software/a la programadora

    _____

7. nosotros/pedir/un plato de pescado/al cocinero

    _____

8. ellas/devolver/el carro/a sus padres

    _____

9. Manolo/mostrar/su nuevo apartamento/a sus amigos

    _____

10. él/decir/la verdad/a su abogado

    _____

Reverse construction verbs. *Complete each sentence with the missing indirect object pronoun to express the equivalent of the English sentence.*

1. *I liked it.* _____ gustó.

2. *Did you (**Ud.**) like them?* ¿_____ cayeron bien?

3. *She didn't care about them.* No _____ importaron.

4. *We loved it.* _____ encantó.

5. *You (**Uds.**) didn't have it.* _____ faltó.

6. *Did you (**tú**) need them?* ¿_____ hicieron falta?

7. *They were interested in it.* _____ interesó.

8. *It was good for her.* _____ convino.

9. *He had more than enough of them.* _____ sobraron.

EJERCICIO
9·8

Reverse construction verbs. *Change the subject from singular to plural in each sentence. Retain the tense—present or preterit—of the original sentence.*

MODELO   Le gusta esta cámara.
            Le gustan estas cámaras.

1. Nos interesa su idea.

   _____

2. Le encantó ese viaje.

   _____

3. Les gustó la obra de teatro.

   _____

4. Me hace falta una camisa.

   _____

5. ¿Te cayó bien el dentista?

   _____

6. Le falta un dólar.

   _____

7. Nos queda un examen.

   _____

8. Les sobra una página.

   _____

Expansión. *Expand each sentence by adding the* **ir a** *+ infinitive construction to the reverse construction verb.*

MODELO   Le gusta la excursión.

Le va a gustar la excursión.

1. Les hace falta más dinero.

_____

2. Me interesa recorrer la ciudad.

_____

3. No nos importa lo que dicen.

_____

4. Le caen mal estos empleados.

_____

5. ¿Te hacen falta dos maletas?

_____

6. No les queda mucho tiempo en el aeropuerto.

_____

7. Me conviene hacer los trámites en línea.

_____

8. No le gustan los planes.

_____

Translation. *Express the following sentences in Spanish.*

1. I arrived in Toledo at 8:00 A.M. and left at 10:00 P.M.

_____

2. The plane took off and twenty minutes later, I unbuckled my seatbelt.

_____

3. Did you (**tú**) like the film?

_____

4. Yes, I loved it.

_____

5. Did they have to make a stopover?

_____

6. Yes. They said it was an endless and exhausting flight.

_____

7. Are you (**Uds.**) interested in traveling around the southwest?

_____

8. We took a trip there three years ago.

_____

9. The passengers asked the flight attendant for water and juice.

_____

10. She liked them but he didn't like them. (use **caer**)

_____

11. I handed her the boarding pass.

_____

12. Did you (**Ud.**) bring the marketing plan to Mr. Salazar?

_____

13. Yes, I gave him the marketing plan the day before yesterday.

_____

14. It didn't matter to us at all.

_____

Talking about your childhood • The imperfect

·10·

The following exercises provide written practice to reinforce your understanding of the corresponding chapter on the CD-ROM.

CD-ROM

Diálogos, análisis, variantes

- ☐ 10.1 Cuando yo era niño...
- ☐ 10.2 En la finca
- ☐ 10.3 De vacaciones en Costa Rica
- ☐ 10.4 Las fotos del cafetal
- ☐ 10.5 Las pirámides
- ☐ 10.6 El profesor explica sus ideas
- ☐ 10.7 Los abuelos
- ☐ 10.8 La historia de la familia
- ☐ 10.9 Merienda al aire libre
- ☐ 10.10 ¡Qué olvidadizos somos!
- ☐ 10.11 Días universitarios
- ☐ 10.12 Se da una propina
- ☐ 10.13 La beca fue suspendida
- ☐ 10.14 Dificultades en la carretera
- ☐ 10.15 Se realizaba un sueño
- ☐ 10.16 Lo que hacíamos
- ☐ 10.17 La dirección electrónica
- ☐ 10.18 ¿Quién tiene el iPod?

Contents

- ◆ the imperfect tense
- ◆ double object pronouns
- ◆ uses of **se**
- ◆ the passive voice
- ◆ long-form possessive adjectives

Communication goals

- ◆ Talking about time, weather, conditions, and repeated actions in the past
- ◆ Describing a trip to Costa Rica
- ◆ Telling about pre-Columbian peoples and the pyramids in Mexico
- ◆ Telling about what you did as a child and your family history
- ◆ Vocabulary: *the university, scholarships and internships, tipping in a restaurant, immigrants*

Write the corresponding imperfect form of the verb for each present tense verb form.

1. hablo _____

2. son _____

3. viajamos _____

4. voy _____

5. crees _____

6. comienzo _____

7. escribe _____

8. ves _____

9. vuelven _____

10. jugamos _____

11. reciben _____

12. puede _____

13. piensas _____

14. damos _____

15. tengo _____

16. oye _____

17. hay _____

18. sé _____

19. dicen _____

20. viene _____

¿Qué hacían? Complete each sentence with the correct imperfect form of the verb in parentheses.

MODELO (abrir) Ella ___*abría*___ las cajas.

1. (trabajar) Ellos _____ en una tienda de deportes.

2. (recorrer) ¿Uds. _____ el cafetal?

3. (ir) Él _____ a dejar de fumar.

4. (reunirse) Nosotros _____ en mi oficina.

5. (Hacer) _____ muy buen tiempo.

6. (ver) Tú _____ montañas y desiertos, ¿no?

7. (ser) Esos inmigrantes _____ de origen griego.

8. (prender) Yo _____ mi celular.

9. (contar) ¿Ud. se lo _____?

10. (servir) Nosotras _____ comida sana.

11. (producir) Se _____ queso en la finca.

12. (interesar) Les _____ mucho las pirámides.

13. (enseñar) Yo les _____ las fotos de mi familia.

14. (dar) El calor nos _____ mucha sed.

15. (vestir) Ella _____ a sus hijas.

16. (pensar) ¿Uds. _____ prestárselo?

17. (querer) Yo _____ reservar los billetes en línea.

18. (saber) Ellas _____ montar a caballo.

19. (tomar) Él y yo _____ una clase a distancia.

20. (aprovechar) Ud. _____ las ofertas de enero.

EJERCICIO
10·3

Todos los días. *Rewrite each sentence in the imperfect, adding the adverb or adverbial phrase of frequency in parentheses.*

MODELO   Gonzalo se despierta a las siete. (todos los días)
Gonzalo se despertaba a las siete todos los días.

1. Yo me reúno con mis amigos. (todos los viernes)

_____

2. Uds. van a esquiar. (todos los inviernos)

_____

3. María Elena almuerza con nosotros. (cada semana)

_____

4. Nosotros asistimos a un concierto. (todos los meses)

_____

5. ¿Comes granos integrales? (a menudo)

_____

6. Paco no duerme la siesta. (generalmente)

_____

7. Se divierten mucho en tus fiestas. (siempre)

_____

8. Veo ese programa. (todas las semanas)

_____

9. Hago un viaje. (todos los años)

_____

10. Le dan una beca. (cada año)

_____

EJERCICIO
10·4

Narratives. *Create narratives by writing the correct imperfect forms of the verbs in parentheses.*

1. Todos los días yo _____ (despertarse) a las siete. Al levantarme, yo

_____ (cepillarse) los dientes, _____ (ducharse) y

_____ (vestirse). Luego yo _____ (desayunar),

_____ (ponerse) el abrigo y _____ (irse). Yo

_____ (llegar) a mi oficina a las nueve. Siempre _____

(tener) mucho trabajo y no _____ (regresar) a casa hasta las diez de la

noche. Yo _____ (comer) algo ligero y _____

(acostarse) en seguida.

2. Todos los días Esteban y Pilar _____ (levantarse) a las seis. Mientras

Esteban _____ (ducharse) y _____ (afeitarse), su esposa

_____ (lavarse) la cabeza y _____ (arreglarse). Luego

Esteban _____ (despertar) a los niños mientras Pilar _____

(preparar) el desayuno. Después de desayunar, Esteban _____ (salir) para

la oficina y Pilar _____ (llevar) a sus hijos al colegio. Después ella

_____ (volver) a la casa donde _____ (trabajar) en su

oficina.

3. Cuando yo era niño, mis papás, mis hermanos y yo _____ (ir) a una finca

que _____ (quedar) en la sierra. A veces nosotros _____

(tomar) las vacaciones en verano, a veces _____ (preferir) tomarlas en

invierno. Es que nos _____ (gustar) los deportes de verano y también los

de invierno. Cuando _____ (hacer) calor, nosotros _____

(poder) nadar y cuando _____ (nevar), nosotros _____

(esquiar). En verano, yo _____ (montar) a caballo todos los días. Mi

caballo favorito _____ (llamarse) Campeón. A mis hermanos menores les

_____ (gustar) darles de comer a los animales que _____

(estar) en la finca.

4. En aquella época _____ (llegar) mucha gente a los Estados Unidos.

Muchos de los inmigrantes _____ (ser) pobres y _____

(soñar) con vivir mejor. Ellos _____ (esperar) encontrar empleo. Muchos

_____ (aprender) inglés para poder trabajar. Ellos _____

(trabajar) en fábricas (*factories*) y tiendas pequeñas. La vida _____ (ser)

difícil para ellos pero ellos _____ (saber) que _____

(vivir) en un país que les _____ (dar) la oportunidad (*opportunity*) de

triunfar en la vida.

5. Ya _____ (ser) las tres de la tarde. _____ (Hacer) cinco

horas que yo _____ (esperar) mi vuelo en el aeropuerto. _____

(Hacer) muy mal tiempo, _____ (llover) y _____ (haber)

niebla. Por eso los aviones no _____ (despegar). _____

(Haber) muchos pasajeros que no _____ (poder) viajar igual que yo. Se

_____ (tener) que cancelar casi todos los vuelos por el mal tiempo.

Mientras yo _____ (esperar), _____ (comer),

_____ (tomar) mucho café, _____ (leer) y

_____ (ver) cosas en las tiendas para pasar el tiempo. Yo

_____ (exasperarse). Mi mejor amiga _____ (casarse)

y yo no _____ (ir) a poder asistir a su boda.

Double object pronouns. *Rewrite each sentence, changing the direct object noun to a pronoun and making any other necessary changes. Retain the tense of the original sentence.*

MODELO   Le explicaba la idea.
                Se la explicaba.

1. Les enseñábamos el cafetal.

   _____

2. Me dieron la beca.

   _____

3. Te hago los pasteles.

   _____

4. ¿Nos prestas tus maletas?

   _____

5. Le entregué la tarjeta de embarque.

   _____

6. Les cuentan el cuento.

   _____

7. Me mandaba los informes.

   _____

8. Le trajimos esas flores.

   _____

9. ¿Te consigue los billetes?

   _____

10. Nos mostraban las pirámides.

   _____

*Double object pronouns: **Algo va a pasar o algo acaba de pasar.** Add the **ir a** + infinitive construction or the **acabar de** + infinitive construction to each sentence. Make the necessary changes. Write each sentence in two ways.*

MODELO   Se lo dice. (ir a)

Va a decírselo.

Se lo va a decir.

1. Me la traen. (acabar de)

   _____

   _____

2. Se las sirvo. (ir a)

   _____

   _____

3. Nos los devuelve. (acabar de)

   _____

   _____

4. Te lo damos. (ir a)

   _____

   _____

5. Me las pides. (acabar de)

   _____

   _____

6. Se lo llevan. (ir a)

   _____

   _____

7. Te los muestro. (acabar de)

   _____

   _____

8. Nos la venden. (ir a)

   _____

   _____

9. Se los haces. (acabar de)

_____

_____

10. Me lo presta. (ir a)

_____

_____

Double object pronouns and reflexive verbs. *Answer each question, changing the direct object noun to a pronoun and making any other necessary changes. Retain the tense of the question in your answer.*

MODELO ¿María se lavaba las manos?

Sí, se las lavaba.

1. ¿Te pusiste la chaqueta?

_____

2. ¿Los pasajeros se abrocharon el cinturón de seguridad?

_____

3. ¿Paula y tú se pintaban los labios?

_____

4. ¿Te cortaste el pelo?

_____

5. ¿El jugador se rompió el dedo?

_____

6. ¿Carlos se quita las botas?

_____

7. ¿Uds. se cepillaban los dientes?

_____

8. ¿Ud. se secó el pelo?

_____

9. ¿Fernanda se maquilló la cara?

_____

10. ¿Los niños se desabrocharon los zapatos?

_____

***Double object pronouns:* Ya se lo lavé.** *Answer each question, saying that you have already helped the children in the ways you are being asked about. Change the direct object noun to a pronoun and make any other necessary changes.*

MODELO   ¿Vas a lavarle el pelo a Juanita?
            Ya se lo lavé.

1. ¿Vas a ponerle las medias a Carlita?

_____

2. ¿Vas a limpiarle los dientes a tu nieto?

_____

3. ¿Vas a lavarles la cabeza a Paquito y Elenita?

_____

4. ¿Vas a quitarles el abrigo a las niñas?

_____

5. ¿Vas a abrocharles los zapatos a tus hijos?

_____

6. ¿Vas a cortarle el pelo a tu sobrinito?

_____

7. ¿Vas a desabrocharles la chaqueta a tus hermanitos?

_____

8. ¿Vas a secarle el pelo a Perlita?

_____

Se construction. *Rewrite each sentence, using the* **se** *construction + verb in the present tense.*

MODELOS   Recorren el país.

Se recorre el país.

Recorren los países.

Se recorren los países.

1. Visitamos el cafetal.

_____

2. Sacas fotos.

_____

3. Cultivan maíz.

_____

4. Realizan el proyecto.

_____

5. Hago los trámites.

_____

6. Construyen un parqueo.

_____

7. Produzco vinos.

_____

8. Resolvemos el problema.

_____

9. Servimos platos vegetarianos.

_____

10. Oímos música.

_____

11. Alquilan furgonetas.

_____

12. Imprimimos los informes.

_____

Se construction. *Rewrite each sentence, using the **se** construction.*

MODELO   Entran por aquí.
            Se entra por aquí.

1. Llegamos a la puerta de embarque.

   _____

2. Viven mejor en este país.

   _____

3. Navegan en la Red.

   _____

4. Hablamos por celular.

   _____

5. Trabajan de lunes a jueves.

   _____

6. Salimos al jardín.

   _____

7. Abren a las diez de la mañana.

   _____

8. Manejamos con cuidado.

   _____

EJERCICIO
10·11

*Expand each sentence with a **se** construction by adding the verb in parentheses.*

MODELO   Se baja del avión. (necesitar)
            Se necesita bajar del avión.

1. Se deja una propina. (deber)

   _____

2. Se pasa por el control de seguridad. (necesitar)

   _____

3. No se encuentra un vuelo directo. (poder)

_____

4. No se fuma. (permitir)

_____

5. Se apaga el celular. (necesitar)

_____

6. Se cambia el vuelo. (poder)

_____

7. Se sube a la pirámide. (permitir)

_____

8. No se come comida basura. (deber)

_____

Passive voice. *Rewrite each sentence, changing the active construction to a passive construction.*

MODELO   El profesor explicó la idea.
            La idea fue explicada por el profesor.

1. El agricultor cultivó el arroz.

_____

2. Los auxiliares de vuelo sirvieron las bebidas.

_____

3. La empresa abrió mil tiendas.

_____

4. La cocinera hizo la torta de cumpleaños.

_____

5. Esos abogados escribieron los contratos.

_____

6. La directora suspendió la reunión.

_____

7. Uno de los turistas tomó las fotos.

_____

8. Unos contadores resolvieron su problema.

_____

9. La mesera puso las mesas.

_____

10. Aquel arquitecto construyó los centros comerciales.

_____

11. Un amigo mío diseñó mi sitio web.

_____

12. El jugador rompió nuestra ventana.

_____

EJERCICIO
10·13

Passive voice. *Complete each passive sentence in the preterit, using the verb in parentheses.*

MODELO   La cena _____*fue preparada*_____ por el cocinero. (preparar)

1. Los cuartos _____ por el pintor. (pintar)

2. Las cartas _____ por el secretario (*secretary*). (entregar)

3. El condominio _____ por los señores Ayala. (vender)

4. La computadora _____ por el programador. (prender)

5. Los niños _____ por sus papás. (acostar)

6. El informe _____ por el estudiante. (imprimir)

7. Los exámenes _____ por la profesora Díaz. (escribir)

8. Esas ciudades _____ por los ingleses. (fundar)

9. Las mesas _____ por los meseros. (poner)

10. Su programa _____ por la universidad. (suspender)

11. Los correos electrónicos _____ por la empleada. (mandar)

12. El Coliseo _____ por los romanos. (construir)

El billetero suyo. *Write phrases using long-form possessive adjectives to tell whom these items belong to.*

MODELO   el billetero/(él) _el billetero suyo_

1. los maletines/(nosotros) _____

2. la cámara/(yo) _____

3. el cartapacio/(él) _____

4. las pulseras/(Ud.) _____

5. el equipaje de mano/(tú) _____

6. la flauta/(ella) _____

7. las tarjetas de embarque/(Uds.) _____

8. el carro/(ellos) _____

9. los discos compactos/(yo) _____

10. la pintura (nosotras) _____

11. los disquetes (ella) _____

12. el celular (Uds.) _____

Translation. *Express the following sentences in Spanish.*

1. How long had you (**Uds.**) been living on the farm?

   _____

2. We had been living there for fifteen years.

   _____

3. There were horses and cows on the farm.

   _____

4. I used to go horseback riding every day.

   _____

5. What were your grandparents like? (**tú**)

   _____

6. They were very loving. We loved each other a lot.

   _____

7. Did I show you (**tú**) the photos?

   _____

8. No, you didn't show them to me.

   _____

9. Then I'm going to send them to you today.

   _____

10. The gift. Did you (**Uds.**) give it to Pablo yet?

    _____

11. Yes, we've just given it to him.

    _____

12. Wines are produced in Spain. (use **se** construction)

    _____

13. You aren't able to change the flight. (use **se** construction)

    _____

14. The tickets were reserved online. (use passive voice)

    _____

15. Our house was built by a team of architects. (use passive voice)

    _____

Health and accidents • The imperfect and the preterit

·11·

The following exercises provide written practice to reinforce your understanding of the corresponding chapter on the CD-ROM.

CD-ROM

Diálogos, análisis, variantes

- ☐ 11.1 En el centro comercial
- ☐ 11.2 Un partido de béisbol
- ☐ 11.3 Al señor Maldonado lo trasladaron
- ☐ 11.4 Compañeros de clase
- ☐ 11.5 Alguien se equivocó de número
- ☐ 11.6 Un niño prodigio
- ☐ 11.7 Paquito estaba enfermo
- ☐ 11.8 Un chequeo médico
- ☐ 11.9 Los mosquitos lo comían vivo
- ☐ 11.10 Aurora tuvo un niño
- ☐ 11.11 Falsa alarma
- ☐ 11.12 Un choque de carros

Contents

- ◆ the imperfect and the preterit: two aspects of past time
- ◆ diminutives

Communication goals

- ◆ Talking about health conditions, accidents, and unplanned events
- ◆ Describing a visit to the doctor
- ◆ Vocabulary: *healthy lifestyle, illnesses, parts of the body*

Imperfect or preterit. *Complete the following sentences, choosing either the imperfect or the preterit for each verb in parentheses. Each sentence has two verbs, one of which will be in the imperfect and the other in the preterit.*

MODELO   Carmen ___*estaba*___ estresada hasta que ___*cambió*___ su estilo de vida. (estar, cambiar)

1. Yo no _____ a nadie en la fiesta hasta que _____ mis amigos. (conocer, llegar)

2. Nosotros _____ en el extranjero cuando _____ la guerra. (estar, estallar)

3. _____ las once de la noche cuando ellos _____ del teatro. (Ser, regresar)

4. Tú _____ veintiocho años cuando _____, ¿no? (tener, casarse)

5. Margarita _____ mientras _____ música. (dormirse, oír)

6. Los mosquitos me _____ hasta que yo _____ el repelente contra mosquitos. (picar, ponerse)

7. Yo _____ las ventanas porque _____ muy fuerte. (cerrar, llover)

8. La policía _____ al ladrón mientras él _____. (atrapar, escaparse)

9. Mientras Teodoro _____ dinero del cajero automático, _____ un atraco. (retirar, haber)

10. ¿Cuántos años _____ (Ud.) cuando _____ en la universidad? (tener, graduarse)

11. Mientras Uds. _____ al béisbol, _____ a llover. (jugar, comenzar)

12. Cuando nosotros _____ al quinto piso, no _____ nadie en la oficina. (subir, haber)

13. Juan Pedro y yo _____ un taxi cuando _____ un accidente de tráfico. (buscar, ver)

14. Franco _____ el colesterol alto hasta que _____ de peso. (tener, bajar)

15. ¿Ud. _____ en esa oficina hasta que los jefes lo _____? (trabajar, trasladar)

16. Julio _____ al médico porque le _____ la garganta. (ir, doler)

17. Yo _____ a comer sano porque _____ mal. (empezar, sentirse)

18. Mientras los paramédicos _____ a las víctimas, _____ la ambulancia. (atender, llegar)

19. Cuando Federico _____, _____ muy mal tiempo. (irse, hacer)

20. Sus tíos _____ a quedarse unos días más, pero no _____. (ir, poder)

EJERCICIO
11·2

Preterit and imperfect: reported speech. *Rewrite each sentence showing reported speech to make it a sentence in the past tense by replacing the present tense verb in the first clause with the preterit and the present tense verb in the second clause with the imperfect.*

MODELO Juan me escribe que está alterado.
Juan me escribió que estaba alterado.

1. Ellos nos dicen que piensan mudarse.

   _____

2. Jimena les cuenta que quiere estudiar en el extranjero.

   _____

3. Nos informan que el avión aterriza.

   _____

4. Sus abuelos les escriben que vienen a verlos.

   _____

5. Isabel nos dice que está embarazada.

   _____

6. Yo les digo que no puedo acompañarlos.

   _____

7. Le informamos que la cámara cuesta trescientos dólares.

   _____

8. Antonio me cuenta que tiene que trabajar en otra sucursal.

   _____

9. Sus papás nos cuentan que Miguelito es un niño prodigio.

   _____

10. Le escribo que a Daniel le duele la espalda.

    _____

11. Me informa que hay mucho tráfico en ese barrio.

_____

12. Le escribimos que no sabemos lo del atraco.

_____

EJERCICIO
11·3

Diminutives. *Rewrite each word as a diminutive ending in* **-ito** *or* **-ita**.

1. el dedo _____

2. la ropa _____

3. la chica _____

4. el joven _____

5. la pierna _____

6. cerca _____

7. Carlos _____

8. el perro _____

9. poco _____

10. la botella _____

11. el pájaro _____

12. Isabel _____

13. el café _____

14. ahora _____

15. la cabeza _____

16. fresco _____

17. la siesta _____

18. la voz _____

19. el hermano _____

20. el calor _____

EJERCICIO
11·4

Augmentatives. *Match each Spanish word with an augmentative to its English translation. Each word derives from a verb and means given to doing the action of the verb.*

1. _____ gritón
2. _____ mirón
3. _____ mandón
4. _____ llorón
5. _____ preguntón
6. _____ dormilón
7. _____ comilón

a. gluttonous
b. always crying, crybaby
c. inquisitive, asking too many questions
d. loud-mouthed, always yelling
e. inclined to sleep a lot
f. bossy
g. given to staring, voyeur

EJERCICIO
11·5

Translation. *Express the following sentences in Spanish.*

1. They waved to us when we were going up the escalator.

_____

2. Laura changed her lifestyle because she always felt tired.

_____

3. Pablo went to the doctor because he had a sore throat.

_____

4. Alberto told us that his wife was pregnant.

_____

5. Did you (**tú**) see Jaime? He has so many mosquito bites.

_____

6. He forgot to put on insect repellent.

_____

7. They told me that a car ran over a pedestrian at this corner.

_____

8. Yes, I was watching while the paramedics tended to the victim.

_____

9. We were sunbathing when suddenly there was a downpour.

_____

10. My little brother always has a stomachache because he's a big eater.

_____

11. Mateo was branch manager until he was transferred.

_____

12. Teresa was forty-eight years old when she retired.

_____

At school and the office • Comparatives and superlatives

·12·

The following exercises provide written practice to reinforce your understanding of the corresponding chapter on the CD-ROM.

CD-ROM

Diálogos, análisis, variantes

- ☐ 12.1 ¿Quién es más terco?
- ☐ 12.2 La primera novela es la mejor de todas
- ☐ 12.3 Busco una nueva computadora
- ☐ 12.4 ¿El traje negro o el gris?
- ☐ 12.5 La contaminación del ambiente
- ☐ 12.6 Un nuevo puesto
- ☐ 12.7 Curso cinco asignaturas

Contents

- ◆ comparative and superlative constructions
- ◆ the absolute superlative (suffix -**ísimo**)
- ◆ pronouns: possessive, demonstrative, prepositional
- ◆ nominalization of adjectives (adjectives used as nouns)

Communication goals

- ◆ Comparing people and things to each other
- ◆ Talking about the university
- ◆ Vocabulary: *environmental pollution, problems of society, school and office supplies*

En comparación. *Combine each pair of sentences into one sentence that shows a comparison of superiority (**más**) and another that shows a comparison of inferiority (**menos**).*

MODELO   Aurora es presumida./Consuelo es más presumida.

Consuelo es más presumida que Aurora.

Aurora es menos presumida que Consuelo.

1. Jaime está entusiasmado./Yo estoy más entusiasmado.

   _____

   _____

2. Los pantalones son caros./La chaqueta es más cara.

   _____

   _____

3. El profesor de matemáticas es exigente./La profesora de física es más exigente.

   _____

   _____

4. La novela alemana es seria./La novela rusa es más seria.

   _____

   _____

5. Uds. son optimistas./Paloma y Gonzalo son más optimistas.

   _____

   _____

En comparación. *Write sentences using the strings of elements to show comparisons of equality.*

MODELO   Timoteo/amable/su hermano

Timoteo es tan amable como su hermano.

1. Pedro/ingenuo/tú

   _____

2. el condominio/amplio/la casa

   _____

3. Patricia/coqueta/su prima

_____

4. las composiciones/largas/los informes

_____

5. su carro japonés/caro/nuestro carro estadounidense

_____

6. nosotros/preocupados/Uds.

_____

7. la película/aburrida/la novela

_____

8. los asesores/ambiciosos/el jefe

_____

9. yo/decepcionado/mis compañeros

_____

10. Marta/rara/su cuñada

_____

EJERCICIO
12·3

Adverbs. *Write sentences using the strings of elements to show comparisons of equality.*

MODELO   Clara/hablar/tímidamente/Carmen
           Clara habla tan tímidamente como Carmen.

1. Alejandro/escuchar/atentamente/Esteban

_____

2. Sergio/trabajar/cuidadosamente/yo

_____

3. la familia Suárez/vivir/cómodamente/la familia Obregón

_____

4. Uds./ir de compras/frecuentemente/nosotros

_____

5. Viviana/manejar/lentamente/tú

_____

6. Antonio/enojarse/fácilmente/Lucía

_____

7. Santiago/correr/rápidamente/Roberto

_____

EJERCICIO
12·4

Nouns. _Write sentences using the strings of elements to show comparisons of equality._

MODELO   Arturo/recibir/correos electrónicos/Celeste
Arturo recibe tantos correos electrónicos como Celeste.

1. yo/tomar/cursos/tú

_____

2. el niño/tener/sueño/su hermanito

_____

3. Beatriz/asistir a/conciertos/María

_____

4. Mateo/comer/comida basura/sus amigos

_____

5. nuestro condominio/tener/dormitorios/su apartamento

_____

6. Inés/tener/paciencia/Guillermo

_____

7. José Luis/necesitar/lápices/Margarita

_____

8. nosotros/tener/hambre/Uds.

_____

¿Cómo son estas personas? *Use the superlative of the adjectives to describe what these members of the family are like. Make all necessary changes.*

MODELO   Camilo/perezoso
Camilo es el más perezoso.

1. Raquel/considerada

_____

2. Rodrigo/cascarrabias

_____

3. Laura y Silvia/calculador

_____

4. Teresa/cortés

_____

5. Alejandro y Miriam/sincero

_____

6. Manolo/egoísta

_____

7. David y Miguel/encantador

_____

The absolute superlative. *Complete each sentence, using the absolute superlative of the adjective in parentheses.*

MODELO   La contaminación del ambiente es ___*malísima*___. (malo)

1. El libro de física es _____. (fácil)

2. Estos platos están _____. (rico)

3. Las composiciones son _____. (largo)

4. La clase de matemáticas es _____. (difícil)

5. La capital es _____. (grande)

6. Este museo de arte es _____. (interesante)

7. Nuestros amigos son _____. (simpático)

8. El profesor Vargas es _____. (bueno)

9. Los paisajes son _____. (hermoso)

10. Esta ropa es _____. (fino)

¿Cuál te gusta más? *Answer each of the following questions, eliminating the nouns that are being compared in your response.*

MODELO   ¿Cuál te gusta más, la primera novela o la segunda novela?

Prefiero la primera, pero me gusta la segunda también.

1. ¿Cuál te gusta más, el abrigo marrón o el abrigo negro?

_____

2. ¿Cuáles te gustan más, los libros de química o los libros de biología?

_____

3. ¿Cuál te gusta más, la oficina que tienes ahora o la oficina anterior?

_____

4. ¿Cuáles te gustan más, los suéteres de lana o los suéteres de algodón?

_____

5. ¿Cuáles te gustan más, los sándwiches de queso o los sándwiches de carne?

_____

6. ¿Cuál te gusta más, la asignatura obligatoria o la asignatura optativa?

_____

7. ¿Cuáles te gustan más, los bolígrafos rojos o los bolígrafos azules?

_____

8. ¿Cuál te gusta más, la mochila grande o la mochila pequeña?

_____

9. ¿Cuál te gusta más, el restaurante que queda en la esquina o el restaurante que queda a dos cuadras de aquí?

_____

10. ¿Cuáles te gustan más, los museos de arte o los museos de ciencias?

_____

Possessive pronouns used in comparisons. *Rewrite each sentence, replacing the italicized phrase with the corresponding possessive adjective.*

MODELO   Mi casa es más grande que *la casa de Fernanda.*
Mi casa es más grande que la suya.

1. Mi computadora es más potente que *tu computadora.*

_____

2. Mis profesores son menos estrictos que *los profesores de Mateo.*

_____

3. Tu puesto es tan interesante como *mi puesto.*

_____

4. Sus cartuchos de tinta cuestan más que *tus cartuchos de tinta.*

_____

5. Sus cursos son más fáciles que *nuestros cursos.*

_____

6. Nuestro apartamento es tan moderno como *el apartamento de Uds.*

_____

7. Tu calle es tan tranquila como *la calle de ellos.*

_____

8. Su equipo juega tan bien como *nuestro equipo.*

_____

9. Nuestra empresa gana más dinero que *la empresa de Ud.*

_____

Demonstrative pronouns. *Answer each question, using demonstrative pronouns to say that you like the first item better than the second.*

MODELO   ¿Qué sopa le gusta más? ¿Esta sopa o esa sopa?
Me gusta ésta más que ésa.

1. ¿Qué zapatería le gusta más? ¿Esta zapatería o aquella zapatería?

_____

2. ¿Qué hotel le gusta más? ¿Aquel hotel o este hotel?

_____

3. ¿Qué cuadernos le gustan más? ¿Esos cuadernos o estos cuadernos?

_____

4. ¿Qué camisas le gustan más? ¿Estas camisas o esas camisas?

_____

5. ¿Qué flauta le gusta más? ¿Aquella flauta o esta flauta?

_____

6. ¿Qué lentes de sol le gustan más? ¿Estos lentes de sol o aquellos lentes de sol?

_____

EJERCICIO

12·10

Te equivocas. *Using prepositional pronouns in your responses, tell your friend that he's wrong about who you were going to do things with or for.*

MODELO   Ibas a almorzar con Rosa, ¿verdad?
          No, con ella, no.

1. Ibas a hablar con tu jefe, ¿verdad?

_____

2. Ibas a comprar unos disquetes para Marta, ¿verdad?

_____

3. Ibas a salir al cine con Emilia y Victoria, ¿verdad?

_____

4. Ibas a trabajar en la tienda de deportes por tu hermano, ¿verdad?

_____

5. Ibas a preparar unos sándwiches para mí, ¿verdad?

_____

6. Ibas a casarte con Mariana, ¿verdad?

_____

7. Ibas a pasar por nosotros, ¿verdad?

_____

8. Ibas a jugar al tenis conmigo, ¿verdad?

_____

Translation. *Express the following sentences in Spanish.*

1. Anita is more conceited than her sister.

_____

2. Jorge is not as weird as his brother.

_____

3. You (**tú**) are as realistic as he is.

_____

4. They (*fem.*) are as disappointed as I.

_____

5. Beatriz is the most sensitive one in her family.

_____

6. That film is the best one of all.

_____

7. Your (**Ud.**) computer is more powerful than ours.

_____

8. Those ink cartridges are as expensive as these.

_____

9. This is the most beautiful city in the world.

_____

10. This house is more spacious than the previous one.

_____

11. They bought as many pens and pencils as I.

_____

12. This dishwasher works better than that one (over there).

_____

13. We're working harder than ever.

_____

14. Enrique travels as frequently as we do.

_____

15. I earned more than $250,000. (*write out the number*)

_____

Business and the cost of living • The present perfect and the past perfect

The following exercises provide written practice to reinforce your understanding of the corresponding chapter on the CD-ROM.

💿 CD-ROM

Diálogos, análisis, variantes

- ☐ 13.1 Un día de mucho ajetreo
- ☐ 13.2 Han empezado el proyecto
- ☐ 13.3 Ha muerto Ramón Fernández
- ☐ 13.4 Son puros chismes
- ☐ 13.5 Antonio no tiene pelos en la lengua
- ☐ 13.6 No nos han invitado
- ☐ 13.7 La mesa está puesta
- ☐ 13.8 Las ventanas están abiertas
- ☐ 13.9 Los informes están impresos
- ☐ 13.10 Los niños no se han acostado
- ☐ 13.11 ¡Cómo ha cambiado la ciudad!
- ☐ 13.12 El costo de la vida
- ☐ 13.13 ¡Cómo había cambiado la ciudad!
- ☐ 13.14 No habían hecho nada

Contents

- ◆ the present perfect
- ◆ the past perfect
- ◆ uses of the past participle

Communication goals

- ◆ Talking about things that have happened in the recent past
- ◆ Talking about things that had happened
- ◆ Describing a business plan
- ◆ Vocabulary: *the cost of living, urban and population growth, kitchen utensils, death and mourning*

Haber *or past participle.* *Using the cue in parentheses, complete each verb phrase with either the missing form of the auxiliary verb* **haber** *or the past participle.*

1. _____ contestado (yo)

2. han _____ (hacer)

3. hemos _____ (oír)

4. _____ comprendido (Ud.)

5. _____ vivido (Uds.)

6. ha _____ (decir)

7. _____ vuelto (tú)

8. he _____ (ver)

9. _____ elaborado (ellas)

10. hemos _____ (escribir)

11. han _____ (incluir)

12. _____ asegurado (nosotros)

Un proyecto. *Create sentences using the present perfect to tell what you and your colleagues have recently done on your project.*

MODELO   nosotros/empezar/el proyecto
          Nosotros hemos empezado el proyecto.

1. el equipo/escribir/el plan de negocios

   _____

2. Alejo y yo/hacer/el presupuesto

   _____

3. los asesores/recoger/los datos

   _____

4. el analista/analizar/los datos

   _____

5. yo/preparar/un informe

   _____

6. tú/mandar/los correos electrónicos

_____

7. Uds./reunirse/en la sala de conferencias

_____

8. Ud./atender/el teléfono

_____

9. Leonardo/diseñar/los folletos

_____

EJERCICIO

13·3

Rewrite each sentence, changing the verb from the present tense to the present perfect.

MODELO   Entran los datos.
              Han entrado los datos.

1. Envío un email.

_____

2. Él muere de una enfermedad.

_____

3. No te atreves a llamar.

_____

4. Llueve todo el día.

_____

5. Recojo los datos.

_____

6. Los meseros ponen las servilletas en la mesa.

_____

7. Es un día estupendo.

_____

8. Los jefes hacen un plan de negocios.

_____

9. Hay poca contaminación del ambiente.

_____

10. Nosotras no se lo decimos.

_____

11. Nadie quiere pagar los impuestos.

_____

12. Se incluyen los ingresos y los gastos.

_____

13. ¿Te despides de tus amigos?

_____

14. Imprimimos los documentos.

_____

15. Van al bautizo.

_____

EJERCICIO

13·4

Ya ha pasado. *Answer the following questions, using the present perfect of the verb in the question to explain that these things have already happened.*

MODELO   ¿Cuándo va María a arreglarse?

Se ha arreglado ya.

1. ¿Cuándo van Uds. a matricularse?

_____

2. ¿Cuándo va Pablo a afeitarse?

_____

3. ¿Cuándo van los Morales a mudarse?

_____

4. ¿Cuándo vas a vestirte?

_____

5. ¿Cuándo va Ud. a reunirse con ellos?

_____

6. ¿Cuándo van Beatriz y Samuel a casarse?

_____

7. ¿Cuándo va Camila a peinarse?

_____

8. ¿Cuándo vas a ducharte?

_____

EJERCICIO

13·5

Ya había pasado. *Write sentences from the strings of elements, using the preterit in the* **cuando** *clause and the past perfect in the main clause.*

MODELO   nosotros/volver del teatro/Uds./salir

Cuando nosotros volvimos del teatro, Uds. ya habían salido.

1. Fernanda/llamar/sus amigas/volver del centro comercial

_____

2. sonar el teléfono/ellos/levantarse

_____

3. despegar el avión/los pasajeros/abrocharse el cinturón de seguridad

_____

4. los invitados/llegar para cenar/Paula/poner la mesa

_____

5. yo/comprar/los cartuchos de tinta/Ud./imprimir el informe

_____

6. nosotros/ver a Antonio/su empresa/trasladarlo

_____

7. Uds./conocer a Claudia/ella/hacerse rica

_____

The past participle used as an adjective. *Complete each phrase by writing the correct adjective form derived from the verb in parentheses.*

MODELO   el documento ___*escrito*___ (escribir)

1. el condominio _____ (alquilar)

2. los carros _____ (descomponer)

3. el programa _____ (descargar)

4. unos días _____ (despejar)

5. la tienda por departamentos _____ (abrir)

6. los datos _____ (guardar)

7. las personas _____ (entusiasmar)

8. el informe _____ (imprimir)

9. el rascacielos _____ (construir)

10. las carreteras _____ (recorrer)

11. el equipaje _____ (facturar)

12. un cine _____ (cerrar)

13. la hipoteca _____ (pagar)

14. las tazas _____ (romper)

15. la invitación _____ (recibir)

16. los informes _____ (actualizar)

Write a sentence using the present perfect and the string of elements. Then write another sentence that shows the resulting condition of the sentence in the present perfect.

MODELO   él/terminar/el informe

Él ha terminado el informe.

El informe está terminado.

1. ellos/vender/su casa

_____

_____

2. ella/apagar/las luces

_____

_____

3. tú/servir/la cena

_____

_____

4. nosotros/abrir/las cajas

_____

_____

5. yo/resolver/esos problemas

_____

_____

6. Uds./elaborar/el presupuesto

_____

_____

7. Ud./recoger/los datos

_____

_____

8. él/poner/la mesa

_____

_____

9. ellas/perder/el dinero

_____

_____

10. tú y yo/lavar/los platos

_____

_____

Translation. *Express the following sentences in Spanish.*

1. Have you (**Ud.**) drawn up the budget?

   _____

2. Yes, I've included income and expenses.

   _____

3. Is the table set?

   _____

4. Yes, and dinner is served.

   _____

5. How the country has grown!

   _____

6. And the population has increased a lot.

   _____

7. Our town has become a big city.

   _____

8. There are almost five million inhabitants.

   _____

9. It has been a very difficult day.

   _____

10. Why? Have you (**tú**) had a lot of work?

    _____

11. Many skyscrapers have been built in the last ten years.

    _____

12. Indeed. Our city is very changed.

    _____

13. There's been a traffic accident in front of the bank.

    _____

14. Has someone called the police?

    _____

15. When we arrived, our friends had already had lunch.

    _____

Giving and following directions • The imperative

•14•

The following exercises provide written practice to reinforce your understanding of the corresponding chapter on the CD-ROM.

CD-ROM

Diálogos, análisis, variantes

Contents

- ◆ the imperative
- ◆ object pronouns in the imperative
- ◆ other ways of giving commands

Communication goals

- ◆ Telling someone to do or not to do something
- ◆ Asking for and giving directions
- ◆ Giving instructions for a recipe
- ◆ Vocabulary: *traffic signs and signals, at the airport, doctor's advice, a hotel emergency*

*Write an affirmative and a negative **Ud.** command for each item.*

MODELO   estacionar en la esquina
Estacione en la esquina.
No estacione en la esquina.

1. doblar a la derecha

   _____

   _____

2. llegar temprano

   _____

   _____

3. andar con cuidado

   _____

   _____

4. manejar lentamente

   _____

   _____

5. cruzar el puente

   _____

   _____

6. seguir por el río

   _____

   _____

7. irse ahora

   _____

   _____

8. salir con ellos

   _____

   _____

9. leer los correos electrónicos

   _____

   _____

10. subir al avión

_____

_____

11. acostarse a las once

_____

_____

12. vestirse

_____

_____

13. jugar al tenis

_____

_____

14. analizar los datos

_____

_____

15. ponerse los lentes de sol

_____

_____

Write an affirmative and a negative **Uds.** *command for each item.*

MODELO   abrir las ventanas

Abran las ventanas.

No abran las ventanas.

1. comer mucho

_____

_____

2. elaborar el presupuesto

_____

_____

3. añadir la sal

_____

_____

4. ver el programa

_____

_____

5. almorzar con ellos

_____

_____

6. pasearse por el parque

_____

_____

7. hacer cola

_____

_____

8. venir en taxi

_____

_____

9. despedirse de él

_____

_____

10. sentarse en el comedor

_____

_____

11. aparcar en este parquímetro

_____

_____

12. navegar en la Red

_____

_____

13. freír las papas

_____

_____

14. asistir a la conferencia

_____

_____

15. bajar en la escalera mecánica

_____

_____

En la oficina. _Write an affirmative or negative_ **Ud.** _or_ **Uds.** _command in response to each question, as indicated. Change direct object nouns to pronouns in your answers._

MODELOS   ¿Debo trabajar en el proyecto? (sí)
Sí, trabaje en el proyecto.

¿Debemos trabajar en el proyecto? (no)
No, no trabajen en el proyecto.

1. ¿Debo recoger los datos? (sí)

_____

2. ¿Debemos analizar los datos? (sí)

_____

3. ¿Debo usar mi BlackBerry? (sí)

_____

4. ¿Debo llamar al gerente de sucursal? (no)

_____

5. ¿Debemos asistir a la reunión? (sí)

_____

6. ¿Debo elaborar el presupuesto? (sí)

_____

7. ¿Debemos hacer el plan de mercadeo? (no)

_____

8. ¿Debemos reunirnos con el jefe? (sí)

_____

9. ¿Debo escribir el informe? (no)

_____

10. ¿Debemos imprimir los documentos? (no)

_____

11. ¿Debo ir a la sala de conferencias? (sí)

_____

12. ¿Debemos seguir los consejos del asesor? (sí)

_____

13. ¿Debo enviar los correos electrónicos? (no)

_____

14. ¿Debemos actualizar el sitio web? (sí)

_____

15. ¿Debo firmar el contrato? (no)

_____

Prepara la comida. *Write an affirmative* **tú** *command in response to each question. Change direct object nouns to pronouns in your answers.*

MODELO   ¿Tengo que comprar fruta?

Sí, cómprala.

1. ¿Necesito leer la receta de cocina?

_____

2. ¿Debo poner la mesa ahora?

_____

3. ¿Tengo que sacar los tenedores de la gaveta?

_____

4. ¿Debo calentar el aceite de oliva?

_____

5. ¿Necesito batir los huevos?

_____

6. ¿Debo añadir este queso?

_____

7. ¿Tengo que echar sal?

_____

8. ¿Debo freír las papas?

_____

9. ¿Debo servir la carne con las papas?

_____

10. ¿Necesito hacer el postre ahora mismo?

_____

EJERCICIO
14·5

¡Ya llega la fiesta! *Tell your nervous and excited friend how to get ready for and enjoy the party. Write an affirmative or negative* **tú** *command for each item.*

MODELO   relajarse
          Relájate.

1. tranquilizarse

_____

2. no ponerse nerviosa

_____

3. arreglarse

_____

4. tener paciencia

_____

5. no ser tonta

_____

6. pintarse la cara

_____

7. vestirse

_____

8. peinarse

_____

9. ir a la fiesta sin preocuparte

_____

10. divertirse mucho

_____

Write an affirmative and a negative **nosotros** *command for each item.*

MODELO   regresar a ese hotel
            Regresemos a ese hotel.
            No regresemos a ese hotel.

1. leer este artículo

_____

_____

2. cruzar la calle

_____

_____

3. pedir perdón

_____

_____

4. buscar un atajo

_____

_____

5. hacer turismo

_____

_____

6. ir al cine

_____

_____

7. divertirse

_____

_____

8. sentarse

_____

_____

9. dormir la siesta

_____

_____

10. traer flores

_____

_____

11. dar consejos

_____

_____

12. registrarse

_____

_____

Write an affirmative **nosotros** *command in response to each question. Express each command in two ways. Change direct object nouns to pronouns in your answers.*

MODELO   ¿Quieres entrar los datos?

Sí, entrémoslos.

Sí, vamos a entrarlos.

1. ¿Quieres ver la telenovela?

_____

_____

2. ¿Quieres discutir las ideas?

_____

_____

3. ¿Quieres descargar los documentos?

_____

_____

4. ¿Quieres conseguir los boletos?

_____

_____

5. ¿Quieres esperar a Juliana?

_____

_____

6. ¿Quieres mandar los paquetes?

_____

_____

7. ¿Quieres hacer la cena?

_____

_____

8. ¿Quieres compartir los gastos?

_____

_____

9. ¿Quieres comenzar el proyecto?

_____

_____

10. ¿Quieres pedir este vino?

_____

_____

11. ¿Quieres aparcar el carro?

_____

_____

12. ¿Quieres oír este disco compacto?

_____

_____

_____

EJERCICIO
14·8

Answer each question with an affirmative command for **Ud.** or **tú**, based on which was used in the question. Change direct object nouns to pronouns and make any other necessary changes in your answers.

MODELOS ¿Le enseño las fotos?
Sí, enséñemelas.

¿Te enseño las fotos?
Sí, enséñamelas.

1. ¿Le entrego el análisis?

_____

2. ¿Le explico mi idea?

_____

3. ¿Te muestro los cuadros?

_____

4. ¿Le doy su pasaporte?

_____

5. ¿Te pongo el abrigo?

_____

6. ¿Te hago la merienda?

_____

7. ¿Te traigo los cartuchos de tinta?

_____

This exercise uses the same questions as the previous one. This time, answer each one with a negative command for **Ud.** *or* **tú.** *Change direct object nouns to pronouns and make any other necessary changes in your answers.*

MODELOS   ¿Le enseño las fotos?

No, no me las enseñe.

¿Te enseño las fotos?

No, no me las enseñes.

1. ¿Le entrego el análisis?

_____

2. ¿Le explico mi idea?

_____

3. ¿Te muestro los cuadros?

_____

4. ¿Le doy su pasaporte?

_____

5. ¿Te pongo el abrigo?

_____

6. ¿Te hago la merienda?

_____

7. ¿Te traigo los cartuchos de tinta?

_____

Answer each question twice, once with an affirmative **tú** *command and once with an affirmative* **Ud.** *command. Change direct object nouns to pronouns and make any other necessary changes in your answers.*

MODELO   ¿Debo mandarle el paquete a Daniel?

Sí, mándaselo.

Sí, mándeselo.

1. ¿Debo darle las llaves a Pilar?

_____

_____

2. ¿Debo escribirles el email a los asesores?

_____

_____

3. ¿Debo prepararles los sándwiches a los niños?

_____

_____

4. ¿Debo pedirles el dinero a mis papás?

_____

_____

5. ¿Debo ponerme los zapatos marrones?

_____

_____

6. ¿Debo cortarme el pelo?

_____

_____

7. ¿Debo lavarle la cara al bebé?

_____

_____

8. ¿Debo quitarme la corbata?

_____

_____

*Answer each question twice, once with an affirmative **nosotros** command and once with an affirmative **Uds.** command. Change direct object nouns to pronouns and make any other necessary changes in your answers.*

MODELO　　　　¿Debemos explicarle el plan a Federico?

Sí, expliquémoselo.

Sí, explíquenselo.

1. ¿Debemos entregarle el informe a Mateo?

_____

_____

2. ¿Debemos darles los regalos a los niños?

_____

_____

3. ¿Debemos servirles el postre a nuestros invitados?

_____

_____

4. ¿Debemos desabrocharnos el cinturón de seguridad?

_____

_____

5. ¿Debemos ofrecerle el puesto a Juan Diego?

_____

_____

6. ¿Debemos mostrarle las raquetas de tenis a Carmen?

7. ¿Debemos devolverle la cámara a Rafael?

8. ¿Debemos venderles la casa a los señores Vega?

EJERCICIO
14·12

Other ways of giving commands. *Express each* **Ud.** *or* **Uds.** *command in another way, using the expression in parentheses.*

MODELOS   Vuelva más tarde. (Favor de)
Favor de volver más tarde.

Vuelvan más tarde. (Favor de)
Favor de volver más tarde.

1. Siéntese aquí. (Haga el favor de)

2. Llámenme. (Tengan la bondad de)

3. Analicen los datos. (Hagan el favor de)

4. Dígamelo. (Favor de)

5. Quédese. (Tenga la bondad de)

6. Hágamelo. (Favor de)

7. Entréguenme los papeles. (Hagan el favor de)

_____

8. Acérquense al quiosco. (Tengan la bondad de)

_____

Translation. *Express the following sentences in Spanish.*

1. Walk four blocks and turn right. (**Ud.**)

_____

2. Don't park on this street. (**Ud.**)

_____

3. Get your boarding pass but don't go to the gate yet. (**Ud.**)

_____

4. Put your hand luggage under your seats. (**Uds.**)

_____

5. The camera? Let's ask them for it.

_____

6. The cell phone? Give it to me. (**tú**)

_____

7. Don't go out. Wait for me. (**tú**)

_____

8. Let's not go to the movies today.

_____

9. Let's see the film another day.

_____

10. Fasten your seat belts. (**Uds.**)

_____

11. Be patient. Don't be in such a hurry. (**tú**)

_____

12. Add a little salt to the soup and warm it. (**Ud.**)

_____

Giving and following directions • The imperative   **135**

Plans for the holidays • The future and the conditional

The following exercises provide written practice to reinforce your understanding of the corresponding chapter on the CD-ROM.

CD-ROM

Diálogos, análisis, variantes

- ☐ 15.1 Planes para el futuro
- ☐ 15.2 Estarán muy contentos
- ☐ 15.3 El organizador de bodas
- ☐ 15.4 Celebraremos la Pascua
- ☐ 15.5 El fin de semana
- ☐ 15.6 ¿Adónde irán Uds.?
- ☐ 15.7 Buscaremos un regalo
- ☐ 15.8 En la sala de recepción
- ☐ 15.9 Habrá reunión a las dos
- ☐ 15.10 Serán las cuatro
- ☐ 15.11 ¿Dónde estará el anillo?
- ☐ 15.12 ¿Cuántos años tendrá?
- ☐ 15.13 No se podrá hacer la ensalada
- ☐ 15.14 ¿Te interesaría ver el partido de béisbol?
- ☐ 15.15 A la comisaría

Contents

- ◆ the future tense
- ◆ the future used to express probability and conjecture
- ◆ the conditional tense

Communication goals

- ◆ Telling what you will do
- ◆ Telling what you would do
- ◆ Expressing probability and conjecturing
- ◆ Vocabulary: *holidays, planning a wedding, post-graduation plans, foods*

¿Qué pasará? *Rewrite each sentence, changing the verb from the present tense to the future tense to tell what will happen.*

MODELO   Navego en la Red.

             Navegaré en la Red.

1. Él termina la maestría.

    _____

2. Uds. corren en la pista.

    _____

3. Ella recibe varios paquetes.

    _____

4. Cierro las ventanas.

    _____

5. ¿Vuelves pasado mañana?

    _____

6. Les digo qué pasó.

    _____

7. Ellos suben al séptimo piso.

    _____

8. Juegan al ajedrez.

    _____

9. Sirvo aceitunas.

    _____

10. Calienta el arroz.

    _____

11. Consigues los boletos.

    _____

12. No vienen hasta el sábado.

    _____

13. Quieren enseñarnos su casa.

    _____

14. Te despiertas a las ocho.

_____

15. ¿Uds. se ponen en contacto?

_____

¿Qué va a pasar? _Rewrite each sentence, using the future tense of the verb instead of the_ **ir a** + _infinitive construction to tell what will happen._

MODELO   Van a comer comida japonesa.
          Comerán comida japonesa.

1. Voy a asistir al concierto.

_____

2. Vamos a tomar una copa.

_____

3. ¿Vas a salir con nosotros?

_____

4. No van a caber en el taxi.

_____

5. Va a haber un desfile.

_____

6. Te va a gustar la película.

_____

7. Van a irse.

_____

8. No vamos a tener ganas de ir.

_____

9. Voy a hacer un viaje.

_____

10. ¿Vas a poder quedarte?

_____

11. Van a casarse en julio.

_____

12. Va a estar de visita.

_____

Future tense: probability and conjecture. *Rewrite each sentence, using the future tense to express probability or conjecture. Remove the word or words that express probability or conjecture in the original sentence.*

MODELO   Probablemente Gustavo vuelve antes de las once.
Gustavo volverá antes de las once.

1. Probablemente Viviana quiere ir al centro comercial.

_____

2. Supongo que hay dificultades con el proyecto.

_____

3. Me imagino que sus colegas saben la hora de la reunión.

_____

4. Probablemente es la una.

_____

5. Me imagino que tu anillo de boda vale mucho.

_____

6. Probablemente hace mucho frío mañana.

_____

7. Supongo que Joaquín está muy contento con su puesto.

_____

8. Me imagino que los gemelos tienen tres años.

_____

9. Probablemente nieva esta semana.

_____

10. Supongo que la casa cuesta más de un millón de dólares.

_____

EJERCICIO 15·4

¿Qué harías? *Complete each sentence with the correct conditional form of the verb in parentheses to tell what would happen.*

MODELO   Los empleados ___*llegarían*___ a las nueve. (llegar)

1. El cocinero _____ más ajo. (añadir)

2. Yo _____ del presupuesto. (ocuparse)

3. Mis colegas _____ español. (aprender)

4. Nosotros _____ los gastos. (compartir)

5. Uds. _____ una copa. (tomar)

6. Nosotros _____ escala en Chicago. (hacer)

7. Tú _____ conmigo. (salir)

8. Samuel _____ suerte. (tener)

9. A Mariana le _____ acompañarnos. (encantar)

10. Ellos no se lo _____ a nadie. (decir)

11. Sus suegros _____ de visita. (estar)

12. Yo _____ jugar al ajedrez. (querer)

EJERCICIO 15·5

Complete each sentence with the correct form of the verb in parentheses. Select the future or the conditional depending on the tense of the verb that appears in the main clause.

MODELOS   (venir) Ella dice que ___*vendrá*___ el lunes.

                (venir) Ella dijo que ___*vendría*___ el lunes.

1. (poder) Él nos informó que ellos no _____ ir.

2. (gustar) Creemos que te _____ este libro.

3. (mudarse) Nos escribieron que (ellos) _____ en el verano.

4. (caber) Están seguros de que todos nosotros no _____ en su furgoneta.

5. (hay) Pensaban que no _____ reunión.

6. (llover) Dicen que _____.

7. (llamar) Ella les aseguró que (ella) los _____.

8. (querer) Saben que yo no _____ llegar tarde.

Translation. *Express the following sentences in Spanish.*

1. How will they celebrate Independence Day?

_____

2. There will be a parade.

_____

3. He says that it will be hot and sunny.

_____

4. She said that it would be cloudy and it would rain.

_____

5. My in-laws will move into their new house in September.

_____

6. I wonder what time it is. (*use future of probability*)

_____

7. It's probably nine o'clock. (*use future of probability*)

_____

8. They wrote that they would take charge of the project.

_____

9. I wonder how old the twins are. (*use future of probability*)

_____

10. It would be her turn.

_____

11. Would you (**tú**) like to go out to have dinner tonight?

_____

12. I'd love to.

_____

13. I can't find my credit card. I wonder where it is.

_____

14. If you (**Uds.**) go back to the hotel, we'll go too.

_____

Talking about relationships; expressing emotions and making judgments • The present subjunctive

The following exercises provide written practice to reinforce your understanding of the corresponding chapter on the CD-ROM.

CD-ROM

Diálogos, análisis, variantes

- ☐ 16.1 La maestra y sus alumnos
- ☐ 16.2 Relaciones familiares: Rosario y su papá
- ☐ 16.3 Relaciones familiares: Jaime y su mamá
- ☐ 16.4 Quieren que me haga médico
- ☐ 16.5 Ojalá que ella cambie de idea
- ☐ 16.6 Es necesario ahorrar más
- ☐ 16.7 Es poco probable que yo pueda ir

Contents

- ◆ the present subjunctive: noun clauses

Communication goals

- ◆ Expressing emotion, value judgment, volition (imposition of will), doubt, and denial
- ◆ Vocabulary: *the classroom*, *family relations*, *choosing a career*

Present subjunctive. *Complete each sentence with the correct form of the present subjunctive of the verb in parentheses.*

MODELO   (imprimir) Quiero que Ud. ___*imprima*___ los documentos.

1. (llegar) Prefiero que Uds. _____ para las ocho.

2. (ser) Esperamos que nuestros hijos _____ muy felices.

3. (abrocharse) Nos piden que _____ el cinturón de seguridad.

4. (hay) No creo que _____ ninguna dificultad.

5. (apoyar) Se alegran de que tú los _____.

6. (poder) Dudo que ella _____ reunirse con nosotros.

7. (dar) Sienten que él no les _____ una beca.

8. (hacer) Insistimos en que Ud. nos _____ caso.

9. (ponerse) Le digo que _____ en forma.

10. (compartir) Les ruega que _____ los gastos.

11. (empezar) Te aconsejo que _____ el proyecto lo antes posible.

12. (almorzar) Nos gusta que ellos _____ con nosotros.

Present subjunctive. *Rewrite the following sentences with impersonal expressions, conjugating the verbs in the subordinate clause with the subjects shown in parentheses.*

MODELO   Es bueno oír música. (nosotros)

Es bueno que oigamos música.

1. Es necesario mantenerse en contacto. (nosotros)

_____

2. Es útil actualizar los datos. (Ud.)

_____

3. Urge ir al médico. (él)

_____

4. Es mejor jugar al tenis por la mañana. (Uds.)

_____

5. Es importante comer granos integrales. (tú)

_____

6. Más vale ir en tren. (ella)

_____

7. Es preciso hacer los trámites hoy. (yo)

_____

8. Hace falta aprender las fechas de memoria. (Uds.)

_____

9. Es imprescindible ponerse el repelente contra mosquitos. (nosotros)

_____

10. Es urgente elaborar el presupuesto hoy. (ellos)

_____

Present subjunctive or present indicative? *Complete each dependent noun clause with either the present subjunctive or the present indicative of the verb in parentheses.*

MODELOS   (mandar) Veo que ellos ___*mandan*___ los correos electrónicos.

(mandar) Necesito que ellos ___*manden*___ los correos electrónicos.

1. (volver) Sé que ellos _____ la semana entrante.

2. (hacer) Me proponen que _____ una pasantía en México.

3. (navegar) Te aconsejamos que _____ en la Red.

4. (decir) Me parece que Uds. _____ puros chismes.

5. (tener) No creo que ella _____ pelos en la lengua.

6. (gustar) Siento que no les _____ mi regalo.

7. (ser) Han oído que _____ un buen club de jazz.

8. (estar) Vemos que tú _____ muy estresado.

9. (perder) Temo que Ud. _____ el tren.

10. (construir) No permiten que se _____ un rascacielos en esta zona.

Present subjunctive or present indicative? *Rewrite each sentence using the cue in parentheses. Choose either the present subjunctive or the present indicative.*

MODELOS   Sacan buenas notas. (es que)

Es que sacan buenas notas.

Sacan buenas notas. (no es que)

No es que saquen buenas notas.

1. Son íntimos amigos. (es verdad)

_____

2. Tiene problemas de dinero. (no es cierto)

_____

3. Se pone el filtro solar. (es bueno)

_____

4. Sabe dónde están. (es dudoso)

_____

5. El sol daña la piel. (es cierto)

_____

6. Hay una reunión en la tarde. (estamos seguros)

_____

7. No se llevan bien. (es una lástima)

_____

8. Buscan casa en este barrio. (no es verdad)

_____

El maestro y sus alumnos. *The teacher insists that his students do things they don't want to do. Write sentences using the present subjunctive to tell the students what they must do.*

MODELO   Marcos: Yo no quiero mirar el mapa.

Marcos, yo insisto en que mires el mapa

1. Arturo: Yo no quiero leer este capítulo.

_____

2. Pilar: Yo no quiero sacar mi computadora.

_____

3. Gilberto: Yo no quiero dibujar con lápiz.

_____

4. Alonso: Yo no quiero sentarme al lado de Javier.

_____

5. Flor: Yo no quiero tomar apuntes.

_____

6. Marisol: Yo no quiero traer mi libro de texto.

_____

7. Andrés: Yo no quiero comenzar la composición.

_____

8. Silvia: Yo no quiero aprender las fechas de memoria.

_____

9. Octavio: Yo no quiero prepararme para el examen.

_____

10. Catalina: Yo no quiero hacer la tarea.

_____

EJERCICIO
16·6

Commands and present subjunctive. *Use the cues in parentheses to express each* **tú** *command as a sentence using the present subjunctive.*

MODELO   Vive la vida plenamente. (Espero)
         Espero que vivas la vida plenamente.

1. Cuídate mucho. (Te aconsejo)

_____

2. Sal con nosotros al cine. (Quiero)

_____

3. Date prisa. (Es necesario)

_____

4. Oye esta música. (Prefiero)

_____

5. Apaga la computadora. (Te pido)

_____

6. Sigue por esta avenida. (Te recomiendo)

_____

7. Ponte los guantes. (Es preciso)

_____

8. Ven a vernos. (Me alegro de)

_____

9. Ve a registrarte. (Es imprescindible)

_____

10. Dime qué pasó. (Insisto en)

_____

11. Ten paciencia. (Te exijo)

_____

12. Sécate el pelo. (Hace falta)

_____

13. Actualiza los datos. (Dudo)

_____

14. Hazme caso. (No creo)

_____

15. Reúnete conmigo lo antes posible. (Es importante)

_____

EJERCICIO
16·7

Translation. *Express the following sentences in Spanish.*

1. Sofía wants to marry Sergio.

_____

2. Her parents prefer that she marry Santiago.

_____

3. Carlitos, I insist that you do your homework now.

_____

4. But I want to go out to play baseball.

   _____

5. We have to prepare for the quiz.

   _____

6. The teacher demands that we memorize all the dates.

   _____

7. I'm glad to be able to stay with you (**Uds.**).

   _____

8. We're glad that you (**tú**) are staying with us.

   _____

9. I doubt there's a meeting this week.

   _____

10. It's important that the students get good grades.

    _____

11. It's necessary that we support our friends.

    _____

12. I advise you (**Ud.**) to save more money.

    _____

13. It's true that I spend an awful lot.

    _____

14. I don't think they're coming on Saturday.

    _____

15. I'm sorry we won't see each other.

    _____

APPENDIX
Grammar summaries

Absolute superlative

The absolute superlative is a Latin term used for the suffix -**ísimo** in Spanish, a suffix that is the equivalent of *very*. The addition of the suffix -**ísimo** creates a new four-form adjective. (See *Adjectives*.) The final vowel of the masculine singular form of the adjective is dropped before the -**ísimo** ending. If the masculine singular form of the adjective ends in a consonant, the suffix -**ísimo** is added directly to the adjective.

caro → carísimo	*very expensive*
contento → contentísimo	*very happy*
raro → rarísimo	*very strange*
tonto → tontísimo	*very silly*
inteligente → inteligentísimo	*very intelligent*
potente → potentísimo	*very powerful*
difícil → dificilísimo	*very difficult*

Adverbs can be formed by adding -**mente** to the feminine singular form of the absolute superlative.

rarísimamente	*very strangely*
tontísimamente	*very stupidly*

Adverbs of quantity also have absolute superlative forms.

mucho → muchísimo	*very much*
poco → poquísimo	*very little*

Adjectives or adverbs of quantity whose last consonant is **c** or **g** change **c** → **qu** and **g** → **gu** before the ending -**ísimo**.

poco → poquísimo	*very little*
simpático → simpatiquísimo	*very nice, very pleasant*
largo → larguísimo	*very long*

Adjectives

Spanish adjectives are part of the noun phrase. They modify or describe the noun that is the head of the noun phrase. Like all modifiers of the noun, Spanish adjectives agree with the noun—most adjectives agree in gender and number, while some agree only in number.

Spanish adjectives are divided into two broad categories: adjectives that have a masculine singular form ending in -**o** and adjectives that have a masculine singular form ending in a consonant or in a vowel other than **o**.

Adjectives that have a masculine singular form ending in -**o** have four forms. They agree with the noun they modify or describe in gender and number.

	MASCULINE	FEMININE
singular	un regalo **caro**	una computadora **cara**
plural	unos regalos **caros**	unas computadoras **caras**

Thus the masculine singular of an adjective having four forms ends in -**o**, the feminine singular in -**a**. An -**s** is added to the singular forms to form the plural. This -**s** is pronounced /s/ like the double *s* in English *class*, not /z/ like the single *s* in English *present*.

Adjectives that have a masculine singular form ending in a consonant or in a vowel other than **o** have two forms. They agree with the noun they modify or describe in number but have the same form for both masculine and feminine.

	MASCULINE	FEMININE
singular	un curso **interesante**	una película **interesante**
plural	unos cursos **interesantes**	unas películas **interesantes**

	MASCULINE	FEMININE
singular	un libro **difícil**	una novela **difícil**
plural	unos libros **difíciles**	unas novelas **difíciles**

Adjectives ending in -**e** add -**s** to form the plural (**interesante** → **interesantes**). Adjectives ending in a consonant add -**es** to form the plural (**difícil** → **difíciles**).

Adjectives of nationality

Some adjectives of nationality do not follow the pattern of other adjectives.

Adjectives of nationality ending in -**o** or -**e** have the expected number of forms. Adjectives of nationality ending in -**o** have four forms; those ending in -**e** have two. Note that adjectives of nationality are not capitalized in Spanish.

	MASCULINE	FEMININE
singular	un restaurante **mexicano**	una comida **mexicana**
plural	unos restaurantes **mexicanos**	unas comidas **mexicanas**

	MASCULINE	FEMININE
singular	un periódico **árabe**	una revista **árabe**
plural	unos periódicos **árabes**	unas revistas **árabes**

Most adjectives of nationality ending in -**e** end in the suffix -**ense**.

	MASCULINE	FEMININE
singular	un periódico **canadiense**	una revista **canadiense**
plural	unos periódicos **canadienses**	unas revistas **canadienses**

Here are some adjectives of nationality ending in vowels other than **e**.

SINGULAR	PLURAL	
belga	belgas	*Belgian*
saudita	sauditas	*Saudi*
iraní	iraníes	*Iranian*
iraquí	iraquíes	*Iraqi*
israelí	israelíes	*Israeli*
hindú	hindúes	*Hindu, Indian*

Adjectives of nationality ending in a consonant have four forms, not two like other adjectives ending in a consonant. Here are the adjectives **español** *Spanish*, **francés** *French*, and **alemán** *German*.

	MASCULINE	FEMININE
singular	español	española
plural	español**es**	español**as**

	MASCULINE	FEMININE
singular	francés	francesa
plural	frances**es**	frances**as**

	MASCULINE	FEMININE
singular	alemán	alemana
plural	aleman**es**	aleman**as**

Note that adjectives of nationality having an accent mark on the final syllable in the masculine singular lose that written accent in the other three forms. (See *Placement of accent marks*.)

Other common adjectives of nationality ending in a consonant:

danés	*Danish*	libanés	*Lebanese*
escocés	*Scottish*	neocelandés	*New Zealander*
finlandés	*Finnish*	portugués	*Portuguese*
holandés	*Dutch*	tailandés	*Thai*
inglés	*English*	taiwanés	*Taiwanese*
irlandés	*Irish*	vietnamés	*Vietnamese*
japonés	*Japanese*		

A citizen of the United States is called **americano** or **norteamericano** in Spanish. **Americano** is common in Spain. In Spanish America, **americano** can also mean *someone from the Americas*. The term **norteamericano** is therefore clearer when referring to a United States citizen. The adjective **estadounidense** may be used in formal language to refer to someone or something from the United States.

Position of adjectives

Adjectives in Spanish normally follow the noun, rather than preceding it as in English.

un hotel **caro**	*an expensive hotel*
una escritora **española**	*a Spanish writer*
un proyecto **importante**	*an important project*

However, certain types of adjectives precede the noun they modify.

1. Adjectives that express quantity

mucho, mucha	*much, a lot of*
muchos, muchas	*many, a lot of*
poco, poca	*little, not much*
pocos, pocas	*few, not many*
bastante, bastantes	*quite a lot of (Latin America); enough (Spain)*
suficiente, suficientes	*enough*
¿cuánto?, ¿cuánta?	*how much?*
¿cuántos?, ¿cuántas?	*how many?*
alguno, alguna, algunos, algunas	*some (See Short forms of adjectives.)*
ninguno, ninguna	*no, none (See Short forms of adjectives.)*
ambos, ambas	*both*
varios, varias	*several*
muchos asesores extranjeros	*many foreign consultants*
pocos restaurantes griegos	*few Greek restaurants*
ambas regiones chilenas	*both Chilean regions*
suficiente dinero	*enough money*

The adjective **todo** also belongs in this category. [See *Todo (adjectives)*.]

todo el pescado	*all the fish*
toda la música	*all the music*
todos los edificios nuevos	*all the new buildings*
todas las enfermeras hispanoamericanas	*all the Spanish-American nurses*

2. Ordinal numbers

el **tercer** día	*the third day*
el **quinto** piso	*the fifth floor*
la **décima** edición	*the tenth edition*

3. Adjectives used in exclamations after **¡Qué!**

¡Qué **hermoso** monumento!	*What a beautiful monument!*
¡Qué **maravilloso** paisaje!	*What a wonderful landscape!*
¡Qué **linda** idea!	*What a lovely idea!*
¡Qué **feos** días!	*What nasty days!*

4. Adjectives that express a subjective judgment made by the speaker rather than an objective description. The adjectives **bueno** *good*, **malo** *bad*, **mejor** *better/best* and **peor** *worse/worst* fall into this category.

una **buena** persona	*a good person*
un **mal** día	*a bad day*
los **peores** problemas posibles	*the worst problems possible*
la **mejor** idea	*the best idea*
un **horrible** chisme	*a horrible piece of gossip*
una **magnífica** oportunidad	*a magnificent opportunity*
un **maravilloso** espectáculo	*a wonderful show*

5. Adjectives that express a quality known to all rather than new information about the noun

la **verde** hierba	*the green grass*
la **blanca** nieve	*the white snow*

6. Some adjectives can appear either before or after the noun, but then the meaning changes depending on the position of the adjective.

nuestro **antiguo** profesor	*our former teacher*
un cementerio **antiguo**	*an ancient cemetery*
cierto análisis	*a certain analysis*
una cosa **cierta**	*a sure thing*
un **nuevo** proyecto	*another project*
un proyecto **nuevo**	*a new project*
este **pobre** país	*this poor country (unfortunate)*
un país **pobre**	*a poor country (economically depressed)*
un **gran** hombre	*a great man*
un hombre **grande**	*a big man*
diferentes posibilidades	*various possibilities*
posibilidades **diferentes**	*different possibilities*
Luis es **medio** brasileño.	*Luis is half Brazilian.*
el brasileño **medio**	*the average Brazilian*
Es el **mismo** programa.	*It's the same program.*
El problema es el programa **mismo**.	*The problem is the program itself.*
Las bebidas allí son **pura** agua.	*The drinks there are nothing but water.*
Hay que beber agua **pura**.	*You should drink pure water.*
un **simple** empleado	*a mere employee*
una muchacha **simple**	*a simple girl*
cualquier persona	*any person*
una persona **cualquiera**	*a vulgar person*
la **única** persona	*the only person*
una persona **única**	*a unique person*

Short forms of adjectives

The adjectives **bueno** *good* and **malo** *bad*, the ordinal numbers **primero** *first* and **tercero** *third*, the indefinite article **uno**, and **alguno** *some* and **ninguno** *no* lose their final -o before a masculine singular noun or before an adjective preceding a masculine singular noun.

un **buen** libro	*a good book*
but	
una **buena** revista	*a good magazine*
un **mal** día	*a bad day*
but	
una **mala** semana	*a bad week*
mi **primer** viaje	*my first trip*
el **tercer** mes	*the third month*

Note however that if these adjectives follow a masculine singular noun the full form is used.

Felipe **Tercero**	*Philip the Third*
el siglo **primero**	*the first century*

Alguno *some* and **ninguno** *no* add an accent mark over the **u** when the final -**o** is dropped. Notice that **alguno** and **ninguno** can stand before other adjectives.

algún buen vino chileno	*some good Chilean wine*
No hay **ningún** restaurante abierto.	*There is no open restaurant.*

The adjective **grande** shortens to **gran** before any singular noun, whether masculine or feminine. **Gran** means *great*.

un **gran** músico alemán	*a great German musician*
una **gran** bailarina rusa	*a great Russian ballet dancer*

Grande does not shorten before plural nouns or when it follows the noun with the meaning *big*.

grandes artistas italianos	*great Italian artists*
un muchacho **grande**	*a big boy*

The adjective **cualquiera** *any* shortens to **cualquier** before any singular noun, whether masculine or feminine.

cualquier postre	*any dessert*
cualquier bebida	*any beverage*

Adverbs

Most adverbs of manner in Spanish are formed by adding the suffix -**mente** to the feminine singular form of the adjective.

MASCULINE SINGULAR	FEMININE SINGULAR	ADVERB	MEANING
cómodo	cómoda	cómodamente	*comfortably*
cuidadoso	cuidadosa	cuidadosamente	*carefully*
generoso	generosa	generosamente	*generously*
lento	lenta	lentamente	*slowly*
nervioso	nerviosa	nerviosamente	*nervously*

If the adjective has only one form for the masculine and feminine singular, then the suffix -**mente** is added to that form.

SINGULAR	ADVERB	MEANING
fácil	fácilmente	*easily*
inteligente	inteligentemente	*intelligently*
regular	regularmente	*regularly*

Adverbs in -**mente** have two stresses in speech, one on the adjective and one on the first **e** of the suffix -**mente**.

Adverbs modify verbs or adjectives. They add the idea of time, place, quantity, doubt, or manner to the sentence. Adverbs of time, place, quantity, and doubt are usually not derived from adjectives in Spanish or in English.

hoy *today*

No sé si vienen **hoy**.   *I don't know if they're coming **today**.*

aquí *here*

Todos se reúnen **aquí**.   *Everyone gets together **here**.*

mucho *a lot*

Ese hombre trabaja **mucho**.   *That man works **a lot**.*

quizás (also: **quizá**) *maybe*

Quizás no pudieron salir.   ***Maybe** they couldn't go out.*

The masculine singular of adjectives is often used as an adverb, especially in informal speech.

¿Es mejor jugar **feo** y ganar o jugar **bonito** y perder?	*Is it better to play dirty and win or play fair and lose?*
No te entienden porque no hablas **claro**.	*They don't understand you because you don't speak **clearly**.*

Spanish often uses a phrase consisting of **con** + a noun instead of an adverb in **-mente**.

Lo hicieron **con cuidado**.	*They did it **carefully**.*
Ella se viste **con elegancia**.	*She dresses **elegantly**.*
Trabajaron **con entusiasmo**.	*They worked **enthusiastically**.*

Al + infinitive

A clause beginning with **cuando** *when* can be replaced by a phrase consisting of **al** + the infinitive of the verb.

Siempre lo veo **cuando salgo**. → Siempre lo veo **al salir**.	*I always see him when I go out.*
Se alegraron **cuando te vieron**. → Se alegraron **al verte**.	*They were happy when they saw you.*
Cuando oí eso, me enojé. → **Al oír eso**, me enojé.	*When I heard that, I got angry.*

The **al** + infinitive phrase can replace a clause beginning with **cuando** when the subjects of the two clauses are the same.

Note that English has a construction consisting of *upon* plus the *-ing* form of the verb that is the equivalent of the Spanish **al** + infinitive phrase:

Upon hearing that, I got angry.

This English construction, however, is typical of formal or literary language. The Spanish **al** + infinitive phrase is used in all levels of language.

Articles

Like English, Spanish has a definite article (equivalent to *the*) and an indefinite article (equivalent to *a, an*). The Spanish articles agree in gender and number with the noun they refer to. Here are the forms of the definite article in Spanish.

	MASCULINE	FEMININE
singular	**el** carro	**la** caja
plural	**los** carros	**las** cajas

The indefinite article in Spanish has plural forms as well. These plural forms are sometimes used in Spanish where in English no article would be used at all, and sometimes they are the equivalent of English *some*. Sometimes the plural indefinite article is used in Spanish before nouns that usually come in pairs, such as *eyes* or *ears*, or nouns that have no singular, such as *scissors*. Here are the forms of the indefinite article in Spanish.

	MASCULINE	FEMININE
singular	**un** carro	**una** caja
plural	**unos** carros	**unas** cajas

Uses of the articles

1. When a noun is used in a general sense it is preceded by the definite article in Spanish. English does not use an article in these cases.

   ### a) abstract nouns

La vida es muy difícil en aquella ciudad.	*Life is very hard in that city.*
La sinceridad es una virtud.	*Sincerity is a virtue.*
No hay nada más importante que **la libertad**.	*There's nothing more important than freedom.*

   ### b) concrete nouns referring to the noun in a general sense

El queso es un buen alimento.	*Cheese is a good food.*
El oro puede ser una buena inversión.	*Gold can be a good investment.*
El español es un idioma importante.	*Spanish is an important language.*

2. Spanish omits the indefinite article before a predicate nominative indicating a person's profession, nationality, or religion.

Ella es **abogada**.	*She's a lawyer.*
Este estudiante es **español**.	*This student is a Spaniard.*
Juan es **católico**.	*Juan's a Catholic.*

   However, if the predicate nominative noun of profession, nationality, or religion is modified, the indefinite article is used, as in English.

Ella es **una abogada muy conocida**.	*She's a very famous lawyer.*
Juan es **un católico practicante**.	*Juan's an observant Catholic.*

Augmentatives

The most common augmentative ending in Spanish is **-ón/-ona**. Augmentatives denote largeness but also other meanings, such as disparagement. When the suffix **-ón/-ona** is added to a verb root it denotes *given to, habitually performing* the action of the verb.

hombre → hombrón	*big man*
preguntar → preguntón	*asking many questions, inquisitive, nosey*

The suffixes **-ote/-ota** and **-azo/-aza** are also used to form augmentatives.

libro → librote	*big book*
grande → grandote, grandota	*very big, enormous*
éxito → exitazo	*smash hit*

Comparative

The comparative of adjectives is relatively simple in Spanish. Here is the basic pattern:

más/menos + adjective + **que**

Más is the equivalent of English *more* + adjective or the suffix *-er*.

más inteligente que	*more intelligent than*
más bonito que	*prettier than*

Menos means *less* but is usually translated as *not as*.

menos interesante que	*less interesting than, not as interesting as*

Spanish uses **tan** + adjective + **como** to express the comparison of equality.

tan terco como	*as stubborn as*
tan aburrido como	*as boring as*

The adjectives **bueno** and **malo** have irregular comparative forms.

mejor	*better*
peor	*worse*
Este hotel es mejor que el otro.	*This hotel is better than the other one.*
Su situación es peor que la nuestra.	*Their situation is worse than ours.*

Más bueno and **más malo** refer to moral qualities.

Ese chico es más bueno que el pan.	*That boy is as good as gold. (literally, better than bread)*
Aquella mujer es más mala que su hermana.	*That woman is worse than her sister.*

The comparatives **más grande** and **más pequeño** are replaced by **mayor** and **menor** when referring to age.

Mi hermano es mayor que yo.	*My brother is older than I.*
Mi hermano es más grande que yo.	*My brother is bigger (taller) than I.*
Su esposa es menor que él.	*His wife is younger than he.*
Su esposa es más pequeña que él.	*His wife is shorter than he.*

Adverbs are compared in the same way as adjectives.

Se viaja más cómodamente en tren que en autobús.	*One travels more comfortably by train than by bus.*
Se viaja menos cómodamente en burro que en carro.	*One travels less comfortably on a donkey than by car.*
Se viaja tan cómodamente en tren como en avión.	*One travels as comfortably by train as by plane.*

When nouns are the object of comparison, **más** + noun + **que** and **menos** + noun + **que** are used.

Él escribe más informes que yo.	*He writes more reports than I.*
Él escribe menos informes que yo.	*He writes fewer reports than I, not as many reports as I.*

Tan changes to **tanto** before a noun, and agrees with the noun in gender and number.

Él escribe tantos informes como yo.	*He writes as many reports as I do.*

Más que, **menos que**, and **tanto como** can also modify verbs.

Ella trabaja **más que** yo.	*She works more than I do.*
Ella trabaja **menos que** yo.	*She works less than I do.*
Ella trabaja **tanto como** yo.	*She works as much as I do.*

Note that colloquial English allows the use of object pronouns after *than*, even when grammatically, a subject pronoun is required: *She works more than me.* This is impossible in Spanish.

After **que** *than*, Spanish uses negative words such as **nada, nadie, nunca** where English uses indefinites.

La salud es más importante **que nada**.	*Health is more important than anything.*
Él estudia más **que nadie**.	*He studies more than anyone.*
Ahora la comida cuesta más **que nunca**.	*Now food costs more than ever.*

Que is replaced by **de** before a numeral.

En esta oficina trabajan **más de cincuenta** personas.	*More than fifty people work in this office.*

However, if the meaning is *only*, **más que** is used. In this case the verb is usually negative.

No cursa más que dos materias.	*He's only taking two subjects.*
No me quedan más que cuatro dólares.	*I have only four dollars left.*

Compound nouns

Many Spanish compound nouns are formed with the preposition **de**. The English equivalent of these compound nouns usually consists of two juxtaposed nouns, but in the opposite order from Spanish.

tienda + zapatos → tienda de zapatos	*store + shoe → shoestore*
tienda + electrodomésticos → tienda de electrodomésticos	*store + appliance(s) → appliance store*
museo + arte → museo de arte	*museum + art → art museum*
base + datos → base de datos	*base + data → database*
libro + texto → libro de texto	*book + text → textbook*
tarjeta + embarque → tarjeta de embarque	*pass + boarding → boarding pass*
tarjeta + crédito → tarjeta de crédito	*card + credit → credit card*

Sometimes other prepositions are used instead of **de**.

la tienda **por** departamentos	*department store*

These compound nouns function as nouns.
They enter into noun phrases:

esas quince nuevas **tiendas de cómputo**	*those fifteen new computer stores*

They can be the subject or object of a verb:

La tienda por departamentos es muy grande.	*The department store is very big.*
Siempre miramos **este programa de televisión**.	*We always watch this television show.*

They can function as the object of a preposition:

Trabajan en **la oficina de turismo**.	*They work at the tourist office.*

Conditional tense

The conditional tense is formed by adding the imperfect tense endings of **-er** and **-ir** verbs to the infinitive. All verbs, including **-ar** verbs, use these endings in the conditional.

Trabajaría.	*I would work.*
Aprendería.	*I would learn.*
Viviría.	*I would live.*

trabajar *to work*

trabajaría	trabajaríamos
trabajarías	trabajaríais
trabajaría	trabajarían

aprender *to learn*

aprendería	aprenderíamos
aprenderías	aprenderíais
aprendería	aprenderían

vivir *to live*

viviría	viviríamos
vivirías	viviríais
viviría	vivirían

The same twelve verbs that have modified infinitive forms in the future have them in the conditional. These verbs have the same endings as the verbs in the charts above. The **yo** form is shown as a model for the entire conjugation.

INFINITIVE	*CONDITIONAL*
poner	**pondría**
salir	**saldría**
tener	**tendría**
valer	**valdría**
venir	**vendría**
caber	**cabría**
haber	**habría**
poder	**podría**
querer	**querría**
saber	**sabría**
decir	**diría**
hacer	**haría**

Compounds of verbs that have modified infinitives in the conditional have the same modification in the conditional: **componer → compondría, mantener → mantendría, convenir → convendría, rehacer → reharía.**

The conditional of **hay**, derived from **haber**, is **habría** *there would be.*

-Ir verbs that have an accent mark in the infinitive, such as **oír** *to hear*, **freír** *to fry*, and **reír** *to laugh*, lose that accent mark in the conditional tense: **freiría, oiría, reiría.**

The conditional is used in hypotheses and statements about what *would* happen.

¿Qué haría Ud.?	*What would you do?*
Yo no diría nada.	*I wouldn't say anything.*
¡Con una prometida como la tuya, yo no me casaría nunca!	*With a fiancée like yours, I would never get married!*

Conjunctions

Conjunctions are words that serve to join sentences together into a single sentence. The most common conjunctions in Spanish are **y, pero, que, porque**, and **si. Y** and **pero** are coordinating conjunctions. They link sentences that are of equal importance in the resultant compound sentence. The two sentences joined by **y** or **pero** can stand as independent sentences.

Él me pidió el libro y yo se lo di.	*He asked me for the book and I gave it to him.*
Mi hija trabaja, pero mi hijo estudia.	*My daughter is working, but my son is studying.*

Que, porque, and **si** are subordinating conjunctions. They incorporate a sentence into a larger sentence as a dependent clause.

Creo que él ha terminado el proyecto.	*I think that he has completed the project.*
Compré agua porque tenía sed.	*I bought water because I was thirsty.*
No sé si los estudiantes se han inscrito.	*I don't know whether the students have registered.*

The conjunction **que** may be followed by the indicative or the subjunctive, depending on the verb of the main clause.

Estoy seguro de **que** él **viene**.	*I'm sure that he's coming.*
No quiero **que** él **venga**.	*I don't want him to come.*

Contractions

The prepositions **a** and **de** contract with the masculine singular definite article **el** to form **al** and **del** respectively.

Voy **al** museo. (**a** + **el**)	*I'm going to the museum.*
Es el cartapacio **del** director. (**de** + **el**)	*It's the director's briefcase.*

The prepositions **a** and **de** do not contract with the other forms of the definite article.

Se lo dije **a los** muchachos.	*I told the boys.*
Salen **de la** heladería.	*They're coming out of the ice cream store.*

The prepositions **a** and **de** do not contract with the pronoun **él** *he, it.*

¿Por qué se lo diste **a él**?	*Why did you give it to him?*
El condominio no es **de él**.	*The condominium doesn't belong to him.*

Dar: idioms with dar

Some of the same idioms that use **tener** (see *Tener: idioms with* **tener**) can also be constructed with **dar** + indirect object to express the idea of *making someone feel something*.

darle hambre a uno	*to make someone hungry*
darle sed a uno	*to make someone thirsty*
darle sueño a uno	*to make someone sleepy*
darle calor a uno	*to make someone feel warm*
darle frío a uno	*to make someone feel cold*
darle miedo a uno	*to make someone feel afraid*
darle la razón a uno	*to admit that someone is right*
El ejercicio **nos da sed**.	*Exercise makes us thirsty.*
La situación política **me da miedo**.	*The political situation frightens me.*
Tuve que **darle la razón**.	*I had to admit he was right.*

Dates

Dates in Spanish, except for the first of the month, are expressed with cardinal numbers, not with ordinal numbers as in English.

el primero de enero, febrero, marzo	*the first of January, February, March*
el tres de abril, mayo, junio	*the third of April, May, June*
el catorce de julio, agosto, septiembre	*the fourteenth of July, August, September*
el veintinueve de octubre, noviembre, diciembre	*the twenty-ninth of October, November, December*

Note that the months begin with lowercase letters in Spanish.

The form **el uno de** *the first of* also exists:

el uno de septiembre	*the first of September*

Demonstrative adjectives and pronouns

Spanish has a set of three demonstratives, whereas English has only two:

este	*this (near the speaker)*
ese	*that (near the person spoken to)*
aquel	*that (removed from both the speaker and the person spoken to)*

These demonstratives correspond to the Spanish division of place:

aquí	*here (near the speaker)*
ahí	*there (near the person spoken to)*
allí	*there (removed from both the speaker and the person spoken to)*

The demonstratives, like the articles, agree with the noun they refer to in gender and number. The masculine singular form is slightly irregular. (It does not end in **-o**.) The remaining three forms look like any other adjective.

MASCULINE SINGULAR	MASCULINE PLURAL	FEMININE SINGULAR	FEMININE PLURAL
este	estos	esta	estas
ese	esos	esa	esas
aquel	aquellos	aquella	aquellas

—**Este** café es muy bueno.	*This café is very good.*
—Sí, pero **aquel** café es menos caro.	*Yes, but that café (over there) is less expensive.*
—**Esos** documentos son muy importantes.	*Those documents are very important.*
—Vamos a guardarlos en **esta** caja fuerte.	*Let's put them away in this safe.*

Demonstrative adjectives may be nominalized (made to function as pronouns) by dropping the noun they precede. A written accent is usually added to the stressed vowel of the demonstrative when it is nominalized. (See *Nominalization*.)

Esta cámara es mejor que **ésa.**	*This camera is better than that one.*
Esos carros son más caros que **aquéllos.**	*Those cars are more expensive than those (over there).*

For many speakers of American Spanish, **aquel** is replaced by **ese**. **Aquel** is often limited to refer to events that happened far back in the past.

Aquella fiesta fue maravillosa.	*That party was wonderful.*
Aquellos años cambiaron mi vida.	*Those years changed my life.*

Each of the demonstratives also has a neuter form: **esto, eso, aquello**. See *Neuters*.

Determiners

Determiners are a small class of words, largely grammatical, whose function is to stand first in a noun phrase. Among the determiners are the articles, demonstrative adjectives, possessive adjectives, and words like *some, no*, etc. In most cases, only one determiner can occur at the head of a noun phrase.

el libro   *esa* tienda
mi amigo   *algunos* restaurantes

Diminutives

Spanish makes great use of diminutives. The most common diminutive ending in Spanish is **-ito/-ita**. Diminutive endings are most commonly added to nouns, but appear also with adjectives.

libro → librito
casa → casita

Diminutives in Spanish express a variety of meanings, not only small size. They can express affection, sarcasm, politeness, reluctance to describe, etc.

Tienen una casita en el campo.	*They have a small house in the country.*
El perrito de ellos es muy cariñoso.	*Their dog is very affectionate.*
La comidita que prepararon fue horrible.	*That dinner they prepared was awful.*
Él es timidito.	*He's somewhat shy.*

Diminutives are very common with proper names. Notice that in spelling the letters **c** and **g** change to **qu** and **gu** before the diminutive ending.

Luis → Luisito
Paco → Paquito
Elena → Elenita
Diego → Dieguito
Sara → Sarita

Words that end in **e, n, r**, or a stressed vowel, as well as words of one syllable, take **-cito/-cita**.

pobre → pobrecito
papá → papacito
tren → trencito
pan → pancito

Nouns of two syllables whose first syllable has **ie** or **ue** and which end in **-o** or **-a** drop the **-o** or **-a** and add **-ecito/-ecita**. The same is true of many one-syllable nouns ending in a consonant.

tienda → tiendecita
puerta → puertecita
flor → florecita

However, the rules vary from country to country, especially for words of one syllable. **Papito, trenecito** and **panecito** also are current.

Direct object

The direct object is a noun or pronoun that completes the thought of a verb by serving as the goal of the action.

Spanish has two kinds of direct objects.

1. Inanimate direct objects. They are connected to the verb without any preposition.

Voy a comprar **este traje**.	*I'm going to buy **this suit**.*
Vimos **la nueva película inglesa**.	*We saw **the new English film**.*

2. Animate direct objects. They are connected to the verb by means of the preposition **a**. This use of **a** is called *personal **a***. The animate object must be specific and identifiable to require the use of *personal **a***.

¿Conoces **a esa señora**?	*Do you know **that woman**?*
No llamé **a Carmen**, pero sí llamé **a su hermano**.	*I didn't call **Carmen** but I did call **her brother**.*

Direct object pronouns

Direct object nouns may be replaced by direct object pronouns once it is clear whom or what they refer to.

Direct object pronouns in standard Latin American usage:

PERSON	SINGULAR	PLURAL
first	me	nos
second	te	(os)
third	lo, la	los, las

Note that **lo** and **la** refer to both people and things. The direct object pronoun **lo** replaces both people and things that are grammatically masculine singular. Thus, **lo** means both *him* and *it*. The direct object pronoun **la** replaces both people and things that are grammatically feminine singular. Thus, **la** means both *her* and *it*. In the plural, note that English *them* refers to both people and things just like Spanish **los** and **las**, but Spanish **los** and **las** reflect the gender of the nouns they replace as well.

Note: The pronoun **os** appears here in parentheses because the **vosotros** form is not used in Latin America. See *Subject pronouns*.

The direct object pronouns **lo, la, los** and **las** also mean *you* when referring to **usted** or **ustedes**.

Creo que **lo** conozco, señor.	*I think I know you, sir.*
Creo que **la** conozco, señora.	*I think I know you, ma'am.*
Creo que **los** conozco, señores.	*I think I know you, gentlemen.*
Creo que **las** conozco, señoras.	*I think I know you, ladies.*

Regional usage: In parts of Spain, **lo** is replaced by **le** when referring to a person, but not when referring to an object. Thus, in these varieties of Spanish the following pairs of sentences use different object pronouns.

¿Qué es ese libro? No lo conocemos.	*What book is that? We are not familiar with it.*
¿Quién es ese señor? No le conocemos.	*Who is that man? We don't know him.*

In Latin America both sentences would read **No *lo* conocemos**.

The plural **los** may be replaced by **les** when referring to people, but this is less common.

In many parts of Latin America **le** and **les** are used as the direct object pronouns corresponding to **Ud.** and **Uds.**, respectively.

Si hay un problema, nosotros **le**   *If there is a problem, we will contact you.*
contactamos.

Double object pronouns

In standard English a direct and indirect object pronoun do not occur together. When a direct and indirect object are present in the same sentence, the indirect object must appear in a prepositional phrase.

I give it *to him.*

In Spanish, however, an indirect object pronoun and a direct object pronoun can appear together, both dependent on the same verb. The indirect object pronoun precedes the direct object pronoun. Here are the possible combinations with a first- or second-person indirect object pronoun.

me lo, me la	*it to me*	nos lo, nos la	*it to us*
me los, me las	*them to me*	nos los, nos las	*them to us*
te lo, te la	*it to you*	os lo, os la	*it to you*
te los, te las	*them to you*	os los, os las	*them to you*

The indirect object pronouns of the third person, **le** and **les**, change to **se** before **lo**, **la**, **los** and **las**.

| **se lo, se la** | *it to him, to her, to you, to them, to you plural* |
| **se los, se las** | *them to him, to her, to you, to them, to you plural* |

If speakers need to focus on the person to whom **se** refers, they add a phrase beginning with the preposition **a**.

Se lo presté **a ella**, no **a él**.   *I lent it to her, not to him.*
Él se los pidió **a Ud.**   *He asked you for them.*

Like single object pronouns, double object pronouns precede the conjugated verb. In verb + infinitive constructions, double object pronouns may either precede the conjugated verb or follow the infinitive. When they follow, they are attached to the infinitive in writing and an accent mark is added to the vowel before the **r** of the infinitive.

¿**Me lo** vas a explicar?   }
¿Vas a explic**ármelo**?   }   *Are you going to explain it to me?*

El with feminine nouns

When a feminine noun begins with a stressed /a/ sound (written **a** or **ha**), it takes the singular article **el**, not **la**.

el agua   *water*
el hambre   *hunger*

Adjectives that modify these nouns are feminine singular.

el agua fría   *cold water*
tanta hambre   *so much hunger*

In the plural **las** is used: **las** aguas.

Estar

Estar *to be* is an irregular **-ar** verb. Its conjugation is as follows.

SINGULAR	PLURAL

Present tense

estoy	estamos
estás	estáis
está	están

Preterit tense

estuve	estuvimos
estuviste	estuvisteis
estuvo	estuvieron

Imperfect tense

estaba	estábamos
estabas	estabais
estaba	estaban

Future tense

estaré	estaremos
estarás	estaréis
estará	estarán

Conditional tense

estaría	estaríamos
estarías	estaríais
estaría	estarían

Present perfect tense

he estado	hemos estado
has estado	habéis estado
ha estado	han estado

Past perfect tense

había estado	habíamos estado
habías estado	habíais estado
había estado	habían estado

Present subjunctive

que esté	que estemos
que estés	que estéis
que esté	que estén

Commands

(nosotros) estemos / no estemos
(tú) está / no estés (vosotros) estad / no estéis
(Ud.) esté / no esté (Uds.) estén / no estén

Forms of address (use of titles)

The following forms are used in Spanish to address a stranger or a person with whom you are not on a first-name basis. They are used more frequently than their American English equivalents.

señor	*Sir*
señora	*Ma'am, Madam*
señorita	*Miss, Ms.*

A young man may be addressed as **joven**.
These words can also function as nouns:

el señor	*man*
la señora	*woman*
la señorita	*young woman*
el joven	*young man*

Spanish uses the surname with **señor, señora** and **señorita** much less frequently than English does.

Buenas tardes, señora.	*Good afternoon, Mrs. (Rodríguez).*

Future tense

The future tense in Spanish, used to express future events, is formed by adding a specific set of endings to the infinitive of the verb. All verbs, regular and irregular, form the future tense in this way.

Trabajaré.	*I will work.*
Aprenderé.	*I will learn.*
Viviré.	*I will live.*

trabajar *to work*

trabajaré	trabajaremos
trabajarás	trabajaréis
trabajará	trabajarán

aprender *to learn*

aprenderé	aprenderemos
aprenderás	aprenderéis
aprenderá	aprenderán

vivir *to live*

viviré	viviremos
vivirás	viviréis
vivirá	vivirán

There are twelve verbs that have modified infinitive forms in the future. These verbs have the same endings as the verbs in the charts above. The **yo** form is shown as a model for the entire conjugation. Compounds (such as **componer, mantener, convenir,** and **rehacer**) of the twelve verbs that have modified infinitives in the future also have the same kind of modification (shortened infinitives) in their own future forms. See also *Conditional tense.*

INFINITIVE	FUTURE
poner	**pondré**
salir	**saldré**
tener	**tendré**
valer	**valdré**
venir	**vendré**
caber	**cabré**
haber	**habré**
poder	**podré**
querer	**querré**
saber	**sabré**
decir	**diré**
hacer	**haré**

The future of **hay**, derived from **haber**, is **habrá** *there will be*.

   -Ir verbs that have an accent mark in the infinitive, such as **oír** *to hear*, **freír** *to fry*, and **reír** *to laugh*, lose that accent mark in the future tense: **freiré, oiré, reiré**.

   In spoken Spanish the **ir a** + infinitive construction and the present tense are used more frequently than the future tense to express future events.

Los veremos el sábado.	*We'll see them on Saturday.*
Vamos a verlos el sábado.	*We're going to see them on Saturday.*
Los vemos el sábado.	*We're seeing them on Saturday.*

   One of the most common uses of the future tense is to express probability or conjecture about the present. Speakers use the *future of probability* when wondering about things that are going on in the present.

¿Qué hora será?	*I wonder what time it is.*
Serán las seis.	*It's probably six o'clock.*
Carlitos tendrá cinco años.	*Carlitos must be five years old.*
¿Qué querrá para su cumpleaños?	*I wonder what she wants for her birthday.*
Estarán de vacaciones todavía.	*They're probably still on vacation.*

Gender of nouns

1. Spanish nouns are divided into two broad classes, traditionally called *masculine* and *feminine*. Most, but not all, nouns referring to males are masculine and most, but not all, nouns referring to females are feminine. Inanimate nouns such as **regalo** and **caja** are assigned to one of the two classes usually (but not always) on the basis of their endings. Most nouns ending in **-o** are masculine, while most nouns ending in **-a** are feminine.

2. Nouns ending in **-e** or a consonant that do not refer to people give no clue as to gender, so their gender must be learned as you learn the noun.

MASCULINE		FEMININE	
el análisis	*analysis*	la clase	*class*
el bar	*bar*	la crisis	*crisis*
el café	*café*	la flor	*flower*
el estante	*shelf*	la llave	*key*
el hospital	*hospital*	la luz	*light*
el informe	*report*	la nariz	*nose*
el juguete	*toy*	la paz	*peace*
el lápiz	*pencil*	la piel	*skin*
el maletín	*suitcase*	la Red	*Web, Internet*
el paquete	*package*	la torre	*tower*
el reloj	*watch*	la tos	*cough*
el mes	*month*	la voz	*voice*
el aceite	*oil*	la catedral	*cathedral*
el automóvil	*car*	la suerte	*luck*
el lugar	*place*	la gente	*people*
el cafetal	*coffee plantation*	la base	*base*
el aire	*air*	la sed	*thirst*
el arete	*earring*	la pirámide	*pyramid*

3. The following suffixes indicate feminine nouns:

-ción, -ión	la nación, la educación, la religión, la habitación, la reunión
-tad, -dad	la amistad, la facultad, la libertad, la nacionalidad, la ciudad, la universidad
-tud	la virtud, la gratitud
-ie	la serie, la superficie

Unpredictable genders

Some nouns have anomalous genders.

la mano	*hand*
la moto (la motocicleta)	*motorcycle*
la foto (la fotografía)	*photograph*
el día	*day*
el mapa	*map*
el tranvía	*trolley*

Many nouns ending in **-ma** (usually international words borrowed from Greek) are masculine.

el clima	*climate*
el drama	*drama*
el problema	*problem*
el tema	*subject*
el trauma	*trauma*

Compound nouns composed of a verb + a plural noun function as masculine singular. In their plural the article changes but the noun remains the same.

el cumpleaños	*birthday*
los cumpleaños	*birthdays*
el aguafiestas	*wet blanket, party pooper*
los aguafiestas	*wet blankets, party poopers*

Getting attention

Words such as **Perdón** *Excuse me* and **Oiga** *Say, Hey* (literally, *Listen*) can be used to get someone's attention when you want to ask a question. They are often followed by the appropriate form of address.

> Perdón/Oiga, señor, señora, señorita.

Hay

The word **hay** is an irregular verb form meaning *there is, there are*. It can be followed by either a singular or a plural noun.

Hay un regalo en la caja.	*There's a gift in the box.*
Hay regalos en la caja.	*There are gifts in the box.*

The noun that follows **hay** is considered to be the *direct object* of the verb.

¿Hay regalos en la caja?	*Are there gifts in the box?*
Sí, los hay.	*Yes, there are.*

Imperative

The imperative, or command, forms are used to tell someone to do something or not to do something. There are imperative forms in Spanish for **tú, Ud., nosotros, vosotros,** and **Uds.**

Most imperative forms involve a change in the vowel of the ending. In other words the **a** in the endings of **-ar** verbs changes to **e** and the **e** or **i** in the endings of **-er** and **-ir** verbs changes to **a**.

Command forms for Ud. and Uds.

Compre (Ud.) esta calculadora.	*Buy this calculator.*
Compren (Uds.) esta calculadora.	*Buy this calculator.*
Lea (Ud.) la propuesta.	*Read the proposal.*
Lean (Uds.) la propuesta.	*Read the proposal.*
Añada (Ud.) un comentario.	*Add a comment.*
Añadan (Uds.) un comentario.	*Add a comment.*

Note that the addition of the pronoun **Ud.** or **Uds.** to an imperative adds a polite tone to the command, much as *please* does in English.

To form the negative imperative for **Ud.** and **Uds.** add **no** before the command form.

No compre (Ud.) esta calculadora.	*Don't buy this calculator.*
No compren (Uds.) esta calculadora.	*Don't buy this calculator.*
No lea (Ud.) la propuesta.	*Don't read the proposal.*
No lean (Uds.) la propuesta.	*Don't read the proposal.*
No añada (Ud.) un comentario.	*Don't add a comment.*
No añadan (Uds.) un comentario.	*Don't add a comment.*

The same vowel changes for **-ar**, **-er**, and **-ir** verbs occur in the command forms for **nosotros**.

Tomemos fotos.	*Let's take pictures.*
No tomemos fotos.	*Let's not take pictures.*
Comamos en este restaurante.	*Let's eat at this restaurant.*
No comamos en este restaurante.	*Let's not eat at this restaurant.*
Escribamos una propuesta.	*Let's write a proposal.*
No escribamos una propuesta.	*Let's not write a proposal.*

Verbs with an irregularity in the first-person singular in the present tense (see *Irregular verbs*) also have that irregular stem in the **Ud.**, **Uds.**, and **nosotros** forms of the imperative.

INFINITIVE	YO FORM	UD. COMMAND	UDS. COMMAND	NOSOTROS COMMAND
decir	digo	**diga**	**digan**	**digamos**
hacer	hago	**haga**	**hagan**	**hagamos**
ofrecer	ofrezco	**ofrezca**	**ofrezcan**	**ofrezcamos**
poner	pongo	**ponga**	**pongan**	**pongamos**
tener	tengo	**tenga**	**tengan**	**tengamos**
traer	traigo	**traiga**	**traigan**	**traigamos**
venir	vengo	**venga**	**vengan**	**vengamos**
conocer	conozco	**conozca**	**conozcan**	**conozcamos**
ver	**veo**	**vea**	**vean**	**veamos**

If the present tense form of a verb has a change in the vowel of the stem, the command forms for **Ud.** and **Uds.** show that change as well (see *Stem-changing verbs*).

INFINITIVE	UD., UDS. FORMS	UD. COMMAND	UDS. COMMAND
cerrar	cierra, cierran	**cierre**	**cierren**
mostrar	muestra, muestran	**muestre**	**muestren**
encender	enciende, encienden	**encienda**	**enciendan**
volver	vuelve, vuelven	**vuelva**	**vuelvan**
convertir	convierte, convierten	**convierta**	**conviertan**
pedir	pide, piden	**pida**	**pidan**
dormir	duerme, duermen	**duerma**	**duerman**

Note that since the present indicative **nosotros** forms of -**ar** and -**er** verbs have no stem change, the **nosotros** form of the imperative does not have a stem change either (see *Stem-changing verbs*).

INFINITIVE	NOSOTROS PRESENT TENSE	NOSOTROS COMMAND
cerrar	cerramos	cerremos
mostrar	mostramos	mostremos
encender	encendemos	encendamos
volver	volvemos	volvamos

However, -**ir** verbs that have changes in the vowel of the stem change the stem vowel to **i** in the **nosotros** form of the imperative. The verb **dormir** has **u** as the stem vowel of the **nosotros** form of the imperative. (Note that the **nosotros** forms of the *present* tense of these verbs do *not* have a stem change—see *Stem-changing verbs*.)

INFINITIVE	NOSOTROS PRESENT TENSE	NOSOTROS COMMAND
convertir	convertimos	convirtamos
pedir	pedimos	pidamos
dormir	dormimos	durmamos

In everyday speech, the affirmative **nosotros** command is often replaced by **vamos a** + infinitive.

compremos → vamos a comprar
hagamos → vamos a hacer
sirvamos → vamos a servir

The negative **nosotros** commands cannot be replaced by **vamos a** + infinitive.

Thus, **vamos a salir** can mean *Let's go out.* or *We're going to go out.* **No vamos a salir**, however, means only *We are not going to go out. Let's not go out* has to be rendered as **No salgamos**.

Several verbs have irregular command forms.

INFINITIVE	UD. COMMAND	UDS. COMMAND	NOSOTROS COMMAND
ir	**vaya**	**vayan**	**vamos / no vayamos**
saber	**sepa**	**sepan**	**sepamos**
ser	**sea**	**sean**	**seamos**

The verbs **dar** and **estar** have an accent mark in the **Ud.** command form. **Estar** also has an accent mark in the **Uds.** command form.

INFINITIVE	UD. COMMAND	UDS. COMMAND	NOSOTROS COMMAND
dar	**dé**	**den**	**demos**
estar	**esté**	**estén**	**estemos**

Negative commands for **tú** and **vosotros** are formed just like the **Ud.**, **Uds.**, and **nosotros** commands—by switching the vowel of the ending.

	NEGATIVE TÚ FORMS		NEGATIVE VOSOTROS FORMS	
INFINITIVE	PRESENT TENSE	COMMAND	PRESENT TENSE	COMMAND
comprar	no compras	**no compres**	no compráis	**no compréis**
leer	no lees	**no leas**	no leéis	**no leáis**
añadir	no añades	**no añadas**	no añadís	**no añadáis**
cerrar	no cierras	**no cierres**	no cerráis	**no cerréis**
mostrar	no muestras	**no muestres**	no mostráis	**no mostréis**
encender	no enciendes	**no enciendas**	no encendéis	**no encendáis**
volver	no vuelves	**no vuelvas**	no volvéis	**no volváis**

Irregularities that appear in the **Ud.**, **Uds.**, and **nosotros** commands also appear in the negative **tú** and **vosotros** commands.

INFINITIVE	NEGATIVE TÚ COMMAND	NEGATIVE VOSOTROS COMMAND
decir	**no digas**	**no digáis**
hacer	**no hagas**	**no hagáis**
poner	**no pongas**	**no pongáis**
tener	**no tengas**	**no tengáis**
venir	**no vengas**	**no vengáis**
conocer	**no conozcas**	**no conozcáis**
ver	**no veas**	**no veáis**
ir	**no vayas**	**no vayáis**
saber	**no sepas**	**no sepáis**
ser	**no seas**	**no seáis**
dar	**no des**	**no déis**
estar	**no estés**	**no estéis**

In **-ir** verbs with changes in the vowel of the stem, the negative **vosotros** command form has the same change in the stem as the **nosotros** command (see *Stem-changing verbs*).

INFINITIVE	PRESENT TENSE	NOSOTROS COMMAND FORM	NEGATIVE VOSOTROS COMMAND FORM
convertir	convertimos/convertís	convirtamos	no convirtáis
pedir	pedimos/pedís	pidamos	no pidáis
dormir	dormimos/dormís	durmamos	no durmáis

Spelling changes in the imperative

In the command forms for **Ud., Uds.,** and **nosotros** and the negative **tú** and **vosotros** commands, the following spelling changes take place.

In **-ar** verbs ending in **-car, -gar** and **-zar** the final consonants of the stem **c, g,** and **z** change to **qu, gu** and **c** respectively before an ending beginning with **e**.

INFINITIVE	UD./UDS. COMMANDS	NOSOTROS COMMAND	NEGATIVE TÚ COMMAND	NEGATIVE VOSOTROS COMMAND
sacar	sa**qu**e(n)	sa**qu**emos	no sa**qu**es	no sa**qu**éis
pagar	pa**gu**e(n)	pa**gu**emos	no pa**gu**es	no pa**gu**éis
almorzar	almuer**c**e(n)	almor**c**emos	no almuer**c**es	no almor**c**éis

-Er and **-ir** verbs whose stem ends in **g** change the **g** to **j** before an ending beginning with **a**.

INFINITIVE	UD./UDS. COMMANDS	NOSOTROS COMMAND	NEGATIVE TÚ COMMAND	NEGATIVE VOSOTROS COMMAND
escoger	esco**j**a(n)	esco**j**amos	no esco**j**as	no esco**j**áis
elegir	eli**j**a(n)	eli**j**amos	no eli**j**as	no eli**j**áis

The command forms for **Ud., Uds.,** and **nosotros** and the negative **tú** and **vosotros** commands all derive from the present subjunctive.

Affirmative commands for **tú** and **vosotros**

Affirmative commands for **tú** and **vosotros** do not show a change in the vowel of the ending of the imperative.

Affirmative commands for **tú** are formed by dropping the final **-s** of the **tú** form of the present tense. Affirmative commands for **vosotros** are formed by replacing the **-r** of the infinitive with **-d**.

INFINITIVE	AFFIRMATIVE TÚ FORMS		AFFIRMATIVE VOSOTROS FORMS	
	PRESENT TENSE	COMMAND	PRESENT TENSE	COMMAND
comprar	compras	**compra**	compráis	**comprad**
comer	comes	**come**	coméis	**comed**
añadir	añades	**añade**	añadís	**añadid**
cerrar	cierras	**cierra**	cerráis	**cerrad**
encender	enciendes	**enciende**	encendéis	**encended**
convertir	conviertes	**convierte**	convertís	**convertid**
pedir	pides	**pide**	pedís	**pedid**
dormir	duermes	**duerme**	dormís	**dormid**
dar	das	**da**	dais	**dad**
estar	estás	**está**	estáis	**estad**

Eight affirmative **tú** commands have irregular one-syllable forms. The corresponding **vosotros** commands are regular.

| | AFFIRMATIVE **TÚ** FORMS | | AFFIRMATIVE **VOSOTROS** FORMS | |
INFINITIVE	PRESENT TENSE	COMMAND	PRESENT TENSE	COMMAND
decir	dices	**di**	decís	decid
hacer	haces	**haz**	hacéis	haced
ir	vas	**ve**	vais	id
poner	pones	**pon**	ponćis	poncd
salir	sales	**sal**	salís	salid
ser	eres	**sé**	sois	sed
tener	tienes	**ten**	tenéis	tened
venir	vienes	**ven**	venís	venid

Imperative: object pronouns in the imperative

In all negative imperative forms object pronouns are placed in their usual position before the verb. This includes reflexive pronouns.

No **me** digas que no puedes venir.	*Don't tell me that you can't come.*
Él quiere dinero. No **se lo** preste Ud.	*He wants money. Don't lend it to him.*
No **nos** mudemos a aquella ciudad.	*Let's not move to that city.*
No **se** vayan Uds.	*Don't go away.*
No **te metas** en estos asuntos.	*Don't butt into these matters.*
Esa camisa está rota. No **te la** pongas.	*That shirt is torn. Don't put it on.*

With affirmative command forms, however, the object pronouns *follow* the command forms and are attached to them in writing. For **tú, Ud.** and **Uds.** commands, if the command form has more than one syllable, an accent mark is added to the stem vowel when an object pronoun (or reflexive pronoun) is added.

Váyanse Uds.	*Go away.*
Escúchame bien. Esto es muy importante.	*Listen to me carefully. This is very important.*
Aquí tienes el informe. **Léelo.**	*Here's the report. Read it.*
Cuídate.	*Take care.*
Él quiere dinero. **Présteselo** Ud.	*He wants money. Lend it to him.*
Necesito los documentos. **Tráigamelos.**	*I need the documents. Bring them to me.*
Alicia tiene la calculadora. **Pídesela.**	*Alicia has the calculator. Ask her for it.*

When an object pronoun is added to the **nosotros** command form, a written accent is placed on the **a** or the **e** of the ending.

| Ellos están enfermos. **Ayudémoslos.** | *They're sick. Let's help them.* |

No accent mark is added to a one-syllable command form when a single object pronoun is added.

Esto es tu trabajo. **Hazlo.**	*This is your work. Do it.*
Ponte el abrigo. Hace frío.	*Put on your coat. It's cold outside.*
Dime si necesitas algo.	*Tell me if you need anything.*

However, the command forms **dé, esté,** and **está** may keep their accents when a pronoun is added.

| **Déme** un consejo. | *Give me some advice.* |
| **Estáte** quieto. | *Keep still, don't move around so much.* |

No accent mark is added to **vosotros** command forms when a single object pronoun is added.

Hacedme caso, niños.	*Pay attention to what I say, children.*
Mandadle un correo eléctronico.	*Send him an e-mail.*

However, all command forms require a written accent mark when two object pronouns are added.

Busca tus guantes y **póntelos**.	*Get your gloves and put them on.*
No entiendo su idea. **Explíquemela**.	*I don't understand your idea. Explain it to me.*
Si terminaron el mensaje, **envíenselo**.	*If you've finished the message, send it to him.*

Additional points:

1. **Nosotros** command forms lose their final **s** before the reflexive pronoun **nos** and before the pronoun **se**.

Levantémonos.	*Let's get up.*
Abrochémonos el cinturón de seguridad.	*Let's fasten our seat belts.*
Divirtámonos.	*Let's have a good time.*
No entienden el problema.	*They don't understand the problem.*
Expliquémoselo.	*Let's explain it to them.*

2. **Vosotros** command forms drop the final **d** before the reflexive pronoun **os**. However, the **d** is retained in **idos** *go away*.

Acostaos ahora mismo.	*Go to bed right now.*
Poneos en contacto con ella.	*Get in touch with her.*
Divertíos en la playa.	*Have a good time at the beach.*

Note the use of the accent mark with **-ir** verbs to indicate that **-ios** is not a diphthong but represents two full syllables. (See *Placement of accent marks*.)

Imperfect tense

The forms of the imperfect tense are almost entirely regular. Two sets of endings are used, one for **-ar** verbs and another for **-er** and **-ir** verbs.

tomar		comer		vivir	
tomaba	tomábamos	comía	comíamos	vivía	vivíamos
tomabas	tomabais	comías	comíais	vivías	vivíais
tomaba	tomaban	comía	comían	vivía	vivían

Only the verbs **ser**, **ir**, and **ver** are irregular in the imperfect.

ser		ir		ver	
era	éramos	iba	íbamos	veía	veíamos
eras	erais	ibas	ibais	veías	veíais
era	eran	iba	iban	veía	veían

The imperfect tense is used for actions that the speaker sees as ongoing in the past.

Imperfect vs. preterit

The imperfect and preterit are both past tenses. The difference between them is not a difference in time but a difference in how past actions are viewed. The preterit views past actions as completed or as having happened once. The imperfect views past actions as ongoing processes in past time.

When Spanish speakers refer to a past action, they have to choose between these two tenses. In English this distinction is not mandatory.

Cuando yo era joven, **dormía** bien.	*When I was young, I **slept** well.*
Anoche **dormí** bien.	*Last night I **slept** well.*

The imperfect has several common translations in English, such as *used to do something* or *was/were doing something*.

Mauricio trabajaba en aquella empresa.	*Mauricio used to work at that firm.*
¿Sabes lo que hacía en México?	*Do you know what he was doing in Mexico?*

The imperfect is the tense most often selected to express repeated actions in the past.

Yo me levantaba temprano todos los días.	*I got up early every day.*
Nosotros siempre pasábamos el verano allí.	*We always spent the summer there.*

The imperfect expresses the background of events. The events themselves are in the preterit. Note that the imperfect is used to tell time in the past.

Eran las tres cuando **terminé** mi informe.	*It was three o'clock when I finished my report.*
Hacía buen tiempo cuando **salieron**.	*The weather was good when they left.*
Empezó a llover mientras **nos paseábamos**.	*It began to rain while we were taking a walk.*
No **fui** a la oficina porque **me sentía** mal.	*I didn't go to the office because I felt sick.*
Yo **entraba** datos en la computadora cuando el jefe me **llamó**.	*I was entering data on the computer when the boss called me.*

Some verbs have very different meanings in the imperfect and the preterit.

Yo **tenía** una idea.	*I had an idea.*
Yo **tuve** una idea.	*I got an idea.*
Sabía su nombre	*I knew his name.*
Supe su nombre.	*I found out his name.*
No **conocíamos** al gerente.	*We didn't know the manager.*
No **conocimos** al gerente.	*We didn't meet the manager.*

Indirect object

The indirect object labels the secondary goal of the action of the verb. The primary goal is the direct object. The direct object is connected directly to the verb without the aid of a preposition. The indirect object is connected to the verb by a preposition (usually *to* or *for* in English). Indirect objects almost always refer to people.

For instance, in the sentence *John sends an e-mail, an e-mail* is the first goal of the action. It is the direct object of the verb. A second goal can be added: *John sends an e-mail to Mary. Mary* is the indirect object, the secondary goal of the action. (Note that in English the indirect object can be placed before the direct object and when this order is used the preposition *to* is omitted: *John sends Mary an e-mail.*)

Indirect object pronouns

The indirect object pronouns in Spanish are:

PERSON	SINGULAR	PLURAL
first	me	nos
second	te	os
third	le	les

Note that the indirect object pronouns for the first two persons are the same as the corresponding direct object pronouns.

Position of indirect object pronouns

Both direct object pronouns and indirect object pronouns follow the same rules for placement in the sentence.

Indirect object pronouns precede the conjugated verb.

¿Por qué **le** contestas así?	*Why do you answer him like that?*
Ella siempre **me** regala cosas bonitas.	*She always gives me nice things (as gifts).*
Yo **les** escribo una vez por semana.	*I write to them once a week.*

In verb + infinitive constructions, the indirect object pronoun may precede the first verb or follow the infinitive. When it follows the infinitive, it is attached to it in writing.

Te quiero mostrar mi carro nuevo.	*I want to show you my new car.*
or Quiero mostrarte mi carro nuevo.	
¿El informe? Se lo vamos a entregar.	*The report? We're going to hand it in to them.*
or ¿El informe? Vamos a entregárselo.	

There is no difference in meaning.

Use of indirect object pronouns

In Spanish an indirect object noun is always accompanied by the corresponding indirect object pronoun, either **le** or **les**.

Le contamos **a Magdalena** lo que pasó.	*We told Magdalena what happened.*
Les expliqué el problema **a mis colegas.**	*I explained the problem to my colleagues.*
Le voy a pedir un aumento de sueldo **al gerente**.	*I'm going to ask the manager for a raise.*

Infinitive

The infinitive is the form of the verb that does not show person or tense. Spanish infinitives end in **-ar, -er**, or **-ir**. The infinitive is the form used for listing verbs in dictionaries and vocabularies.

The Spanish infinitive can be used as a noun and function as the subject or object of a sentence. It can be preceded by the masculine definite article **el**.

El nadar es un buen ejercicio.	*Swimming is a good exercise.*
Han prohibido **fumar** en el metro.	*They have forbidden smoking in the subway.*
Me gusta **alquilar** películas.	*I like renting films.*

The Spanish infinitive is the form used after prepositions.

Hablan **de abrir** otra sucursal de la tienda.	*They're talking about opening another branch of the store.*
Nos lo dijo **al entrar.**	*He told it to us upon entering (=when he came in).*
Se fueron **sin decir** nada a nadie.	*They left without saying anything to anyone.*

Notice that English uses the *-ing* form in the above cases (used as a noun and after prepositions).

The infinitive as an alternate command form

The infinitive is often used to express a command, both in speech and in formal style, as in written instructions. In speech it is often preceded by the preposition **a.**

Niños, a levantarse.	*Get up, kids.*
Agitar antes de usar.	*Shake before using.*

Intransitive verbs

Intransitive verbs in Spanish are those which cannot take a direct object. Examples of intransitive verbs are **ir** *to go* and **llegar** *to arrive.*

Other verbs can be either intransitive or transitive, but English equivalents are very different.

intransitive

Ellos subieron al tercer piso.	*They went up to the third floor.*

transitive

Ellos subieron las maletas.	*They took the suitcases up.*

Irregular verbs

Many verbs do not follow the standard pattern of formation in the present tense. These are called irregular verbs. The most common pattern for irregular verbs in the present tense is for the **yo** form to be irregular while the rest of the forms are regular. The most common **yo**-form irregularity is a **-g-** inserted before the ending **-o.** Verbs with this irregularity are called **g** verbs.

caer *to fall*		**hacer** *to make, do*		**poner** *to put*	
cai**g**o	caemos	ha**g**o	hacemos	pon**g**o	ponemos
caes	caéis	haces	hacéis	pones	ponéis
cae	caen	hace	hacen	pone	ponen

salir *to go out, leave*		**traer** *to make, do*		**valer** *to be worth, cost*	
sal**g**o	salimos	trai**g**o	traemos	val**g**o	valemos
sales	salís	traes	traéis	vales	valéis
sale	salen	trae	traen	vale	valen

Some **g** verbs show other irregularities or have stem changes in the present.

decir *to say, tell*		**oír** *to hear*	
di**g**o	decimos	oi**g**o	oímos
dices	decís	oyes	oís
dice	dicen	oye	oyen

tener *to have*		**venir** *to come*	
tengo	tenemos	vengo	venimos
tienes	tenéis	vienes	venís
tiene	tienen	viene	vienen

A variant of **g** verbs are those which show an anomalous -**zc**- before the **o** ending of the **yo** form. These verbs have infinitives that end in -**cer** or -**cir**, preceded by a vowel.

conocer *to know*		**traducir** *to translate*	
cono**zc**o	conocemos	tradu**zc**o	traducimos
conoces	conocéis	traduces	traducís
conoce	conocen	traduce	traducen

A few verbs have other irregularities in the first-person singular, but regular forms in the rest of the conjugation.

caber *to fit*		**saber** *to know*		**ver** *to see*	
quepo	cabemos	**sé**	sabemos	veo	vemos
cabes	cabéis	sabes	sabéis	ves	veis
cabe	caben	sabe	saben	ve	ven

Verbs ending in -**uir** add a -**y**- before the ending in the singular conjugations and in the third person plural.

construir *to build*	
constru**y**o	construimos
constru**y**es	construís
constru**y**e	constru**y**en

The irregularity of the first person for -**g**- verbs, -**zc**- verbs, verbs with -**uy**-, and **caber**, **saber**, and **ver** appears in all forms of the present subjunctive (see *Present subjunctive of irregular verbs*.)

A small number of verbs end in -**oy** in the first-person singular (**dar, estar, ir,** and **ser**). The ending -**oy** is stressed. There are other irregularities in the conjugations of **estar** and **ser**. Notice that in **vosotros** forms of one syllable (**dais, vais, sois** and also **veis**, above), the written accent mark is omitted.

dar *to give*		**estar** *to be*		**ir** *to go*		**ser** *to be*	
doy	damos	**estoy**	estamos	**voy**	vamos	**soy**	somos
das	dais	estás	estáis	vas	vais	eres	sois
da	dan	está	están	va	van	es	son

For irregular forms in other tenses, see *Imperfect tense, Present perfect, Present subjunctive of irregular verbs, Preterit tense.*

Negative sentences

Spanish sentences are made negative by placing **no** before the verb.

No salen hoy.	*They're not going out today.*

The word **no** stands before object pronouns and before the auxiliary verb **haber**.

No se lo di.	*I didn't give it to him.*
No hemos hecho nada esta tarde.	*We haven't done anything this afternoon.*

The word **no** stands before the first verb in verb + infinitive constructions.

Creo que **no** van a venir. *I think they're not going to come.*
No se atreve a decírtelo. *He doesn't dare to tell it to you.*

No is both the equivalent of the English response *no* and a marker of negation. Therefore, many sentences have two occurrences of **no**.

—¿Quieres comer? *Do you want to eat?*
—**No, no** tengo hambre. *No, I'm not hungry.*

Negative words

Nada *nothing* and **nadie** *no one* are negative words. They have negative meaning when used in isolation.

—¿Qué buscas? *What are you looking for?*
—Nada. *Nothing.*
—¿Quién hace la comida? *Who's making the meal?*
—Nadie. *No one.*

Nada and **nadie** can function as either the subject or object of a verb. When **nadie** is the direct object of a verb it is preceded by the personal **a**. When a negative word follows the verb in Spanish, **no** must be used before the verb.

Nada es imposible. *Nothing is impossible.*
Nadie habla inglés aquí. *No one speaks English here.*
No hago **nada** hoy. *I'm not doing anything today.*
Ellos **no** ayudan **a nadie**. *They don't help anyone.*

Here is a list of the most common negative words in Spanish and their affirmative counterparts.

nada	*nothing*	algo	*something*
nadie	*no one, nobody*	alguien	*someone, somebody*
ninguno (ningún), ninguna	*no, none*	alguno (algún), alguna	*some*
		algunos, algunas	*some*
nunca, jamás	*never*	algunas veces, a veces, alguna vez	*sometimes*
		siempre	*always*
		muchas veces, a menudo	*often*
tampoco	*neither*	o	*or*
ni... ni	*neither . . . nor*	o... o	*either . . . or*
ya no	*no longer*	todavía	*still*

Ninguno and **alguno** are used before nouns as adjectives or as pronouns. For the forms **ningún** and **algún** before a masculine singular noun, see *Adjectives: short forms* under *Adjectives*.

Note that **ninguno** is not used in the plural unless the following noun is inherently plural and has no singular, such as **las tijeras** *scissors*: **ningunas tijeras**. For all other nouns the singular is used.

ningún médico *no doctor, no doctors*
ninguna calle *no street, no streets*

Note these expressions:

en/por **ningún** lado	*nowhere*
en/por **ninguna** parte	*nowhere*
de **ninguna** manera	*in no way, not at all*
de **ningún** modo	*in no way, not at all*

Neuters

Spanish has several forms ending in **-o** that are called *neuters*.

There are three neuter demonstrative pronouns: **esto, eso,** and **aquello**. These pronouns refer to situations or ideas, not to specific nouns. They are written without an accent mark.

—Mi hijo estudia muy poco.	*My son is studying very little.*
—**Eso** es muy malo.	*That's very bad.* (**eso** = *the fact that he doesn't study*)
—Miguel está resentido porque lo despidieron.	*Miguel is resentful because they fired him.*
—Pero **aquello** fue hace mucho tiempo.	*But that was a long time ago.* (**aquello** = *the fact that he was fired*)

Spanish also has a neuter article, **lo**, which can be used before the masculine singular of adjectives. **Lo** + adjective means *the part, the aspect, etc.*

Lo difícil es terminar el proyecto a tiempo.	*The hard part is finishing the project on time.*
Lo interesante es su conclusión.	*The interesting part is his conclusion.*

Lo is very common before long-form possessive adjectives.

Lo mío es esperar.	*What I have to do is wait.*
Lo nuestro es sufrir.	*Our lot (in life) is to suffer.*

The neuter demonstrative pronouns and **lo** can also stand before a phrase beginning with **de** to mean *the matter of, that business about.*

¿Oíste **lo de Eduardo**?	*Did you hear the business about Eduardo?*
Esto de no hablar cortésmente es inaceptable.	*This business of not speaking politely is unacceptable.*
Aquello de no respetar la ley tendrá consecuencias graves.	*That matter of not respecting the law will have serious consequences.*

Lo may appear before adverbs.

lo antes posible	*as soon as possible*
Lo hice **lo mejor posible**.	*I did it as best I could.*

Nominalization

Nominalization is the process by which a part of speech, such as an adjective, is made to function as a noun or pronoun. In English there are several processes that accomplish this. In Spanish, however, there is only one—deletion of the noun. Nominalization takes place in various types of structures:

1. A noun may be deleted from a phrase consisting of a determiner + noun + adjective. In this structure, the adjective plus the definite article (or other determiner) can function as a noun. The definite article is not stressed in the nominalized phrase, but the indefinite article is.

el modelo nuevo y el **modelo** antiguo	*the new model and the old model*
→ el modelo nuevo y **el antiguo**	*the new model and **the old one***
las ciudades grandes y las **ciudades** pequeñas	*big cities and little cities*
→ las ciudades grandes y **las pequeñas**	*big cities and **little ones***
una computadora barata y una **computadora** cara	*a cheap computer and an expensive computer*
→ una computadora barata y **una cara**	*a cheap computer and **an expensive one***

2. A noun may be deleted in a prepositional phrase begining with **de** (this includes phrases expressing possession). In this structure, the definite article (or other determiner) becomes a pronoun and is stressed.

la casa de María y la **casa** de Juan	*María's house and Juan's house*
→ la casa de María y **la de Juan**	*María's house and **Juan's***
los zapatos de cuero y los **zapatos** de tela	*leather shoes and cloth shoes*
→ los zapatos de cuero y **los de tela**	*leather shoes and **cloth ones***

3. A noun may be deleted after a demonstrative adjective. In this structure, an accent mark is usually added to the demonstrative adjective when the noun is deleted, and the resultant structure is called a demonstrative pronoun in traditional grammatical descriptions.

ese vuelo y este **vuelo**	*that flight and this flight*
→ ese vuelo y **éste**	*that flight and **this one***
estas dietas y esa **dieta**	*these diets and that diet*
→ estas dietas y **ésa**	*these diets and **that one***
estos documentos y aquellos **documentos**	*these documents and those documents*
→ estos documentos y **aquéllos**	*these documents and **those***
aquella sucursal y estas **sucursales**	*that branch and these branches*
→ aquella sucursal y **éstas**	*that branch and **these***

4. A noun may be deleted from a phrase containing a long-form possessive. The resultant structure is called a possessive pronoun in traditional grammatical descriptions.

el tráfico nuestro y el **tráfico** suyo	*our traffic and their traffic*
→ el tráfico nuestro y **el suyo**	*our traffic and **theirs***
la universidad tuya y la **universidad** mía	*your university and my university*
→ la universidad tuya y **la mía**	*your university and **mine***
los consejos suyos y los **consejos** tuyos	*his advice and your advice*
→ los consejos suyos y **los tuyos**	*his advice and **yours***
la pasantía mía y las **pasantías** de Uds.	*my internship and your internships*
→ la pasantía mía y **las de Uds.**	*my internship and **yours***

Noun clauses

A clause is a sentence incorporated into a larger sentence. Clauses may function as nouns, in which case they may be the subject or object of the main verb of the sentence. Such clauses are called noun clauses. Compare these two English sentences.

> I know *the answer*.
> I know *that he's here*.

The answer is a noun that is the direct object of the verb *know*. *That he's here* also functions as the direct object of the verb *know* and is therefore a noun clause.

When a clause is embedded in a larger sentence it is seen as subordinate to, or dependent on, the main clause, and is called a *subordinate* or *dependent clause*. To embed a clause into a sentence, a conjunction is used. In the above sentence, *that* is the subordinating conjunction that embeds the sentence *he's here* into the sentence *I know*. *I know* is the main clause of the sentence.

Noun phrases

Noun phrase components

A noun and the words directly associated with it (articles or other determiners, numbers, demonstratives, possessives, adjectives) form a *noun phrase*. In Spanish, almost all of the components of noun phrases change their form to match the gender and number of the noun. This change in form to match the noun is called *agreement*. Thus we say that in Spanish an adjective *agrees* in gender and number with its noun.

la maleta	*the suitcase*
una pulsera	*a bracelet*
unos ingenieros norteamericanos	*some American engineers*
mi casa	*my house*
este barrio	*this neighborhood*
cien vuelos diarios	*one hundred daily flights*
aquellos quince edificios viejos	*those fifteen old buildings*

A proper noun can be a noun phrase all by itself: **Roberto**.

Noun phrase functions

Nouns and noun phrases function as the subject or object of the verb, as the object of a preposition, or as a short answer to a question.

Here are examples of a noun phrase functioning as the object of a preposition.

en + **la maleta**	*in the suitcase*
para + **Carmen**	*for Carmen*

A noun phrase may function as a short answer to a question.

—¿Qué hay en la maleta?	*What's in the suitcase?*
—**Una pulsera.**	*A bracelet.*

Numbers

Numerals in Spanish present few problems.

Here are the numbers from one to twenty.

1	uno, una	11	once
2	dos	12	doce
3	tres	13	trece
4	cuatro	14	catorce
5	cinco	15	quince
6	seis	16	dieciséis
7	siete	17	diecisiete
8	ocho	18	dieciocho
9	nueve	19	diecinueve
10	diez	20	veinte

The numbers **uno** and **una** are identical with the indefinite article and agree in gender with the noun that follows them.

The numbers 16 through 19 may be written as three words each, but this is less and less common: **diez y seis, diez y siete, diez y ocho, diez y nueve**.

Here are the numbers from twenty-one to thirty-nine:

21	veintiuno, veintiuna	31	treinta y uno, treinta y una
22	veintidós	32	treinta y dos
23	veintitrés	33	treinta y tres
24	veinticuatro	34	treinta y cuatro
25	veinticinco	35	treinta y cinco
26	veintiséis	36	treinta y seis
27	veintisiete	37	treinta y siete
28	veintiocho	38	treinta y ocho
29	veintinueve	39	treinta y nueve
30	treinta		

All numbers ending in *one* have a masculine and a feminine form: **veintiuno, veintiuna; treinta y uno, treinta y una**.

The numbers 21 through 29 may be written as three words each, but this is less and less common: **veinte y uno/una, veinte y dos, veinte y tres,** etc.

The numbers 31 through 39 are occasionally written as one word each in some countries: **treintiuno/treintiuna, treintidós, treintitrés,** etc.

Note that the forms **veintidós, veintitrés, veintiséis** have written accent marks according to the rules for the placement of accent marks in Spanish.

The numbers from 40 to 99 follow these patterns:

40	cuarenta	70	setenta
41	cuarenta y uno/una	71	setenta y uno/una
42	cuarenta y dos	80	ochenta
43	cuarenta y tres	81	ochenta y uno/una
50	cincuenta	90	noventa
51	cincuenta y uno/una	91	noventa y uno/una
52	cincuenta y dos	99	noventa y nueve
60	sesenta		
61	sesenta y uno/una		

Numbers ending in -**ún, y un** become -**una, y una** before a feminine noun:

veintiuna, treinta y una páginas   *twenty-one, thirty-one pages*

However, the masculine form is used colloquially before feminine nouns as well.
Here are the hundreds in Spanish.

100	cien
200	doscientos/doscientas
300	trescientos/trescientas
400	cuatrocientos/cuatrocientas
500	quinientos/quinientas
600	seiscientos/seiscientas
700	setecientos/setecientas
800	ochocientos/ochocientas
900	novecientos/novecientas

The forms **quinientos/as, setecientos/as, novecientos/as** are irregular in their formation.

The numeral **cien** becomes **ciento** before another number. **Ciento** has no feminine form. **Ciento** + number is used before both masculine and feminine nouns.

101	ciento uno
102	ciento dos
110	ciento diez
155	ciento cincuenta y cinco

The word **y** is not used between **ciento** and a following number.

Multiples of **cien** agree in gender and number with the noun they refer to. They agree even when another number intervenes.

doscien**tos** cafés	*two hundred cafés*
doscien**tos** cincuenta y ocho cafés	*two hundred and fifty-eight cafés*
doscien**tas** tiendas	*two hundred stores*
doscien**tas** cincuenta y ocho tiendas	*two hundred and fifty-eight stores*
quinien**tos** pesos	*five hundred pesos*
quinien**tos** dieciocho pesos	*five hundred and eighteen pesos*
quinien**tas** computadoras	*five hundred computers*
quinien**tas** dieciocho computadoras	*five hundred and eighteen computers*
novecien**tos** archivos	*nine hundred files*
novecien**tos** treinta y un archivos	*nine hundred and thirty-one files*
novecien**tas** calles	*nine hundred streets*
novecien**tas** treinta y un**a** calles	*nine hundred and thirty-one streets*

The word for 1,000 is **mil**.

1,000	mil	6,000	seis mil
1,050	mil cincuenta	7,000	siete mil
1,200	mil doscientos/as	8,000	ocho mil
1,278	mil doscientos/as setenta y ocho	9,000	nueve mil
2,000	dos mil	10,000	diez mil
2,100	dos mil cien	20,000	veinte mil
2,912	dos mil novecientos/as doce	100,000	cien mil
3,000	tres mil	200,000	doscientos/as mil
4,000	cuatro mil	500,000	quinientos/as mil
5,000	cinco mil	1,000,000	un millón

The word **un** is not used before **cien** or **mil** to mean 100 or 1,000—contrast English *one hundred, one thousand.*

Agreements of multiples of 100,000 take place across intervening numbers.

trescient**os** mil mensajes	*three hundred thousand messages*
trescient**os** cincuenta mil mensajes	*three hundred and fifty thousand messages*
trescient**as** mil viviendas	*three hundred thousand dwellings*
trescient**as** cincuenta mil viviendas	*three hundred and fifty thousand dwellings*

According to grammarians, **un** and **una** do not agree with the noun when they precede **mil** directly—only **un** is used, even if the noun is feminine.

trescient**as** cincuenta y un mil viviendas	*three hundred fifty-one thousand dwellings*

However, agreement with a feminine noun is common.

treinta y una mil cuentas de banco	*thirty-one thousand bank accounts*

In Spain and most South American countries, a period is used instead of a comma in writing thousands. (The comma, on the other hand, serves as the equivalent of the English decimal point.)

1.500.000	un millón quinientos mil

The word **millón** is a masculine noun. It is preceded by **un** and followed by **de** when a noun follows directly. It is made plural (**millones**) after numbers higher than *one.*

un millón de dólares	*a million dollars*
diez millones de dólares	*ten million dollars*

The preposition **de** is not used if another number intervenes.

un millón quinientos mil dólares	*one million five hundred thousand dollars*
diez millones quinientos mil dólares	*ten million five hundred thousand dollars*

In most Spanish-speaking countries, **un billón** means *a trillion.* A billion is **mil millones**.

Ordinal numbers

The ordinal numbers in Spanish, from first to tenth, are:

primero	*first*		sexto	*sixth*
segundo	*second*		séptimo	*seventh*
tercero	*third*		octavo	*eighth*
cuarto	*fourth*		noveno	*ninth*
quinto	*fifth*		décimo	*tenth*

1. The ordinals **primero** and **tercero** are shortened to **primer** and **tercer**, respectively, before a masculine singular noun. See *Adjectives: short forms* under *Adjectives.*

el **primer** mensaje	*the first message*
el **tercer** mes	*the third month*

2. The ordinal numbers, except for **primero**, are not used in giving the date. The cardinal numbers are used instead: **dos, tres, cuatro, cinco**, etc. (see *Numbers*).

el **cuatro** de julio	*the fourth of July*
el **once** de enero	*January eleventh*
el **veinticinco** de agosto	*August twenty-fifth*
el **seis** de junio	*June sixth*
el **veintinueve** de marzo	*March twenty-ninth*

but

el **primero** de febrero	*February first*

Some speakers say **el uno de febrero**.

3. After **décimo** *tenth*, Spanish usually uses the cardinal number in place of the ordinal.

Ellos viven en el piso **doce**.	*They live on the twelfth floor.*

Note the use of ordinals with centuries and monarchs:

el siglo segundo	*the second century*
Carlos Quinto	*Charles the Fifth*
Isabel Segunda	*Elizabeth the Second*

El siglo dos is also common.

Para vs. por

The prepositions **para** and **por** are often confusing to English-speaking students of Spanish because both of them can be translated as *for* in certain contexts.

Para labels the goal of an action. This goal may be the destination of motion, the time by which something is done, or the beneficiary of the action.

Daniel salió **para** la oficina.	*Daniel left for the office.*
Tiene que terminar el informe **para** el jueves.	*He has to finish the report by Thursday.*
El anillo es **para** Fernanda.	*The ring is for Fernanda.*
Lo hice **para** ti.	*I did it for you. (=for your benefit)*

Para is used before an infinitive to label the purpose of an action.

Estudio mucho **para** sacar buenas notas.	*I study a lot in order to get good grades.*

Para appears in several idiomatic expressions.

para siempre	*forever*
para variar	*for a change*

Por expresses motion through a place or imprecise location.

Caminé **por** el parque.	*I walked through the park.*
Creo que viven **por** aquí.	*I think they live around here.*

Por expresses duration in time.

Trabajó con nosotros **por** muchos meses.	*He worked with us for many months.*

Por expresses the cause or reason for an action.

Se enoja **por** cualquier cosa.	*He gets angry for any little thing.*
No nos gusta vivir aquí **por** el frío.	*We don't like living here because of the cold.*
Lo hice **por** ti.	*I did it because of you.*

Por appears in many idiomatic expressions.

por ahora	*for now*
por aquí	*around here*
por casualidad	*by chance*
por ciento	*percent*
por desgracia	*unfortunately*
por eso	*therefore, that's why*
por favor	*please*

Passive voice

The passive voice in both Spanish and English consists of a form of **ser** / *to be* + the past participle. The past participle agrees in gender and number with the subject of the sentence (see *Past participles*).

La computadora va a ser reparada hoy.	*The computer will be fixed today.*
Los empleados fueron despedidos por el jefe.	*The employees were fired by the boss.*
El mensaje electrónico fue leído por la secretaria.	*The e-mail was read by the secretary.*

The phrase beginning with **por** is called the agent phrase. It is not essential in passive sentences.

| Los cheques han sido cobrados. | *The checks have been cashed.* |

The passive is used to move the focus of the sentence to the direct object of the verb, by making it the subject.

El jefe despidió **a los empleados**. → **Los empleados** fueron despedidos por el jefe.

The passive voice thus deemphasizes the performer of the action. The passive voice is much more common in English than in Spanish. Spanish prefers to use the **se** construction to remove the focus from the performer of the action.

| Aquí **se habla** español. | *Spanish is spoken here.* |
| **Se alquilaron** todos los apartamentos. | *All the apartments were rented.* |

Past participles
Formation of the past participle

The past participle in Spanish ends in **-do**; some irregular verbs have past participles in **-to** or **-cho**.

The past participle consists of the following elements:

*for -**ar** verbs:*	verb stem + the vowel **a** + **do**
*for -**er** and -**ir** verbs:*	verb stem + the vowel **i** + **do**
tomar → tom + a + do → **tomado**	*taken*
comer → com + i + do → **comido**	*eaten*
vivir → viv + i + do → **vivido**	*lived*

The past participles of **ir** and **ser** are regular.

> **ir → ido**
> **ser → sido**

-**Er** and -**ir** verbs whose stems end in a vowel add an accent mark over the **i**.

> caer → caído
> creer → creído
> leer → leído
> oír → oído
> traer → traído

The following verbs have irregular past participles:

> abrir → **abierto**
> cubrir → **cubierto**
> decir → **dicho**
> escribir → **escrito**
> freír → **frito**
> hacer → **hecho**
> imprimir → **impreso**
> morir → **muerto**
> poner → **puesto**
> resolver → **resuelto**
> romper → **roto**
> ver → **visto**
> volver → **vuelto**

When a prefix is added to these verbs the participle of the new verb shows the same irregularities.

> contradecir → **contradicho**   *to contradict*
> describir → **descrito**   *to describe*
> descubrir → **descubierto**   *to discover*
> devolver → **devuelto**   *to give back*
> prever → **previsto**   *to foresee*
> rehacer → **rehecho**   *to redo*
> suponer → **supuesto**   *to suppose*

Uses of the past participle

1. The past participle is frequently used as an adjective. It may follow a noun or a form of **estar** or **ser**. When used as an adjective it agrees in gender and number with the noun it refers to.

> un documento **roto**   *a torn document*
> los mensajes **escritos**   *the written messages*
> una reunión **aburrida**   *a boring meeting*
> las puertas **cerradas**   *the closed doors*
> El profesor está **enojado**.   *The teacher is angry.*
> La cena está **servida**.   *Dinner is served.*
> Los turistas están **cansados**.   *The tourists are tired.*
> Las ventanas están **abiertas**.   *The windows are open.*

The past participle expresses positions of the body such as *sitting, standing*. See *Ser vs. estar*, point 7.

2. The past participle is used with **ser** to form the passive voice. See *Passive voice*. In the passive voice the past participle agrees in gender and number with the noun it refers to.

3. The past participle is used with **haber** to form the present perfect, the past perfect and the other perfect tenses. In the perfect tenses the past participle is invariable—it does not agree in gender or number.

Past perfect (pluperfect)

The past perfect tense in Spanish consists of the imperfect tense of the auxiliary verb **haber** + the past participle. In the perfect tenses the past participle is invariable—it does not agree in gender or number with any element of the sentence. The Spanish past perfect corresponds to the English past perfect *had* + past participle.

singular

había tomado, comido	*I had taken, eaten*
habías tomado, comido	*you had taken, eaten*
había tomado, comido	*he, she, you (**Ud.**) had taken, eaten*

plural

habíamos tomado, comido	*we had taken, eaten*
habíais tomado, comido	*you had taken, eaten*
habían tomado, comido	*they, you (**Uds.**) had taken, eaten*

No words can be placed between the auxiliary verb and the past participle. The negative word **no** precedes the form of **haber**.

No habían regresado cuando yo llegué.	*They hadn't returned when I arrived.*
¿**No** había llamado todavía?	*Hadn't she called yet?*

Object pronouns, including reflexive pronouns (see *Reflexive verbs*), precede the form of **haber** in the perfect tenses. The negative word **no** precedes the object pronouns.

¿La cámara? **Se la hemos** devuelto.	*The camera? We've returned it to them.*
No me había probado el traje.	*I hadn't tried on the suit.*

Placement of accent marks

Spanish uses three accent marks in its spelling system:

- ´ el acento
- ~ la tilde
- ¨ la diéresis

El acento (the written accent) (´) appears over vowels, whether lowercase or uppercase:

á Á é É í Í ó Ó ú Ú

Panam**á**	*Panama*
cort**é**s	*polite*
israel**í**	*Israeli*
avi**ó**n	*airplane*
m**ú**sica	*music*

The **tilde** (~) appears over the letter **n** to form **ñ**, **Ñ**. The **ñ**, called **eñe**, is considered a separate letter of the Spanish alphabet and represents a sound similar to the *ni* in *onion*, but with the *n* pronounced as part of the second syllable: *o - nion*.

año	*year*
sueño	*dream*
hondureño	*Honduran*

The **diéresis** (¨) appears over the letter **u** after **g** to indicate that the **u** is pronounced as /w/.

verg**ü**enza	*shame*
ling**ü**ística	*linguistics*
nicarag**ü**ense	*Nicaraguan*

The placement of the written accent (´) is determined by the rules of stress and rules of syllable formation in Spanish.

Rules of stress

1. In Spanish, a word that ends in a vowel, **-n** or **-s** is normally stressed on the next-to-last syllable:

boda	restau**ran**tes
cine	**sa**bes
comen	bille**te**ro
es**tan**te	nece**si**tan
pul**se**ra	

2. A word ending in a consonant other than **-n** or **-s** is normally stressed on the final syllable.

ho**tel**	re**loj**
compren**der**	celu**lar**
canti**dad**	a**zul**
us**ted**	inte**rior**

3. If a word violates one of these rules, a written accent is placed over the stressed vowel. The following words end in a vowel, **-n** or **-s**, but are not stressed on the next-to-last syllable. An accent mark is therefore added over the vowel of the stressed syllable.

cámara	**có**modo
ciberca**fé**	habita**ción**
male**tín**	cham**pú**
come**rás**	**fí**sica
cómputo	man**dón**
te**lé**fono	di**rás**
electró**ni**ca	

4. The following words end in a consonant other than **-n** or **-s** but are not stressed on the final syllable. An accent mark is therefore added over the vowel of the stressed syllable.

a**zú**car	**fá**cil
lápiz	in**ú**til
por**tá**til	di**fí**cil

The plurals of these words retain the accent mark because they end in **-s** but are not stressed on the next-to-last syllable. (See rule 3, on page 192.)

az**ú**cares	f**á**ciles
l**á**pices	in**ú**tiles
port**á**tiles	

Accent marks are also used to indicate that two consecutive vowels belong to two different syllables.

The five vowels of Spanish are divided into two categories.

STRONG VOWELS	WEAK VOWELS
a	i
e	u
o	

When two strong vowels come together they always form two separate syllables.

paseo	pa - se - o
poeta	po - e - ta
peatonal	pe - a - to - nal

When a strong and a weak vowel come together, they normally form a diphthong, which means that they are pronounced as part of one syllable.

farmacia	far - ma - cia
restaurante	res - tau - ran - te
armario	ar - ma - rio
tienda	tien - da
veinte	vein - te
siete	sie - te
oiga	oi - ga
Europa	eu - ro - pa
cuatro	cua - tro

When a strong and a weak vowel come together and form two syllables, an accent mark is placed over the weak vowel to indicate that it is not part of a diphthong.

peluquer**í**a	pe - lu - que - r**í** - a
ba**ú**l	ba - **ú**l
re**ú**ne	re - **ú** - ne
re**í**mos	re - **í** - mos
pa**í**s	pa - **í**s

Note that when the two weak vowels come together they form a single syllable and the pronunciation varies:

mu**y** (**i** *is written* **y** *at the end of one-syllable words*)
ciudad

Plural of nouns

Spanish forms the plural of nouns by adding **-s** to nouns ending in a vowel and **-es** to nouns ending in a consonant. The **s** of the plural is always pronounced /s/, never /z/.

SINGULAR	PLURAL
cuarto	cuartos
oficina	oficinas
estante	estantes
cibercafé	cibercafés
señor	señores
catedral	catedrales

When the last syllable of a noun ending in a consonant has an accent mark, that accent mark is eliminated when the **-es** plural ending is added.

SINGULAR	PLURAL
maletín	maletines
reunión	reuniones
invitación	invitaciones
autobús	autobuses
francés	franceses

Note that **el país** is an exception: **los países**.

Nouns ending in a consonant but stressed on the next-to-last syllable in the singular add a written accent on the vowel of that syllable when the **-es** plural ending is added.

SINGULAR	PLURAL
joven	jóvenes
examen	exámenes
origen	orígenes

These apparent irregularities follow the rules for the placement of accent marks in Spanish.

Possessive adjectives

The possessive adjectives in Spanish are:

PERSON	SINGULAR	PLURAL
first	mi(s)	nuestro(s)/nuestra(s)
second	tu(s)	vuestro(s)/vuestra(s)
third	su(s)	su(s)

The possessive adjectives **mi, tu** and **su** are used before singular nouns. They add an **-s** before plural nouns: **mis, tus, sus**.

mi carpeta	mis carpetas
tu mensaje	tus mensajes
su perro	sus perros

The possessive adjectives **nuestro** *our* and **vuestro** *your* are four-form adjectives. They agree in gender and number with the following noun.

nuestro/vuestro mensaje	nuestros/vuestros mensajes
nuestra/vuestra carpeta	nuestras/vuestras carpetas

The possessive adjective **su(s)** refers to all third persons, both singular and plural. It can therefore mean *his, her, its, their, your, your (plural)*. Be careful not to make the mistake of assuming that **su** means *his/her* and that **sus** means *their*. **Su** and **sus** agree with the following noun, not with the possessor.

su perro	*his/her/your/their dog*
sus perros	*his/her/your/their dogs*

To focus on the referent of **su/sus**, a phrase beginning with **de** is used.

el perro de él/de ella/de Ud./de ellos/de ellas/de Uds.
los perros de él/de ella/de Ud./de ellos/de ellas/de Uds.

Long-form possessive adjectives

Most Spanish speakers don't stress possessive adjectives the way we do in English to contrast them:

He likes *his* computer, not *my* computer.
Your house is bigger than *their* house.

In order to stress possessive adjectives, Spanish uses long-form possessives. These consist of the definite article + noun + long-form possessive. All the long-form possessive adjectives agree with the noun in gender and number.

el boleto mío	la oficina mía	el boleto nuestro	la oficina nuestra
los boletos míos	las oficinas mías	los boletos nuestros	las oficinas nuestras
el boleto tuyo	la oficina tuya	el boleto vuestro	la oficina vuestra
los boletos tuyos	las oficinas tuyas	los boletos vuestros	las oficinas vuestras
el boleto suyo	la oficina suya	el boleto suyo	la oficina suya
los boletos suyos	las oficinas suyas	los boletos suyos	las oficinas suyas

A prepositional phrase beginning with **de** can replace forms of **suyo** to focus on the person referred to.

el boleto de él/de ella/de Ud./de ellos/de ellas/de Uds.
los boletos de él/de ella/de Ud./de ellos/de ellas/de Uds.

In noun phrases with long-form possessive adjectives, the indefinite article, a demonstrative adjective, or a numeral can replace the definite article.

una oficina nuestra	*an office of ours*
estos boletos suyos	*these tickets of yours*
dos amigos míos	*two friends of mine*

For possessive pronouns, see *Nominalization*.

Predicate

The predicate consists of everything in a sentence except the subject. Thus, in the sentence *Caroline writes children's books* the words *writes children's books* form the predicate of the sentence. The predicate contains the verb and its objects, prepositional phrases adding to the meaning of the verb, adverbs, etc.

Predicate nominative

Noun phrases can follow forms of the verb **ser** *to be* in the predicate of a sentence. In traditional grammar this function is called the *predicate nominative*.

Es **una fiesta** para Esteban.	*It's a party for Esteban.*
Son **los amigos** de mi hijo.	*They're the friends of my son.*

Prepositions

Prepositions are words (such as *to, for, in, at, from* in English) that link nouns or pronouns to other elements of the sentence. The group of words consisting of a preposition + noun or pronoun is called a prepositional phrase. The prepositions of one language rarely correspond exactly to the prepositions of another. See also *Prepositional pronouns*.

Here are some of the most common Spanish prepositions and their English equivalents:

A (to)

Voy **a** la oficina.	*I'm going to the office.*
Le di los documentos **a** mi colega.	*I gave the documents to my colleague.*

Other uses:

English *away from, at a distance of (often no preposition in English translation)*

La estación está **a tres cuadras** del hotel.	*The station is three blocks from the hotel.*
El centro comercial está **a diez minutos** de aquí.	*The mall is ten minutes from here.*

The preposition **a** is used to connect many verbs to a following infinitive (see *Verb + infinitive construction*).

Comienzan **a** entender.	*They're beginning to understand.*
Yo iba **a** inscribirme al curso.	*I was going to register for the course.*

The preposition **a** labels animate, definite direct objects (see *Direct object*, point 2).

¿Viste **a** tus amigos?	*Did you see your friends?*
Vi **a** algunos de ellos.	*I saw some of them.*

The preposition **a** occurs in a number of idiomatic expressions.

a pie	*on foot*
clase a distancia	*online course, distance learning course*
a lo mejor	*maybe*
a veces	*sometimes*

The preposition **a** contracts with the masculine singular definite article **el** to form **al** (see *Contractions*).

Con (with)

El gerente llegó **con** los asesores.	*The manager arrived with the consultants.*
Abrió la puerta **con** su llave.	*He opened the door with his key.*

The preposition **con** is used to connect a few verbs to a following infinitive (see *Verb + infinitive construction*).

Cuenten con nosotros.	*Count on us.*

De (of, from, about)

Conozco al gerente **de** esta sucursal.	*I know the manager of this branch.*
Ellos llegan **del** supermercado ahora.	*They're coming from the supermarket now.*
Siempre hablan **de** política.	*They're always talking about politics.*

Notes:

De expresses possession, origin, material.

Estos libros son **de** la señora Valdivia.	*These are Mrs. Valdivia's books.*
Aquí se venden muchos vinos **de** España.	*Many wines from Spain are sold here.*
Ella lleva una pulsera **de** diamantes.	*She is wearing a diamond bracelet.*

The preposition **de** is used to form compound nouns.

la raqueta **de** tenis	*tennis racket*
la tienda **de** cómputo	*computer store*
la base **de** datos	*database*

The preposition **de** is used to connect many verbs and verbal expressions to a following infinitive (see *Verb + infinitive construction*).

Acabamos **de** terminar el proyecto.	*We've just finished the project.*
Traté **de** ponerme en contacto con ellos.	*I tried to contact them.*

A prepositional phrase beginning with **de** can replace forms of **su** and **suyo** to focus on the person referred to (see the section on long-form possessive adjectives under *Possessive adjectives*).

The preposition **de** contracts with the masculine singular definite article **el** to form **del** (see *Contractions*).

Other uses:

¿Qué pides **de** postre?	*What are you ordering for dessert?*
morir **de** miedo	*to die of fright*
trabajar **de** día, **de** noche	*to work days, nights*

The preposition **de** occurs in a number of idiomatic expressions.

de todas formas	*anyway, in any case*
de veras	*really*
de repente	*suddenly*
de nada	*you're welcome*

En (in, at, on)

Nosotros vivimos **en** el campo.	*We live in the country.*
Él trabaja **en** el aeropuerto.	*He works at the airport.*
Hay lápices y papel **en** la mesa.	*There are pencils and paper on the table.*

To specify position, **en** can be replaced by **dentro de** *inside of* or **encima de** *on, on top of*.

En specifies the period of time *within which* something happens:

Regresamos **en** diez minutos.	*We're coming back in ten minutes.*

En appears in various expressions:

en serio	*seriously*
ir **en** avión, **en** barco, **en** carro	*to go by plane, boat, car*

The preposition **en** is used to connect a few verbs to a following infinitive (see *Verb + infinitive construction*):

Insiste en quedarse una semana más.   *He insists on staying one more week.*

Sin (*without*)

Ellos vinieron **sin** sus padres.   *They came without their parents.*
Mi hermano está **sin** trabajo.   *My brother is out of work.*

Prepositions with expressions of time

With the days of the week Spanish does not use the preposition **en**.

Te veo el martes.   *I'll see you on Tuesday.*
Él no trabaja los viernes.   *He doesn't work on Fridays.*

Prepositional pronouns

Spanish has a special set of pronouns used after prepositions. These pronouns are identical to the subject pronouns except in the first and second persons singular.

Here is the set of prepositional pronouns after **para**.

para **mí**   para **nosotros/nosotras**
para **ti**   para **vosotros/vosotras**
para **él/ella**   para **ellos/ellas**
para **Ud.**   para **Uds.**

Note that the prepositional pronoun **mí** has a written accent while the prepositional pronoun **ti** does not.

After **con** there are two irregular forms:

con + mí → conmigo   *with me*
con + ti → contigo   *with you*

Present perfect

The present perfect tense in Spanish consists of the present tense of the auxiliary verb **haber** + the past participle. In the perfect tenses the past participle is invariable—it does not agree in gender or number with any other element of the sentence. The Spanish present perfect usually corresponds to the English present perfect, which consists of *have* + past participle.

singular

he tomado, comido   *I have taken, eaten*
has tomado, comido   *you have taken, eaten*
ha tomado, comido   *he, she has, you (**Ud.**) have taken, eaten*

plural

hemos tomado, comido   *we have taken, eaten*
habéis tomado, comido   *you have taken, eaten*
han tomado, comido   *they, you (**Uds.**) have taken, eaten*

No words can be placed between the auxiliary verb and the past participle. The negative word **no** precedes the form of **haber**.

¿Por qué **no** han llegado?	*Why haven't they arrived?*
Hoy **no** he visto a nadie.	*Today I haven't seen anyone.*

Object pronouns, including reflexive pronouns (see *Reflexive verbs*), precede the form of **haber** in the perfect tenses. The negative word **no** precedes the object pronouns.

¿El iPod? **Se lo he** dado a Lorenzo.	*The iPod? I have given it to Lorenzo.*
Los niños **no se han** acostado todavía.	*The children have not gone to bed yet.*

Present subjunctive in noun clauses

Spanish distinguishes between two types of noun clauses: those that express an action that is part of reality and/or the speaker's experience and those that express an action that is not yet part of reality and/or the speaker's experience and that is therefore in the realm of desire or wish. Those subordinate noun clauses that express unrealized actions appear in the subjunctive.

In most cases the verbs in the main clause that trigger a subjunctive in the subordinate clause make the use of the subjunctive obligatory. Here are the major categories of verbs that must be followed by dependent clauses in the subjunctive.

1. imposition of will: **desear que, esperar que, necesitar que, preferir que, querer que**. The negative of these verbs is also followed by a clause in the present subjunctive.

Queremos que **te quedes** un poco más.	*We want you to stay a little longer.*
Espero que **puedan** venir.	*I hope they'll be able to come.*
No necesitamos que nos **ayudes**.	*We don't need for you to help us.*

2. getting someone to do something: **aconsejarle a uno que, exigirle a uno que, insistir en que, mandarle a uno que, pedirle a uno que**. The indirect object may be omitted when a subjunctive clause follows.

¿Por qué (me) pides que venga?	*Why are you asking me to come?*
Te aconsejo que le **hagas** caso.	*I advise you to pay attention to what he says.*
Me exigen que **trabaje** los fines de semana.	*They demand that I work on weekends.*
Siempre nos pide que le **prestemos** dinero.	*He always asks us to lend him money.*
Insisto en que Ud. **coma** con nosotros.	*I insist that you eat with us.*

An infinitive clause is also possible with **aconsejar, exigir, mandar, pedir**.

Te aconsejo **hacerle** caso.	*I advise you to pay attention to what he says.*

3. doubt, uncertainty: **dudar que, no creer que, no pensar que**.

Dudo que ella lo **sepa**.	*I doubt she knows it.*
No creen que **seamos** capaces de hacerlo.	*They don't think we're capable of doing it.*

Note that the negative of **dudar** and the affirmative of **creer** and **pensar** are followed by the indicative, not the subjunctive.

No dudamos que te **ama**.	*We don't doubt that he loves you.*
Pienso que **es** una tienda muy cara.	*I think it's a very expensive store.*

4. emotions and subjective value judgments: **alegrarse (de) que, (no) gustarle a uno que, (no) parecerle a uno bien/mal que, sentir que, es una lástima que**

Me alegro de que me **comprendas**.	*I'm glad you understand me.*
Sentimos que él **esté** enojado.	*We're sorry that he's angry.*
No les gusta que su hija **salga** con Álvaro.	*They don't like that their daughter is going out with Álvaro.*
Me parece bien que **tengamos** vacaciones.	*I think it's good that we'll have a vacation.*

Expressions consisting of **es** + adjective + **que** (impersonal expressions) with meanings similar to the verbs in 1-4 above, i.e, imposition of will, emotion, subjective value judgments, or doubt, are also followed by the subjunctive.

Es necesario que **vengas**.	*It's necessary for you to come.*
Es importante que ella **hable** con su esposo.	*It's important for her to talk with her husband.*
Es poco probable que me **conozcan**.	*It's improbable that they will know me.*
Es triste que no **encuentren** empleo.	*It's sad that they can't find work.*
Es mejor que las **llamemos** mañana.	*It's better for us to call them tomorrow.*

The following impersonal expressions are followed by the subjunctive only when negative: **no es cierto que, no es evidente que, no es verdad que, no estoy seguro (de) que**.

No es verdad que él **sea** médico.	*It's not true that he's a doctor.*
Es verdad que él **es** médico.	*It's true that he's a doctor.*
No estoy seguro de que **quieran** salir.	*I'm not sure they want to go out.*
Estoy seguro de que **quieren** salir.	*I'm sure they want to go out.*

When these expressions are affirmative they are followed by the indicative.

Es cierto que él **es** médico.	*It's true that he's a doctor.*
Es evidente que tú la **amas**.	*It's evident that you love her.*

The expression **es dudoso que** is followed by the subjunctive when affirmative but by the indicative when negative.

Es dudoso que se **pueda** terminar este proyecto.	*It's doubtful that this project can be completed.*
No es dudoso que se **puede** terminar este proyecto.	*It's not doubtful that this project can be completed.*

Note:

1. The English equivalent of a Spanish subjunctive clause is often an infinitive clause, rather than a subordinate clause beginning with *that*. This is common after the verbs **dejar, hacer, impedir, mandar, ordenar, permitir,** and **prohibir.** All of these verbs take an indirect object except for **dejar**, which takes a direct one.

Nadie te impide estudiar.	*No one is keeping him from studying.*
No lo dejé salir.	*I didn't let him go out.*

2. If the subject of both clauses is the same, Spanish uses the infinitive, not the subjunctive.

Yo quiero que él **vaya**.	*I want him to go.*
Yo quiero **ir**.	*I want to go.*

3. The expressions **tal vez** *perhaps* and **quizás** *perhaps* can be followed either by the indicative or the subjunctive depending on the degree of certainty the speaker has about the action.

Tal vez nieve esta noche.   *Perhaps it will snow tonight.*
Quizás juegan al golf mañana.   *Perhaps they'll play golf tomorrow.*

Present subjunctive of irregular verbs

Verbs that have an irregularity such as **-g-**, **-zc-**, or **-y-** in the *yo* form of the present indicative have that irregularity in all persons of the present subjunctive. These irregularities occur only in **-er** and **-ir** verbs and therefore all the affected present subjunctive endings have the vowel **-a-**.

INFINITIVE	*YO* FORM PRESENT INDICATIVE	SUBJUNCTIVE					
		YO	TÚ	ÉL, ELLA, UD.	NOSOTROS	VOSOTROS	ELLOS, ELLAS, UDS.
caber	**quep**o	quepa	quepas	quepa	quepamos	quepáis	quepan
caer	**caig**o	caiga	caigas	caiga	caigamos	caigáis	caigan
conocer	**conozc**o	conozca	conozcas	conozca	conozcamos	conozcáis	conozcan
construir	**construy**o	construya	construyas	construya	construyamos	construyáis	construyan
decir	**dig**o	diga	digas	diga	digamos	digáis	digan
hacer	**hag**o	haga	hagas	haga	hagamos	hagáis	hagan
oír	**oig**o	oiga	oigas	oiga	oigamos	oigáis	oigan
poner	**pong**o	ponga	pongas	ponga	pongamos	pongáis	pongan
salir	**salg**o	salga	salgas	salga	salgamos	salgáis	salgan
tener	**teng**o	tenga	tengas	tenga	tengamos	tengáis	tengan
traer	**traig**o	traiga	traigas	traiga	traigamos	traigáis	traigan
venir	**veng**o	venga	vengas	venga	vengamos	vengáis	vengan
ver	**ve**o	vea	veas	vea	veamos	veáis	vean

Other irregular verbs in the present subjunctive:

INFINITIVE	SUBJUNCTIVE					
	YO	TÚ	ÉL, ELLA, UD.	NOSOTROS	VOSOTROS	ELLOS, ELLAS, UDS.
dar	dé	des	dé	demos	deis	den
estar	esté	estés	esté	estemos	estéis	estén
haber	haya	hayas	haya	hayamos	hayáis	hayan
ir	vaya	vayas	vaya	vayamos	vayáis	vayan
saber	sepa	sepas	sepa	sepamos	sepáis	sepan
ser	sea	seas	sea	seamos	seáis	sean

Present subjunctive of regular verbs

The present subjunctive is formed by switching the characteristic vowels of the conjugations. **-Ar** verbs change the **-a-** of the present indicative to **-e-** while **-er** and **-ir** verbs change the vowels **-e-** and **-i-** of the present indicative to **-a-** in the subjunctive. Regular **-er** and **-ir** verbs share the same set of endings for the different persons of the subjunctive.

trabajar

Quiere que trabaj**e** con él.   *He wants me to work with him.*
Quiere que trabaj**es** con él.   *He wants you to work with him.*
Quiere que trabaj**e** con él.   *He wants her to work with him.*

Quiere que trabaj**emos** con él.	*He wants us to work with him.*
Quiere que trabaj**éis** con él.	*He wants you to work with him.*
Quiere que trabaj**en** con él.	*He wants them to work with him.*

aprender

Espera que aprend**a** español.	*She hopes I'll learn Spanish.*
Espera que aprend**as** español.	*She hopes you'll learn Spanish.*
Espera que aprend**a** español.	*She hopes he'll learn Spanish.*
Espera que aprend**amos** español.	*She hopes we'll learn Spanish.*
Espera que aprend**áis** español.	*She hopes you'll learn Spanish.*
Espera que aprend**an** español.	*She hopes they'll learn Spanish.*

escribir

Prefieren que les escrib**a** un email.	*They prefer that I write them an e-mail.*
Prefieren que les escrib**as** un email.	*They prefer that you write them an e-mail.*
Prefieren que les escrib**a** un email.	*They prefer that he write them an e-mail.*
Prefieren que les escrib**amos** un email.	*They prefer that we write them an e-mail.*
Prefieren que les escrib**áis** un email.	*They prefer that you write them an e-mail.*
Prefieren que les escrib**an** un email.	*They prefer that they write them an e-mail.*

Notes:

1. In the present subjunctive the **yo** form and the **él** form are identical.

2. **-Ar** and **-er** verbs that have changes in the vowel of the stem in the present indicative have these same changes in the present subjunctive.

Quiero que c**ie**rres la puerta.	*I want you to close the door.*
Quieren que cerremos la puerta.	*They want us to close the door.*
Prefiero que no v**ue**lvas muy tarde.	*I prefer that you not come back very late.*
¿A qué hora quiere Ud. que v**o**lvamos?	*What time do you want us to come back?*

3. **-Ir** verbs that have the change **e → ie** or **e → i** in the present indicative also have these changes in the present subjunctive. But these verbs also change the **e** of the stem to **i** in the **nosotros** and **vosotros** forms of the present subjunctive.

sentir		pedir	
sienta	sintamos	pida	pidamos
sientas	sintáis	pidas	pidáis
sienta	sientan	pida	pidan

4. **Dormir** and **morir** change **o** to **u** in the stem of the **nosotros** and **vosotros** forms.

   ### dormir

d**ue**rma	d**u**rmamos
d**ue**rmas	d**u**rmáis
d**ue**rma	d**ue**rman

5. Verbs that end in **-iar** or **-uar** and that have an accent mark on the **í** or the **ú** in the singular and third-person plural of the present tense have the accent mark in the same four persons of the present subjunctive. The **nosotros** and **vosotros** forms do not have an accent mark. For example: **enviar:** envíe, envíes, envíe, enviemos, enviéis, envíen; **continuar:** continúe, continúes, continúe, continuemos, continuéis, continúen.

Present tense

The Spanish verb system

The Spanish verb system is characterized by a large number of forms, each one of which shows person and tense. This is very different from English, where person and tense are signaled by separate words (often contracted).

SPANISH	ENGLISH
iré	*I'll go ← I will go*

Spanish verbs are divided into three classes, called conjugations, shown by the vowel of the infinitive. The infinitive is the form of the verb that does not show person or tense and is the form used for listing verbs in dictionaries and vocabularies. Spanish infinitives may end in **-ar**, **-er**, or **-ir**. When the infinitive ending is removed, the stem of the verb is left. Endings are added to the stem.

Formation of the present tense

The present indicative tense in Spanish is formed by adding the present tense endings to the stem of the verb. Here is a sample verb for each of the conjugations. The endings are in boldface.

COMPRAR *TO BUY*		**COMER** *TO EAT*		**ABRIR** *TO OPEN*	
compr**o**	compr**amos**	com**o**	com**emos**	abr**o**	abr**imos**
compr**as**	compr**áis**	com**es**	com**éis**	abr**es**	abr**ís**
compr**a**	compr**an**	com**e**	com**en**	abr**e**	abr**en**

Note that the endings of the **-er** and **-ir** verbs are identical except in the first- and second-person plural (**nosotros** and **vosotros**) forms. (For an explanation of these terms see *Subject pronouns*.) The endings of the three conjugations are similar—the characteristic difference is the vowel of the ending: **-ar** verbs have the vowel **a** in five of the six endings while **-er** verbs have the vowel **e**. **-Ir** verbs have the same endings as **-er** verbs in all but two persons, as explained above.

There are variations in the above pattern of the present tense. A large number of Spanish verbs with the vowel **e** or **o** in the stem modify that vowel in four out of the six forms of the present tense. See *Stem-changing verbs*.

Verbs that don't follow the above pattern are called irregular verbs.

The present indicative is used for normal statements in main clauses and subordinate clauses. The present indicative (as opposed to the present subjunctive) implies that the speaker sees the action as a fact, as part of reality or of his or her experience.

Preterit tense

Preterit formation

The preterit tense in Spanish expresses completed actions in the past.

The preterit is signaled by sets of endings added to the verb stem. The characteristic feature of the preterit of regular verbs is that its endings are all stressed.

The preterit of **-er** and **-ir** verbs have the same endings. They differ from the preterit endings of the **-ar** verbs in having **i** rather than **a** as the characteristic vowel.

Here are the preterit conjugations of regular verbs.

comprar *to buy*

compré	compramos
compraste	comprasteis
compró	compraron

vender *to sell*

vendí	vendimos
vendiste	vendisteis
vendió	vendieron

escribir *to write*

escribí	escribimos
escribiste	escribisteis
escribió	escribieron

Note that in the **nosotros** form of -**ar** and -**ir** verbs the preterit forms are identical with those of the present tense.

present and preterit

compramos	*we buy* or *we bought*
escribimos	*we write* or *we wrote*

Context clarifies whether the verb form is present or preterit.
For -**er** verbs, the present and preterit forms are distinct.

PRESENT	PRETERIT
vend**emos**	vend**imos**

Preterit of verbs with stem changes

In the preterit there are no stem changes in -**ar** and -**er** verbs even if they have a stem change in the present. (See *Stem-changing verbs*.)

pensar *to think*

PRESENT		PRETERIT	
pienso	pensamos	pensé	pensamos
piensas	pensáis	pensaste	pensasteis
piensa	piensan	pensó	pensaron

volver *to return*

PRESENT		PRETERIT	
vuelvo	volvemos	volví	volvimos
vuelves	volvéis	volviste	volvisteis
vuelve	vuelven	volvió	volvieron

-**Ir** verbs that have a change in the vowel of the stem in the present also have a vowel change in the third-person forms of the preterit. Verbs that change **e → ie** or **e → i** in the present have -**i**- in the third persons singular and plural of the preterit. The verbs **morir** and **dormir** have -**u**- in the third persons singular and plural of the preterit.

sentirse *to feel*

PRESENT		PRETERIT	
me s**ie**nto	nos sentimos	me sentí	nos sentimos
te s**ie**ntes	os sentís	te sentiste	os sentisteis
se s**ie**nte	se s**ie**nten	se s**i**ntió	se s**i**ntieron

pedir *to ask for*

PRESENT		PRETERIT	
p**i**do	pedimos	pedí	pedimos
p**i**des	pedís	pediste	pedisteis
p**i**de	p**i**den	p**i**dió	p**i**dieron

morir *to die*

PRESENT		PRETERIT	
m**ue**ro	morimos	morí	morimos
m**ue**res	morís	moriste	moristeis
m**ue**re	m**ue**ren	m**u**rió	m**u**rieron

dormir *to sleep*

PRESENT		PRETERIT	
d**ue**rmo	dormimos	dormí	dormimos
d**ue**rmes	dormís	dormiste	dormisteis
d**ue**rme	d**ue**rmen	d**u**rmió	d**u**rmieron

Preterit of verbs with spelling changes

-**Ar** verbs whose stem ends in **c, g**, or **z** change those letters to **qu, gu**, and **c**, respectively in the **yo** form of the preterit. These forms are regular in speech but have these changes in order to accord with the rules of Spanish spelling.

INFINITIVE	**YO** FORM OF THE PRETERIT
sacar	sa**qué**
tocar	to**qué**
jugar	ju**gué**
pagar	pa**gué**
almorzar	almor**cé**
comenzar	comen**cé**

Preterit of -er and -ir verbs with stems ending in a vowel

-**Er** and -**ir** verbs whose stems end in a vowel change the endings -**ió** to -**yó** and -**ieron** to -**yeron**. These verbs (except verbs whose stems end in -**u**) also add a written accent to the **i** of the endings of the **tú, nosotros**, and **vosotros** forms of the preterit.

caer *to fall*

caí	caímos
caíste	caísteis
cayó	cayeron

leer *to read*

leí	leímos
leíste	leísteis
leyó	leyeron

construir *to build*

construí	construimos
construiste	construisteis
construyó	construyeron

oír *to hear*

oí	oímos
oíste	oísteis
oyó	oyeron

Verbs in -**guir** do not follow this pattern.

seguir *to follow*

seguí	seguimos
seguiste	seguisteis
siguió	siguieron

Irregular preterits

A number of common verbs in Spanish have irregular preterit forms. Almost all of these verbs have the following characteristics:

1. The preterit is formed from an irregular stem.

2. The endings are the same as those of -**er** and -**ir** verbs except in the **yo** and **él/ella/Ud.** forms.

3. The **yo** and **él/ella/Ud.** forms are stressed on the stem, not on the endings.

4. The ending for the **yo** form is -**e** and the ending for the **él/ella/Ud.** form is -**o**.

5. In most cases the irregular stem has the vowel -**i**- or -**u**-.

venir *to come*

vine	vinimos
viniste	vinisteis
vino	vinieron

tener *to have*

tuve	tuvimos
tuviste	tuvisteis
tuvo	tuvieron

The verbs **decir, traer,** and verbs ending in -**ducir** have preterit stems ending in **j**. In the **ellos/ellas/Uds.** form of these verbs the ending is -**eron**, not -**ieron**.

decir *to say, tell*

dije	dij**imos**
dij**iste**	dij**isteis**
dij**o**	dij**eron**

traer *to bring*

traje	traj**imos**
traj**iste**	traj**isteis**
traj**o**	traj**eron**

conducir *to drive*

conduj**e**	conduj**imos**
conduj**iste**	conduj**iste**
conduj**o**	conduj**eron**

The verb **dar** is conjugated like an **-er/-ir** verb in the preterit. The preterit forms of **dar** and **ver** have no accent marks.

dar *to give*

di	d**imos**
d**iste**	d**isteis**
d**io**	d**ieron**

ver *to see*

vi	v**imos**
v**iste**	v**isteis**
v**io**	v**ieron**

The verbs **ser** *to be* and **ir** *to go* share the same conjugation in the preterit. Context clarifies which verb is intended.

ser/ir

fui	fuimos
fuiste	fuisteis
fue	fueron

For the full preterit conjugations of other verbs with irregular preterits, see the verb charts.

Pronunciation

Spanish spelling is a reasonable indicator of pronunciation.

Spanish has five vowels: **a**, **e**, **i**, **o**, **u**. These vowels are short and pronounced with more tension of the articulatory muscles than is used in English. They are pronounced the same whether stressed or unstressed.

casa
leche
tipo
mono
luna

The Spanish diphthongs **ai (ay)**, **au**, **ei (ey)**, **eu**, **oi (oy)**, and **uy** are pronounced as combinations of the two vowels they are written with and merge into a single syllable.

The letters **b/v** (**b** and **v** represent the same sound in Spanish), **d**, and **g** represent sounds that change according to their position in the stream of speech.

After a pause and after a nasal consonant (**m** or **n**), these sounds are hard. The letters **b/v** represent the English *b* of boy. **D** represents a sound similar to the English *d* in dot and **g** represents a sound similar to the letter *g* in English goat.

vaca	donde
ambos	dando
invitar	ganga

D is also hard after **l**, as in **falda**. In all other positions **b/v**, **d**, and **g** are soft. **B/v** is pronounced like English *w*, but with the lips not rounded.

cabo
robusto
cerveza

D is pronounced like the *th* in English *other*.

cada	padre
modo	pierden
podemos	

G is pronounced almost like the hard **g**, but with the air forced through the back of the tongue and the hard palate.

amigo	seguimos
digo	pagamos
hago	

The softening of **b/v**, **d**, and **g** happens between vowels even when the vowels are in two different words.

me voy	lo difícil
la boca	no gasto
le damos	la galleta

Spanish has two **r** sounds represented by the letter **r**.

A single **r** between vowels or after a consonant indicates a single flap of the tip of the tongue against the gum ridge behind the upper teeth. The closest English sound is the *d* in *ladder*.

caro	triste
pero	grande
duro	

A double **rr** between vowels, or a single **r** at the beginning of a word, represents a trill, three or four of the flaps made in producing the single **r**.

rápido	carro
ropa	perro
ruso	zorro
rico	correo
receta	guerra

The letter **c** represents two sounds in Spanish. Before the letters **e** and **i** it is pronounced like the English *s* in *some*. (In Spain, it is pronounced like the English *th* in *think* in this position; see next page.) In all other positions, the letter **c** represents the sound **k**.

cereza	casa
cerrar	cosa
cero	curioso
cielo	clase
cinco	creer

In Latin American Spanish, the letter **z** represents a sound like the English *s* in *some*. In Spain, the letter **z**, like the letter **c** before the letters **e** and **i**, represents a sound similar to the *th* in English *think*.

zapato	luz
zona	lápiz
plaza	

In Spanish, the letter **j** and the letter **g** when it comes before **e** and **i** represent a sound that is made by pronouncing /k/ but forcing air between the arched back of the tongue and the roof of the mouth. This sound is found in the name *Bach*.

jardín	joven
gente	jueves
gira	

Spanish **ll** and **y** both represent a sound similar to English *y* but pronounced with more articulatory tension.

allá	ya
llave	yo
llevar	apoyo
lluvia	construye

Spanish **l** is pronounced similar to English *l*, except that the tip of the tongue touches the back of the upper teeth. Spanish **l** is clearly pronounced, even in final position.

lata	el
luna	azul
baile	Brasil

The letters **p**, **t**, and **k** represent sounds similar to the ones they represent in English, except that before a stressed vowel Spanish **p**, **t** and **k** are not followed by a puff of air as they are in English.

pan	toma
postre	cama
tema	queso

The letter **ñ** in Spanish spelling represents a sound similiar to the *ni* in *onion* but with the *n* pronounced as part of the second syllable.

año	cariñoso
baño	diseñar

The letters **f**, **m**, **n**, and **ch** represent sounds similar to the ones they represent in English. The letter **h** in Spanish spelling is always silent.

Note that the sounds **t**, **d**, **l**, and **n** in Spanish are made with the tip of the tongue touching the back of the upper teeth, not the gum ridge above the upper teeth as in English.

Punctuation

Punctuation in Spanish is similar to that of English except in questions and exclamations. Spanish uses an inverted question mark and an inverted exclamation point at the beginning of these sentences in addition to the standard question mark and exclamation point at the end.

¿Adónde va Luisa?	*Where is Luisa going?*
¡Qué día más bonito!	*What a lovely day!*

¿Qué?

See *Question words (interrogatives).*

¡Qué! in exclamations

The word **¡qué!** can be used before nouns and adjectives to form an exclamation.

¡Qué panorama!	*What a view!*
¡Qué susto!	*What a scare!*
¡Qué bonito!	*How lovely!*
¡Qué aburrido!	*How boring!*

To emphasize a characteristic of a noun, the pattern **¡qué!** + adjective + noun may be used.

¡Qué buen amigo!	*What a good friend!*
¡Qué mala suerte!	*What bad luck!*
¡Qué ridículas ideas!	*What ridiculous ideas!*

Perhaps more common in the above function is the pattern **¡qué!** + noun + **más/tan** + adjective.

¡Qué cuadro más interesante!	*What an interesting painting!*
¡Qué salsa tan rica!	*What a delicious sauce!*
¡Qué muchachas más inteligentes!	*What intelligent girls!*
¡Qué niños más traviesos!	*What mischievous children!*

Question formation

There are two types of questions. *Yes/no questions* ask for confirmation or denial.

Is Susan here yet?

They expect the answer *yes* or *no.*

Information questions begin with a question word. (See *Question words.*)They expect a piece of information as an answer.

What time is it?
Who is that man?
Where does your sister work?
How did you do that?

In Spanish, all questions are written with an inverted question mark at the beginning of the sentence and a regular question mark at the end.

¿Qué hora es**?**

The most common way to ask a yes/no question in Spanish is to change the intonation from statement intonation to rising question intonation. This is shown in writing by enclosing the sentence in question marks.

Marcos es chileno.	*Marcos is Chilean.*
¿Marcos es chileno?	*Is Marcos Chilean?*

The subject can also be placed after the verb.

Elena trabaja en esta oficina.	*Elena works in this office.*
¿Trabaja Elena en esta oficina?	*Does Elena work in this office?*

When a question includes a form of the verb **ser** + an adjective, the subject is placed at the end of the sentence. The pattern of the question is thus verb + adjective + subject.

El hotel es cómodo.	*The hotel is comfortable.*
¿Es cómodo el hotel?	*Is the hotel comfortable?*

Placing the subject at the end of the sentence is also possible in questions containing **estar** + adjective.

¿Está abierta la tienda?	*Is the store open?*
¿Está terminado el proyecto?	*Is the project finished?*

Question words (interrogatives)

Question words introduce information questions. These questions ask for a piece of information as an answer.

Question words are always written with an accent mark in Spanish and they carry stress in questions.

The most important question words in Spanish are:

¿cuál?, ¿cuáles?	*which one(s)?*
¿cuándo?	*when?*
¿cuánto?, ¿cuánta?	*how much?*
¿cuántos?, ¿cuántas?	*how many?*
¿cómo?	*how?*
¿dónde?	*where? (location)*
¿adónde?	*where? (with verbs of motion)*
¿de dónde?	*from where?*
¿qué?	*what?*
¿para qué?	*for what purpose?*
¿por qué?	*why?*
¿quién?, ¿quiénes?	*who?*
¿a quién?, ¿a quiénes?	*whom?*
¿de quién?, ¿de quiénes?	*whose?*

Notes:

¿Qué? may be used before a verb or a noun.

¿Qué hay en la gaveta?	*What's (there) in the drawer?*
¿Qué tienda buscas?	*What store are you looking for?*

¿Cómo? asks for repetition when you don't hear something clearly.

—Él llega mañana.	*He's arriving tomorrow.*
—**¿Cómo?** No oigo. ¿Cuándo llega?	*What? I can't hear. When is he arriving?*

¿**Cómo?** is also used to express astonishment.

—Han despedido a María Elena. *They've fired María Elena.*
—¿**Cómo?** No lo puedo creer. *What? I can't believe it.*

Reflexive verbs

Reflexive verb formation

Reflexive verbs are a class of verbs in Spanish that always appear with an object pronoun that refers to the subject. This pronoun is called the *reflexive pronoun*. English also has reflexive verbs. In English, reflexive pronouns end in -*self* or -*selves*: *I hurt myself., They hurt themselves.* English reflexive verbs are a limited class and stress that the subject performs the action upon him- or herself. In Spanish, however, reflexive verbs are a broad category with several different functions that do not correspond at all to English reflexives.

Study the conjugation of the reflexive verb **levantarse** *to get up* in the present and preterit. Note that the reflexive pronouns are the same as the direct and indirect object pronouns in the first and second persons (**yo, tú, nosotros, vosotros**). In the third person, the reflexive pronoun is **se** both in the singular and in the plural.

Reflexive verbs appear in vocabulary lists with -**se** attached to the infinitive: **despertarse, enojarse, lavarse, calmarse**, etc.

PRESENT		PRETERIT	
me levanto	**nos** levantamos	**me** levanté	**nos** levantamos
te levantas	**os** levantáis	**te** levantaste	**os** levantasteis
se levanta	**se** levantan	**se** levantó	**se** levantaron

When a reflexive verb appears in the infinitive in verb + infinitive constructions, the **se** of the infinitive must change to agree with the subject of the sentence. Like other object pronouns, the reflexive pronoun may be placed either before the first verb or after the infinitive, in which case it is attached to it in writing.There is no difference in meaning.

Me debo calmar.	Debo calmar**me**.
Te debes calmar.	Debes calmar**te**.
Se debe calmar.	Debe calmar**se**.
Nos debemos calmar.	Debemos calmar**nos**.
Os debéis calmar.	Debéis calmar**os**.
Se deben calmar.	Deben calmar**se**.

Reflexive verb uses

1. Spanish reflexive verbs correspond most often to intransitive verbs or verb phrases in English. Their English equivalents often contain *get* or *be.*

aburrirse	*to get/be bored*
asustarse	*to get scared*
divertirse	*to have a good time*
enojarse	*to get angry*
marearse	*to get dizzy*
ofenderse	*to become insulted*
pasearse	*to stroll*
sorprenderse	*to be surprised*
tranquilizarse	*to calm down, stop worrying*

Me aburro en la oficina.	*I get bored at the office.*
Ella se mareó en el avión.	*She got dizzy on the plane.*
Él se ofende por tonterías.	*He gets insulted at silly things.*
Me divertí mucho en Costa Rica.	*I had a very good time in Costa Rica.*

2. Spanish reflexive pronouns are often the equivalent of English possessive adjectives when used with parts of the body or articles of clothing. Note that in this case, the reflexive pronoun is an indirect object and the definite article is used before the noun. The part of the body or article of clothing in sentences such as these is the direct object.

lastimarse el pie	*to hurt one's foot*
lavarse las manos	*to wash one's hands*
limpiarse los dientes	*to brush (=clean) one's teeth*
ponerse los zapatos	*to put on one's shoes*
quitarse el abrigo	*to take off one's coat*
romperse el brazo	*to break one's arm*
Si tienes calor, debes quitarte el suéter.	*If you're warm you should take off your sweater.*
Javier se rompió la pierna.	*Javier broke his leg.*

3. Many reflexive verbs have a nonreflexive counterpart. The nonreflexive verb is transitive and is used with a direct object. Compare the following pairs of expressions.

acostar a los niños	*to put the children to bed*	acostarse	*to go to bed*
asustar al gato	*to scare the cat*	asustarse	*to get scared*
calmar a las víctimas	*to calm the victims down*	calmarse	*to calm down*
lavar el carro	*to wash the car*	lavarse	*to wash up*
pasear al perro	*to walk the dog*	pasearse	*to take a walk*
sentar a la gente	*to seat people*	sentarse	*to sit down*

Acosté a los niños y después me acosté.	*I put the children to bed and then I went to bed.*
Juan se despertó y luego despertó a su hermana.	*Juan woke up and then woke his sister up.*

4. A small number of Spanish verbs exist only as reflexives.

atreverse (a hacer algo)	*to dare (to do something)*
desmayarse	*to faint*
divorciarse	*to get divorced*
jactarse (de algo)	*to boast (about something)*
quejarse (de algo)	*to complain (about something)*
suicidarse	*to commit suicide*
No me atrevo a pedirle nada.	*I don't dare ask him for anything.*
Esos empleados se quejan de todo.	*Those employees complain about everything.*

5. Reflexive verbs used in the plural may convey a reciprocal meaning equivalent to *each other*.

Pablo y Beatriz se ven todos los días.	*Pablo and Beatriz see each other every day.*
Ellos se quieren.	*They love each other.*
¿Por qué no nos tuteamos?	*Why don't we use the **tú** form with each other?*
Nos enviamos correos electrónicos.	*We send each other e-mails.*

Relative pronouns

Relative pronouns introduce relative clauses. A relative clause is a sentence incorporated into a larger sentence that functions as an adjective within the larger sentence. In other words, it describes a noun. Relative clauses are also called *adjective clauses*. Look at the following English example.

> They live in a *new* house.
> They live in a house *that they bought last year*.

Note that *new* and *that they bought last year* both modify the noun *house*. *New* is an adjective; *that they bought last year* is a relative clause.

The Spanish relative pronoun **que** can refer to people or things and can be either the subject or object of its clause.

mi amigo que trabaja en Inglaterra	*my friend who works in England*

(**que** is the subject of the verb **trabaja**)

la señora que voy a llamar	*the woman I am going to call*

(**que** is the direct object of the verb **llamar**)

un programa que es innovador	*a program which is innovative*

(**que** is the subject of the verb **es**)

los sitios Web que diseñan	*the websites that they design*

(**que** is the direct object of the verb **diseñan**)

In English, when the relative pronoun is the object of the verb in the relative clause, the pronoun is often omitted. It may never be omitted in Spanish.

la casa **que** compraron	*the house they bought*
los asesores **que** contratamos	*the consultants we hired*

When **que** is the object of the verb in the relative clause and it refers to people, it may be replaced by **a quien** or **a quienes**, depending on whether it refers to a singular or plural noun.

el empleado **a quien** despidieron	*the employee they fired*
los asesores **a quienes** contratamos	*the consultants we hired*

A quien and **a quienes** are more formal in style than **que**.

Reverse construction verbs

Reverse construction verbs usually appear with an indirect object pronoun. They are called reverse construction verbs because the English subject in equivalent sentences corresponds to the Spanish indirect object and the English direct object corresponds to the subject of the corresponding Spanish sentence.

For instance, the verb **gustar** is the equivalent of English *to like*, but the structure of sentences containing **gustar** is very different from those containing *to like* in English. In the English sentence

> *I like this computer.*

The subject of the sentence is *I*. The noun phrase *this computer* is the direct object of the verb *like*.

The Spanish equivalent of the above sentence is

Me gusta esta computadora.

In the Spanish sentence **me** is the indirect object of the verb **gustar**. The subject is **esta computadora.** Therefore, the verb is in the third-person singular, to agree with the subject. Note that the verb changes to the third-person plural when the subject is plural.

I like these computers.
Me gustan estas computadoras.

Reverse construction verbs are usually in the third-person singular or plural, and appear only rarely in the other persons.

When an infinitive is the subject of a reverse construction verb (or even when several infinitives are), the verb is in the third-person singular.

Me gusta ver las noticias antes de acostarme.	*I like to watch the news before going to bed.*
¿Te interesaría trabajar en Chile?	*Would you be interested in working in Chile?*
Me hace falta salir y comprar comida.	*I need to go out and buy food.*

Note that subject nouns used with **gustar** are usually preceded by the definite article or some other determiner.

Le gusta **el** helado.	*He likes ice cream.*
Nos gustan **los** documentales.	*We like documentaries.*

Here are some common reverse construction verbs. The phrase **a uno** represents the indirect object.

convenirle a uno	*to be suitable for someone*
encantarle a uno	*to love (something)*
entusiasmarle a uno	*to be/get excited about something*
faltarle a uno	*to be short of something, to not have something*
hacerle falta a uno	*to need something*
importarle a uno	*to matter to someone*
interesarle a uno	*to be interested in something*
quedarle a uno	*to have something left*
sobrarle a uno	*to have more than enough of something*
tocarle a uno	*to be someone's turn*

Me encanta el café en este país.	*I love the coffee in this country.*
Nos entusiasmó mucho el partido.	*We got very excited about the game.*
Le falta paciencia.	*He has no patience.*
Me hace falta tu apoyo.	*I need your support.*
¿No te importa el medio ambiente?	*Don't you care about the environment?*
Me interesan los altibajos de la economía.	*I'm interested in the fluctuations of the economy.*
¿Cuánto dinero les queda?	*How much money do you have left?*
Me sobra trabajo.	*I have more than enough work.*
A ti te toca ahora.	*It's your turn now.*

To focus on the person involved in sentences with reverse construction verbs, a phrase consisting of the preposition **a** + a prepositional pronoun is used.

A mí me importa el futuro, pero **a él**, nada.	*I care about the future, but he doesn't at all.*

Some reverse construction verbs can be used in other constructions as well, but with a difference in meaning.

reverse construction: A ella le falta paciencia.	*She lacks patience.*
regular construction: Ella falta mucho a clase.	*She is often absent from class.*
reverse construction: Me quedó poco dinero.	*I had little money left.*
regular construction: Quedé en verlo mañana.	*I agreed to see him tomorrow.*
reverse construction: Les toca jugar ahora.	*It's their turn to play now.*
regular construction: Ellos tocan la guitarra.	*They play the guitar.*

Saber vs. conocer

Spanish has two verbs meaning *to know*: **saber** and **conocer**.

Saber means to know something you have learned or can repeat or state.

Sé la fecha.	*I know the date.*
Sabemos la respuesta.	*We know the answer.*

Saber, and not **conocer**, is used before a following clause beginning with **si** or **que**.

¿**Sabes** si van a venir?	*Do you know whether they are going to come?*
Sé que ella enseña en esta escuela.	*I know that she teaches at this school.*

Saber is used before an infinitive with the meaning *to know how to do something*.

Esta niña ya **sabe** nadar.	*This child already knows how to swim.*

Conocer means *to be familiar with*, *to have an acquaintance with*. It is used with people and places.

¿**Conocen** Uds. a mi primo Javier?	*Do you know my cousin Javier?*
Él **conoce** muy bien Madrid.	*He knows Madrid very well.*

Note also:

No **conozco** la República Dominicana.	*I haven't been to the Dominican Republic.*

Se construction

To understand **se** constructions it is important to understand the difference between the subject of the verb and the performer of the action. The subject is a grammatical category. The subject determines the ending of the verb. Usually, the subject is also the performer of the action, but not always.

In sentences such as *The water boiled.*, *The meat was cooking.*, the nouns *water* and *meat* are the subjects of the sentence but are not the performers of the actions. The performers of the actions are left unspecified.

Spanish removes the focus from the performer of the action by using the **se** construction. The **se** construction consists of the pronoun **se** and the third-person singular or plural of the verb, depending on whether the grammatical subject is singular or plural. The usual translation of the **se** construction in English is the passive voice.

Se terminó el proyecto.	*The project was finished.*
Se va a alquilar este apartamento.	*This apartment is going to be rented.*
Se tomaron unas decisiones importantes.	*Important decisions were made.*
Se vendieron las computadoras viejas.	*The old computers were sold.*

The **se** construction is very common on commercial signs.

Se alquila oficina.	*Office for rent.*
Se venden carros.	*Cars for sale.*

For intransitive verbs, the verb is always in the third-person singular in the **se** construction.

¿Por dónde se sale?	*Where is the exit?*
Se come bien en Madrid.	*The food is good in Madrid. In Madrid you eat well.*

If the verb has a reflexive **se**, then the **se** construction cannot be used. **Uno** is used instead.

Uno se divierte mucho en Barcelona.	*People have a great time in Barcelona.*
Uno se aburre mucho en esta zona.	*People get very bored in this region.*

Ser (*to be*)

The verb **ser** is one of the two Spanish verbs meaning *to be*. Its conjugation is as follows:

Present tense

SINGULAR	PLURAL
soy	somos
eres	sois
es	son

Preterit tense

SINGULAR	PLURAL
fui	fuimos
fuiste	fuisteis
fue	fueron

Note that in the preterit its forms are the same as those of **ir** *to go*.

Imperfect tense

SINGULAR	PLURAL
era	éramos
eras	erais
era	eran

Future

SINGULAR	PLURAL
seré	seremos
serás	seréis
será	serán

Conditional

SINGULAR	PLURAL
sería	seríamos
serías	seríais
sería	serían

Present perfect tense

SINGULAR	PLURAL
he sido	hemos sido
has sido	habéis sido
ha sido	han sido

Past perfect (pluperfect)

SINGULAR	PLURAL
había sido	habíamos sido
habías sido	habíais sido
había sido	habían sido

Present subjunctive

SINGULAR	PLURAL
que sea	que seamos
que seas	que seáis
que sea	que sean

Commands

	(nosotros) seamos / no seamos
(tú) sé / no seas	(vosotros) sed / no seáis
(no) sea (Ud.)	(no) sean (Uds.)

Ser vs. estar

The verbs **ser** and **estar** both mean *to be*, but they are not interchangeable. They are used in different contexts (see *Ser*; see *Estar*).

1. **Ser** links nouns and pronouns.

El señor García **es** el profesor.	*Mr. García is the teacher.*
Yo **soy** ingeniero.	*I'm an engineer.*
Alicia y José **son** nuestros amigos.	*Alicia and José are our friends.*

2. **Ser** is used before (or, in questions, after) a phrase beginning with **de** that expresses possession, origin, or material.

¿De quién **es** esta bufanda?	*Whose scarf is this?*
Esta oficina **es** del jefe.	*This office is the boss's.*
Marta **es** de Honduras.	*Marta is from Honduras.*
El reloj **es** de plata.	*The watch is made of silver.*

3. **Ser** is used with colors and nationalities.

Mi coche nuevo **es** rojo.	*My new car is red.*
Nosotros **somos** norteamericanos.	*We are American.*

4. **Ser** is used to tell time and to give the date.

¿Qué hora **es**?	*What time is it?*
Es la una.	*It's one o'clock.*
Son las dos y media.	*It's two thirty.*
Hoy **es** el diez de septiembre.	*Today is September tenth.*

5. **Estar** is used to express location.

Mis hijos **están** en el parque ahora.	*My children are at the park now.*
Buenos Aires **está** en Argentina.	*Buenos Aires is in Argentina.*

Note, however, that only **ser** can be used to indicate the location of an event.

La conferencia **es** en el salón 229.	*The lecture is in room 229.*
La fiesta **va a ser** en mi casa.	*The party is going to be at my house.*

6. **Estar** is used to express states of health.

Estamos acatarrados.	*We're sick with colds.*
La secretaria no está hoy. **Está** enferma.	*The secretary isn't in today. She's sick.*
¿Cómo **está** Ud.?	*How are you?*
Estoy bien, mal, perfectamente.	*I'm fine, sick, feeling fine.*

7. **Estar** is used with the past participle to express positions of the body. English uses the *-ing* form for this purpose.

Los invitados **están** sentados.	*The guests are sitting.*
Mi tío **está** acostado.	*My uncle is lying down.*

In the above cases, **ser** and **estar** do not contrast. The structure of the sentence determines which one is used.

    Ser and **estar** may also be used, with most adjectives, in contrast with each other. **Estar** is used to show that the quality designated by the adjective results from a change in the speaker's perception. Examine the following contrasts.

Alfredo **es** nervioso.	*Alfredo is nervous (= a nervous person).*
El paciente **está** nervioso.	*The patient is nervous (=seems nervous, feels nervous, is acting nervous).*
El niño **es** gordo.	*The child is fat.*
El niño **está** gordo.	*The child has gotten fat.*
Este profesor **es** muy aburrido.	*This teacher is very boring.*
Los estudiantes **están** aburridos.	*The students are bored.*

    Estar can signal a subjective statement, as opposed to **ser**, which signals an objective assessment.

Luis tiene noventa años. Es viejo.	*Luis is ninety years old. He's old.*
Luis tiene solamente sesenta años, pero está viejo.	*Luis is only sixty years old, but he acts, seems, looks old.*

Often, the adjective has a different meaning in English depending on whether it is used with **ser** or **estar**.

Ella **es** viva.	*She's lively, quick-witted.*
Ella **está** viva.	*She's alive.*
Estos chicos **son** listos.	*These kids are smart.*
Estos chicos **están** listos.	*These kids are ready.*

Note the difference between **ser** and **estar** when describing food.

Los vegetales **son** buenos para la salud.	*Vegetables are good for your health.*
Estos vegetales **están** buenos.	*These vegetables are good (=taste good).*
El pescado **es** rico.	*Fish is delicious. (general statement)*
El pescado **está** rico.	*The fish is delicious.*

Special cases:
Only **estar** is used with **contento**.

Estamos contentos porque tenemos el día libre.	*We're glad because we have the day off.*

Both **ser** and **estar** may be used with **casado** *married* and with **feliz** *happy*.

Soy/Estoy casado.	*I'm married.*

Spelling rules

After **g** and **q** and before the vowels **e** and **i**, the letter **u** does not represent a vowel but is merely a spelling convention. The combinations of letters **gue** and **gui** represent the spoken syllables /ge/ and /gi/ (with the *g* pronounced as in English *go*), respectively: ju**gue**te. The combinations of letters **que** and **qui** represent the spoken syllables /ke/ and /ki/, respectively: pa**que**te, a**quí**. These spelling changes appear in the verb system and with certain noun suffixes. See *Absolute superlative*, *Diminutives*, *Imperative*, *Present subjunctive*, and *Preterit tense*.

Nouns ending in -**z** change -**z** to -**c** when the plural ending -**es** is added.

el lápiz → los lápi**ces**
la voz → las vo**ces**

Stem-changing verbs

Many Spanish verbs which have the vowel **e** or **o** in the stem show a change in that vowel in those persons of the present tense where the stem is stressed. The most common changes are **e** → **ie** and **o** → **ue**. Some -**ir** verbs have the change **e** → **i** (see **servir**, below).

pensar (**e** → **ie**)
volver (**o** → **ue**)
servir (**e** → **i**)

pensar *to think*

p**ie**nso	pensamos
p**ie**nsas	pensáis
p**ie**nsa	p**ie**nsan

contar *to tell, count*

c**ue**nto	contamos
c**ue**ntas	contáis
c**ue**nta	c**ue**ntan

perder *to lose*

pierdo	perdemos
pierdes	perdéis
pierde	pierden

volver *to go back*

vuelvo	volvemos
vuelves	volvéis
vuelve	vuelven

sentirse *to feel*

me siento	nos sentimos
te sientes	os sentís
se siente	se sienten

dormir *to sleep*

duermo	dormimos
duermes	dormís
duerme	duermen

servir *to serve*

sirvo	servimos
sirves	servís
sirve	sirven

The present subjunctive of **-ar** and **-er** verbs has the same stem changes as the present indicative.

pensar

que piense	que pensemos
que pienses	que penséis
que piense	que piensen

contar

que cuente	que contemos
que cuentes	que contéis
que cuente	que cuenten

perder

que pierda	que perdamos
que pierdas	que perdáis
que pierda	que pierdan

volver

que vuelva	que volvamos
que vuelvas	que volváis
que vuelva	que vuelvan

-Ir verbs with stem changes also change the vowel of the **nosotros** and **vosotros** forms of the present subjunctive. In those forms **e** changes to **i** and **o** changes to **u**. Thus they have a stem change in every person of the present subjunctive, even in those persons (the **nosotros** and **vosotros** forms) where the stem is not stressed.

sentirse

que me sienta	que nos sintamos
que te sientas	que os sintáis
que se sienta	que se sientan

servir

que sirva	que sirvamos
que sirvas	que sirváis
que sirva	que sirvan

dormir

que duerma	que durmamos
que duermas	que durmáis
que duerma	que duerman

Note that the verb **jugar** is conjugated as if it had **o** as its stem vowel. In Old Spanish its infinitive was **jogar**.

jugar

present indicative

juego	jugamos
juegas	jugáis
juega	juegan

present subjunctive

que juegue	que juguemos
que juegues	que juguéis
que juegue	que jueguen

For stem changes in the preterit, see *Preterit*.

Subject pronouns

Spanish and English have different sets of personal pronouns. The English subject pronouns by person and number are:

PERSON	SINGULAR	PLURAL
first	I	we
second	you	you
third	he, she, it	they

Here are the Spanish subject pronouns:

PERSON	SINGULAR	PLURAL
first	yo	nosotros, nosotras
second	tú	vosotros, vosotras
third	él, ella, usted	ellos, ellas, ustedes

1. The pronoun **yo** in Spanish is not capitalized unless it is the first word of a sentence.

2. The Spanish equivalents of *we* make a gender distinction that English does not require. **Nosotros** is used for groups of two or more males or males and females. **Nosotras** is used for groups of two or more females.

3. Spanish has four equivalents for English *you*. The pronouns **tú** and **vosotros/vosotras** are informal. **Tú** is used to address one person with whom you have a relationship that Hispanic culture defines as informal: family members, children, fellow students, etc. In Spain, **vosotros/vosotras** is used to address two or more people with whom you have an informal relationship. Note that **vosotros/vosotras** makes the same gender distinction as **nosotros/nosotras**, above.

   Usted and **ustedes** are used in formal situations. **Usted** is used to address one person with whom you have a relationship that Hispanic culture defines as formal: strangers, superiors at work, people seen as not part of your "in-group," etc. **Ustedes** is used to address two or more people with whom you have a formal relationship.

4. The equivalents of *you* described in #3, above, reflect the usage of Spain only. In Spanish America, **vosotros/vosotras** is not used. Instead, **ustedes** is used as the plural of both **tú** and **usted**.

5. **Usted** is used with a third-person singular verb. **Ustedes** is used with a third-person plural verb. In writing, **usted** is usually written **Ud.** and **ustedes** is usually written **Uds.** These abbreviations are pronounced **usted** and **ustedes**, respectively.

6. The standards of formality that condition the choice between **tú** and **usted** vary over the Spanish-speaking world. Informal address is more frequent in Spain than in countries such as Mexico or Ecuador. Rural aristocratic milieus use **usted** much more than modern urban milieus.

7. When in doubt, foreigners should use formal address until asked to switch to **tú** by the native speaker they are talking to. American culture places a high value on informality, but in Spanish-speaking cultures the inappropriate use of **tú** is rude, not friendly.

8. Spanish has no equivalent for English *it* as a subject pronoun. All masculine nouns, whether referring to people or things, are replaced by **él**. All feminine nouns are replaced by **ella**.

9. In the third person plural, groups of two or more males or males and females are referred to as **ellos**. Groups of two or more consisting entirely of females are referred to as **ellas**.

10. In many parts of Spanish America **tú** is replaced by the pronoun **vos**, which has its own set of verb endings. This phenomenon, called **el voseo**, is characteristic of the speech of Argentina, Uruguay, Paraguay, Bolivia, Chile (in informal speech only), Central America except for Panamá, and in parts of Venezuela and Colombia. In Argentina, Uruguay and Nicaragua, **vos** is acceptable in both speech and writing and has become the normal second-person singular form.

11. In Spanish, personal pronouns are not used as much as in English because the ending of the verb shows who the subject is. The pronouns are used for focus or contrast, as in sentences such as the following:

Él es asesor, pero **nosotros** somos abogados.	*He's a consultant, but **we** are lawyers.*
Ella fue al campo, pero **yo** fui a la playa.	*She went to the country, but **I** went to the beach.*

    In the English equivalent of the above sentence, the subject pronouns are stressed.

12. The pronoun **usted** is used more than other pronouns to add a note of politeness or formality to sentences.

Subjunctive

See *Present subjunctive*.

Superlative

The superlative in Spanish is not different in form from the comparative, except that a definite article is usually present in the noun phrase. Compare:

un libro más interesante	*a more interesting book*
el libro más interesante	*the most interesting book*
un libro menos interesante	*a less interesting book*
el libro menos interesante	*the least interesting book*

Spanish uses **de**, not **en**, when a phrase of location follows a superlative.

el museo más famoso **de** la ciudad	*the most famous museum in the city*
las mejores tiendas **del** barrio	*the best stores in the neighborhood*
la peor carretera **de** la región	*the worst highway in the region*

See also *Absolute superlative*.

Tag questions

Spanish adds phrases such as **¿no?, ¿verdad?, ¿no es verdad?**, and **¿no es cierto?** to statements to turn them into questions. These phrases are called *tags*. Tag questions signal that the speaker expects the answer *yes*. (If the statement to be agreed with is negative, only **¿verdad?** can be used as a tag.) English also uses tags such as *isn't it?* and *are you?* to turn statements into questions.

Pablo ya se fue, ¿no?	*Pablo left already, didn't he?*
No hay vuelo directo, ¿verdad?	*There's no direct flight, is there?*
Uds. harán un viaje a Chile, ¿no es cierto?	*You'll take a trip to Chile, won't you?*

Telling time

To ask what time it is in Spanish one says **¿Qué hora es?** (**¿Qué horas son?** is also used, especially in the Americas.) Phrases telling time in Spanish begin with **Son las** + the hour except for **Es la una.** *It's one o'clock.*

Here is the way Spanish tells time on the traditional analog clock.

Son las cinco.	*It's five o'clock.*
Son las cinco y cinco.	*It's five past five.*
Son las cinco y diez.	*It's ten past five.*
Son las cinco y cuarto.	*It's a quarter past five.*
Son las cinco y veinte.	*It's twenty past five.*
Son las cinco y veinticinco.	*It's twenty-five past five.*
Son las cinco y media.	*It's half past five.*
Son las seis menos veinticinco.	*It's twenty-five to six.*
Son las seis menos veinte.	*It's twenty to six.*
Son las seis menos cuatro.	*It's a quarter to six.*
Son las seis menos diez.	*It's ten to six.*
Son las seis menos cinco.	*It's five to six.*
Son las seis.	*It's six o'clock.*

The preceding system is typical of Spain and Argentina. In the rest of Spanish America the times from the half hour to the following hour are usually expressed as follows.

Faltan veinticinco para las seis.	*It's twenty-five to six.*
Faltan veinte para las seis.	*It's twenty to six.*
Faltan quince para las seis.	*It's a quarter to six.*
Faltan diez para las seis.	*It's ten to six.*
Faltan cinco para las seis.	*It's five to six.*

As in the United States, the use of digital clocks and watches in Spanish-speaking countries has changed the way people tell time. Phrases such as the following are replacing the traditional analog times.

Son las cinco y quince.	*It's five fifteen.*
Son las cinco y treinta.	*It's five thirty.*
Son las cinco (y) cuarenta y cinco.	*It's five forty-five.*

Notice that the conjunction **y** may be left out from thirty-one to fifty-nine past the hour.

To specify the time at which something happens, the preposition **a** is used.

—¿A qué hora llega el avión?	*What time is the plane arriving?*
—A las ocho cincuenta.	*At eight fifty.*

Spanish has two ways of expressing A.M. and P.M.

1. In everyday speech the phrases **de la mañana, de la tarde, de la noche** are added to the expression of time.

Salí de la oficina a las nueve de la noche.	*I left the office at nine P.M.*

2. For official time—train schedules, plane schedules, movie and show times, and class times—a twenty-four-hour clock is used.

Hay un tren a las dieciocho (y) veinte.	*There's a train at six twenty P.M.*
El avión llegará a las veintidós (y) cuarenta.	*The plane will arrive at ten forty P.M.*

Tener: idioms with tener

Many English phrases that consist of *to be* + adjective and that refer to mental or physical states have Spanish equivalents consisting of **tener** + noun. These expressions are used only for people, not for things.

NOUN		IDIOM	
el hambre	*hunger*	tener hambre	*to be hungry*
la sed	*thirst*	tener sed	*to be thirsty*
el calor	*heat*	tener calor	*to be warm*
el frío	*cold*	tener frío	*to be cold*
la prisa	*hurry, haste*	tener prisa	*to be in a hurry*
la vergüenza	*shame*	tener vergüenza	*to be ashamed*
el éxito	*success*	tener éxito	*to be successful*
el cuidado	*care, caution*	tener cuidado	*to be careful*
la razón	*right, reason*	tener razón	*to be right*
la suerte	*luck*	tener suerte	*to be lucky*
el sueño	*sleep, sleepiness*	tener sueño	*to be sleepy*
las ganas	*desire*	tener ganas de + *infinitive*	*to feel like doing something*

Since the word following **tener** in these idioms is a noun, it cannot be modified by **muy** but rather by quantity words such as **mucho**, **poco**, **tanto**, or **demasiado**, which agree with the noun in gender and number.

¿Tienes mucha sed?	*Are you very thirsty?*
Hoy tengo poca hambre.	*Today I'm not very hungry.*
Tenemos muchas ganas de conocerla.	*We are very eager to meet her.*
¡Tengo tanto sueño!	*I am so sleepy!*
Tengo demasiado frío aquí.	*I am too cold here.*
Debes tener mucho cuidado.	*You must be very careful.*
¿Por qué tiene Ud. tanta prisa?	*Why are you in such a hurry?*

See also *Dar: idioms with **dar**.*
For **hambre**, see *El with feminine nouns*; for **sed**, see *Gender of nouns.*

Todo (adjective)

When **todo** is used as an adjective it is usually followed by the definite article. Notice the different translations in English.

todo el, toda la	*the whole, all the*
todos los, todas las	*every, all the*
todo el día	*all day long*
todos los días	*every day*
toda la historia	*the entire story*
todas las historias	*all the stories, every story*

The forms **todo** and **toda** may precede a singular noun with the meaning *every*, especially in more formal style.

todo documento = todos los documentos	*every document*
toda tienda = todas las tiendas	*every store*

Todo (pronoun)

Todo as a pronoun in Spanish means *everything.*

Todo es impresionante aquí.	*Everything is impressive, awesome here.*
Todo cuesta una fortuna en esta tienda.	*Everything costs a fortune in this store.*

When the pronoun **todo** is the object of a verb, the pronoun **lo** precedes the verb. Notice that **todo** as direct object may sometimes precede the verb.

Ese profesor **lo** explica **todo**.	*That teacher explains everything.*
Ahora **lo** comprendo **todo**.	*Now I understand everything.*
¿Qué regalo le podemos comprar?	*What gift can we buy for him? He has everything.*
Todo lo tiene.	

Transitive verbs

Transitive verbs in Spanish are those which must appear with a direct object. If the direct object is a definite, animate being then it will be preceded by the personal **a**. (See *Direct object.*)

Vimos la nueva película.	*We saw the new film.*
Vimos a nuestros amigos.	*We saw our friends.*

When a transitive verb in Spanish has no object in the sentence it often becomes reflexive.

Él enoja a su jefe.	*He makes his boss angry.*
El jefe se enoja.	*The boss gets angry.*

One could analyze the reflexive pronoun in the last example as occupying the place of the mandatory direct object.

Uses of the present tense

1. The present tense is used in Spanish to express actions beginning in the past but continuing into the present (English *have/has been doing something*). The period of time during which the action has been going on is expressed in a phrase beginning with **hace**.

Hace tres años que trabajo aquí.	*I have been working here for three years.*
Él estudia español hace un año.	*He's been studying Spanish for a year.*

   Note that the time phrase with **hace** can be placed either at the beginning of the sentence or at the end. When it is placed at the beginning the conjunction **que** is used to connect it to what follows.

   The question form for this construction is: **¿Cuánto (tiempo) hace que** + verb in present tense?

   ¿Cuánto (tiempo) hace que Ud. busca empleo? *How long have you been looking for work?*

2. The **yo** form and the **nosotros** form of the present tense are used to ask for instructions.

¿Entrego los documentos hoy?	*Shall I submit the documents today?*
¿Llamamos a Daniela Chávez?	*Shall we call Daniela Chávez?*

3. After **¿Por qué no ... ?** the present tense is used to make a suggestion.

   ¿Por qué no cenas con nosotros? *Why don't you have dinner with us?*

4. The present tense may be used to express the future when another element of the sentence (such as an adverb of time) makes the future reference clear.

   Mañana salgo para Honduras. *I'll leave for Honduras tomorrow.*

Verb + infinitive construction

In both Spanish and English the infinitive can follow a conjugated verb. In this function the infinitive serves as a complement, or completion form, much like an object. Depending on the first verb (the conjugated verb) in this construction, the infinitive may follow the verb directly or be connected to it by a connector, most commonly the preposition **a** or **de**. The prepositions **con** and **en** are also used as connectors, as is the word **que**.

Here are some of the most common verbs followed directly by the infinitive.

deber *should, ought to, must*

Debemos ayudarlo.	*We must, should, ought to help him.*

dejar *to let, allow to*

¿Por qué no lo dejaste hablar?	*Why didn't you let him speak?*

esperar *to hope to*

Esperamos graduarnos en mayo.   *We hope to graduate in May.*

lograr *to succeed in, manage to*

A ver si logro salir un poco antes.   *Let's see if I can get out a little early.*

necesitar *to need to*

Necesitas estudiar un poco más.   *You have to study a little more.*

pensar *to intend to*

Pienso ir de vacaciones en junio.   *I intend to go on vacation in June.*

poder *can, to be able to*

¿Ud. no puede terminar el informe hoy?   *Can't you finish the report today?*

preferir *to prefer to*

Preferimos quedarnos en casa.   *We prefer to stay home.*

querer *to want to*

Quiero buscar otro empleo.   *I want to look for another job.*

saber *to know how to*

Esos niños ya saben nadar.   *Those children already know how to swim.*

sentir *to regret*

Siente no poder venir.   *She regrets not being able to come.*

Here are some of the most common verbs that are followed by **a** + infinitive.

aprender a *to learn to*

¿Dónde aprendió Ud. a hablar español?   *Where did you learn to speak Spanish?*

atreverse a *to dare to*

¿Él se atrevió a decirte eso?   *He dared to say that to you?*

ayudar (a uno) a *to help (someone) to*

Ayúdeme a elaborar el presupuesto.   *Help me draw up the budget.*

comenzar a *to begin to, start to*

¿Cuándo comienza Ud. a trabajar?   *When do you start to work?*

empezar a *to begin to, start to*

Empiezo a comprender el problema.   *I'm beginning to understand the problem.*

enseñar (a uno) a *to teach (someone) to*

Mi padre me enseñó a montar en bicicleta.   *My father taught me to ride a bicycle.*

invitar (a uno) a *to invite (someone) to do something*

Me invitaron a presentar mi plan de   *They invited me to present my business plan.*
negocios.

ponerse a *to begin to*

Hay que ponerse a trabajar.   *We have to start to work.*

Note some special cases of verb + **a** + infinitive.

1. Verbs of motion are usually followed by **a** before an infinitive.

bajar a hacer algo	*to go down to do something*
entrar a hacer algo	*to go in to do something*
regresar a hacer algo	*to go/come back to do something*
salir a hacer algo	*to go out to do something*
subir a hacer algo	*to go up to do something*
venir a hacer algo	*to come to do something*

2. **Ir** + **a** + infinitive is a frequent substitute for the future tense.

—¿Cuándo vamos a cenar?	*When are we going to have dinner?*
—Voy a servir la cena a las ocho.	*I'm going to serve dinner at eight o'clock.*

3. **Vamos a** + infinitive often means *let's do something.*

Vamos a jugar al tenis.	*Let's play tennis.*

4. **Volver a** + infinitive means *to do something again.*

¿Por qué no vuelves a llamarlos?	*Why don't you call them again?*
Volví a verlo en el concierto.	*I saw him again at the concert.*

Here are some of the most common verbs that are followed by **de** + infinitive.

acabar de to have just done something

Acabo de entregarle los datos.	*I have just submitted the data to him.*

dejar de to stop doing something

¿Por qué no dejas de molestarme?	*Why don't you stop bothering me?*

olvidarse de to forget to do something

Se olvidó de ponerse el filtro solar.	*She forgot to put on sunscreen.*

tener ganas de to feel like doing something

No tenemos ganas de salir esta noche.	*We don't feel like going out tonight.*

tratar de to try to do something

Trate Ud. de comprenderme.	*Try to understand me.*

There are two cases where **que** is used to connect a verb to a following infinitive.

hay que one must

Hay que estudiar idiomas.	*One must study languages.*

tener que to have to

¿Qué tienes que hacer hoy?	*What do you have to do today?*

The verb **soñar** *to dream* is connected by **con** to a following infinitive:

Sueñan con mejorar su vida.	*They dream of improving their lives.*

Verbs differing in the type of object they take

Some English verbs that require a preposition before the object have Spanish equivalents that are followed by a direct object.

buscar otro empleo	*to look for another job*
escuchar música	*to listen to music*
esperar el autobús	*to wait for the bus*
mirar los contratos	*to look at the contracts*

If the direct object is a definite animate being, it is preceded by the personal **a**.

Buscaba **a** la programadora.	*I was looking for the computer programmer.*
Escuchamos **al** cantante.	*We're listening to the singer.*
Espere **a** sus colegas.	*Wait for your colleagues.*
Mira **a** estos niños.	*Look at these kids.*

Weather expressions

Spanish uses the verb form **hace** in most weather expressions.

¿Qué tiempo hace?	*What's the weather like?*
Hace buen tiempo.	*The weather is good.*
Hace mal tiempo.	*The weather is bad.*
Hace calor.	*It's warm.*
Hace frío.	*It's cold.*
Hace fresco.	*It's cool.*
Hace sol.	*It's sunny.*
Hace viento.	*It's windy.*
¿Qué temperatura hace?	*What's the temperature?*
¿Cuántos grados hace?	*How many degrees is it?*
Hace ochenta grados.	*It's eighty degrees.*

With the nouns **sol** and **viento** the verb **hay** may also be used.

Hay sol.	*It's sunny.*
Hay viento.	*It's windy.*

Since the words **calor, frío, fresco, sol,** and **viento** are nouns, **mucho** is used as the equivalent of *very*.

Hace **mucho** calor/frío.	*It's very warm/cold.*
Hace **mucho** sol/viento.	*It's very sunny/windy.*

But **muy** is used before the adjectives **buen, mal**.

Hace **muy** buen/mal tiempo.	*The weather is very good/bad.*

In some weather expressions other verbs are used.

Está nublado.	*It's cloudy.*
Está húmedo.	*It's humid.*
Está despejado.	*The sky is clear.*
Llueve. (**llover** o → ue *to rain*)	*It's raining, it rains.*
Nieva. (**nevar** e → ie *to snow*)	*It's snowing, it snows.*
Truena. (**tronar** o → ue *to thunder*)	*It's thundering, it thunders.*

Word order

The typical Spanish word order in a sentence is the same as English: subject-verb-object.

Los asesores escribieron un informe.   *The consultants wrote a report.*

However, word order in Spanish often appears freer than word order in English. Spanish uses word order the way English uses intonation—to focus on the new information or key information in a sentence. English word order is relatively fixed, so a rise in intonation signals the focus of the sentence.

I think *Mary* arrived.
No, *John* arrived.

In Spanish, new information is placed at the end of the sentence, even if it is the subject.

Creo que llegó María.   *I think María arrived.*
No, llegó Felipe.   *No, Felipe arrived.*

The word **llegó** goes at the end of the sentence when the verb is what is focused on.

¿Felipe salió?   *Did Felipe leave?*
No, Felipe llegó.   *No, Felipe arrived.*

Answer key

1 Finding your way around • *Hay*

1·1   1. la/una   2. el/un   3. el/un   4. la/una   5. el/un   6. la/una   7. el/un
    8. el/un   9. la/una   10. el/un   11. el/un   12. el/un   13. el/un   14. la/una
    15. el/un

1·2   1. las maletas/unas maletas   2. los cines/unos cines   3. los relojes/unos relojes
    4. las librerías/unas librerías   5. los hoteles/unos hoteles   6. las oficinas/unas oficinas
    7. los teatros/unos teatros   8. los restaurantes/unos restaurantes   9. las cámaras/unas
cámaras   10. los paquetes/unos paquetes   11. los teléfonos/unos teléfonos   12. los
bares/unos bares   13. los cibercafés/unos cibercafés   14. las farmacias/unas farmacias
    15. los maletines/unos maletines

1·3   1. la tienda de ropa/las tiendas de ropa   2. la tienda de cómputo/las tiendas de cómputo
    3. la oficina de turismo/las oficinas de turismo   4. la tienda de electrodomésticos/las
tiendas de electrodomésticos   5. la tienda de deportes/las tiendas de deportes   6. la
tienda por departamentos/las tiendas por departamentos

1·4   1. ¿Qué hay en el armario?   2. ¿Es un regalo?   3. ¿Hay una heladería por aquí?
    4. ¿Qué tiendas hay?   5. ¿Es un cibercafé?   6. ¿Hay dos zapaterías en la esquina?
    7. ¿Qué libros hay en el estante?   8. ¿Hay una tienda de cómputo en el centro?

1·5   1. No, no es una agenda electrónica.   2. No, no hay quince libros en el estante.
    3. No, el reloj no es para Carlos.   4. No, no hay una tienda de deportes en el centro
comercial.   5. No, no es un regalo para Rosario.   6. No, no hay ropa en la maleta.
    7. No, no hay un cartapacio en la oficina.   8. No, la computadora no es para Mario.

1·6   1. Es un billetero.   2. Es una cartera.   3. Es un reloj.   4. Es una agenda electrónica.
    5. Es un bolso.   6. Es una cámara.   7. Es un iPod.   8. Es un cartapacio.

1·7   1. El billetero no es para José. Es para Juan.   2. La cartera no es para Matilde. Es para
Julia.   3. El reloj no es para Jorge. Es para Alberto.   4. La agenda electrónica no es para
Lorenzo. Es para Nora.   5. El bolso no es para Rosa. Es para Margarita.   6. La cámara
no es para Luz. Es para Daniel.   7. El iPod no es para Susana. Es para Guillermo.
    8. El cartapacio no es para Carlos. Es para Roberto.

1·8   1. una computadora   2. dos zapaterías   3. tres relojes   4. cuatro maletas
    5. cinco cines   6. seis oficinas de turismo   7. siete hoteles   8. ocho regalos
    9. nueve cámaras   10. diez heladerías   11. once cajas   12. doce cibercafés
    13. trece mochilas   14. catorce teléfonos   15. quince estantes   16. dieciséis
supermercados   17. diecisiete peluquerías   18. dieciocho tiendas por departamentos
    19. diecinueve paquetes   20. veinte deportes

2 Describing places and things • Adjectives

2·1   1. El barrio es comercial también.   2. La empresa es nueva también.   3. La heladería
es animada también.   4. La tienda por departamentos es grande también.   5. El
cartapacio es pequeño también.   6. El BlackBerry es importante también.   7. La calle
es peatonal también.   8. El inglés es útil también.

2·2 1. Los relojes son hermosos también. 2. Los cines son animados también. 3. Las maletas son negras también. 4. Las zapaterías son grandes también. 5. Los documentos son fáciles también. 6. Los periódicos son aburridos también. 7. Los folletos son cortos también. 8. Las cajas son chiquitas también.

2·3 1. los restaurantes del centro 2. la farmacia de la esquina 3. el interior del carro 4. el armario del cuarto 5. los juguetes de la juguetería 6. las mesas de las oficinas 7. la peluquería del hotel 8. el color del billetero

2·4 1. La avenida es larga y muy bonita. 2. Las habitaciones son muy grandes y muy claras. 3. La música es hermosa y muy interesante. 4. El bar es chiquito y feo. 5. Los hoteles son modernos y muy cómodos. 6. Las calles son ruidosas y muy transitadas. 7. El informe es muy pesado y malo. 8. El garaje es muy pequeño y oscuro.

2·5 1. ¿Cómo es el centro comercial?/Es grande y animado. 2. ¿Cómo son los libros?/Son difíciles pero muy interesantes. 3. ¿Cómo es el carro?/Es pequeño y bastante cómodo. 4. ¿De qué color es el carro?/ Es rojo y el interior es azul.

2·6 1. ¿Hay un regalo en la caja? 2. ¿Es para Susana? 3. ¿Es grande? 4. ¿Es azul? 5. ¿Es bastante útil? 6. ¿Es muy bonito? 7. ¿Es de una tienda por departamentos? 8. ¿Es de una librería? 9. ¿Es ropa? 10. ¿Es un iPod?

2·7 1. ¿Es animado tu barrio?/No, mi barrio es bastante tranquilo. 2. ¿Son interesantes sus libros de química?/No, nuestros libros de química son aburridos. 3. ¿Es nueva su empresa?/Sí, su empresa es nueva y muy importante. 4. ¿Son negras sus maletas?/No, sus maletas son marrones. 5. ¿Son difíciles sus artículos?/No, sus artículos son fáciles.

2·8 1. Los armarios son muy grandes. 2. Las calles son bastante ruidosas. 3. El centro es muy animado. 4. Las habitaciones son bastante cómodas. 5. La música es muy hermosa. 6. Los libros de economía son muy interesantes. 7. Los teléfonos portátiles son muy útiles. 8. La empresa es bastante importante.

3 Talking about nationalities and professions, food, and films • *Ser*

3·1 1. este/ese/aquel pollo 2. estas/esas/aquellas hamburguesas 3. esta/esa/aquella ensalada 4. este/ese/aquel arroz 5. estos/esos/aquellos huevos 6. estas/esas/aquellas quesadillas 7. esta/esa/aquella fruta 8. estos/esos/aquellos sándwiches 9. este/ese/aquel té 10. estas/esas/aquellas legumbres 11. esta/esa/aquella cerveza 12. estos/esos/aquellos jugos

3·2 1. esta/esa/aquella región 2. este/ese/aquel cine 3. estos/esos/aquellos países 4. estas/esas/aquellas ciudades 5. este/ese/aquel coche 6. esta/esa/aquella cámara 7. estos/esos/aquellos relojes 8. estas/esas/aquellas cajas

3·3 1. esos restaurantes mexicanos 2. unas tiendas caras 3. todos los platos auténticos 4. muchos jardines hermosos 5. dieciséis estudiantes franceses 6. varios carros azules 7. toda la zona comercial 8. varias películas diferentes

3·4 1. Lucie es francesa. 2. Marcos es peruano. 3. Lidia y Greta son alemanas. 4. Javier y Pedro son españoles. 5. María es griega. 6. Margarita y Antonio son polacos. 7. Graciela es china. 8. Alberto y Nora son japoneses. 9. Raúl es puertorriqueño. 10. Silvia y Daniel son dominicanos.

3·5 1. ¿De qué origen es Patricia? 2. ¿Cómo es la película? 3. ¿De dónde eres?/¿De qué país eres? 4. ¿Qué hay en la caja? 5. ¿De qué color es su carro? 6. ¿De dónde son?/¿De qué ciudad son? 7. ¿Qué es Mario? 8. ¿Cómo son los actores?

3·6 1. Ud. es de Chile. 2. Nosotros somos de Argentina. 3. Ella es de Japón. 4. Yo soy de Italia. 5. Uds. son de Francia. 6. Ellas son de Canadá. 7. Tú eres de Israel. 8. Él es de Escocia.

3·7 1. Yo soy de origen italiano. 2. Eduardo es de origen iraní. 3. Juanita y su hermana son de origen español. 4. Tú eres de origen japonés. 5. Nosotros somos de origen polaco. 6. Ud. es de origen portugués. 7. Gabriela es de origen griego. 8. Ud. y yo somos de origen inglés.

3·8 1. ¿De qué país eres? 2. Soy de México. 3. ¿De la capital? 4. No, no soy de Ciudad de México. Soy de Guadalajara. 5. ¿De dónde son Uds.? 6. Mi esposo y yo somos chilenos. 7. ¿De qué origen son? 8. Yo soy de origen escocés y Rafael es de origen alemán. 9. ¿Juan Miguel es contador? 10. No, es asesor. 11. ¿Y su esposa es abogada? 12. No, Isabel es ingeniera. 13. ¿Cómo es la comida de este restaurante italiano? 14. Todos los platos son buenos. 15. ¿Son sabrosas la pizza y la pasta? 16. Ah sí. Y la salsa es muy auténtica.

4 Describing people, emotions, and health • *Ser* and *estar*

4·1 1. Yo estoy bien. 2. Mi mamá está entusiasmada. 3. Tú estás regular. 4. Mi cuñada está molesta. 5. Mis hermanos y yo estamos emocionados. 6. Mis sobrinas están estresadas. 7. Nuestros tíos están cansados. 8. El abuelo está preocupado. 9. La tía está enferma. 10. Las hijas están resfriadas. 11. Mi papá está nervioso. 12. Los nietos están acatarrados.

4·2 1. El restaurante mexicano está cerca del teatro. 2. El museo de arte está en frente del hotel. 3. La tienda de cómputo está al lado de la librería. 4. El taller mecánico está detrás de la gasolinera. 5. El cine está a la izquierda del club de jazz. 6. El colegio está a cinco cuadras del parque. 7. El estacionamiento está delante de la tienda por departamentos. 8. La autopista está lejos del centro.

4·3 1. es 2. están 3. son 4. eres 5. están 6. es 7. estamos 8. Es 9. son 10. está 11. estás 12. soy 13. estamos 14. estoy 15. somos

4·4 1. Pedro es aburrido./Pedro está aburrido. 2. ¿Dónde están los informes?/¿Dónde es la reunión? 3. Sus tíos son molestos./Sus tíos están molestos. 4. ¿De quién es la cámara?/¿Para quién es la cámara? 5. ¿Cómo son Eva y Vicente?/¿Cómo están Eva y Vicente? 6. Su hermana es alegre./Pero no está alegre hoy. 7. ¿Qué hora es?/ ¿A qué hora es?

4·5 1. ¿Cómo están Uds.? 2. ¿Qué hora es? 3. ¿Dónde está el museo? 4. ¿Dónde es la fiesta? 5. ¿A qué hora es el examen? 6. ¿Por qué está Rosario contenta? 7. ¿Cómo son los hermanos Reyes? 8. ¿De qué es el abrigo? 9. ¿Qué día es hoy? 10. ¿De dónde son Uds.?/¿Cuál es su nacionalidad? 11. ¿Para quiénes son los regalos? 12. ¿Cómo está el pollo?

4·6 1. El director es inteligente./¿Es inteligente el director? 2. La impresora está descompuesta./¿Está descompuesta la impresora? 3. Los espectáculos son aburridos./¿Son aburridos los espectáculos? 4. El museo de arte es moderno./¿Es moderno el museo de arte? 5. Estas regiones son hermosas./¿Son hermosas estas regiones? 6. La carne está muy hecha./¿Está muy hecha la carne? 7. Los dentistas están deprimidos./¿Están deprimidos los dentistas? 8. El actor es rubio./¿Es rubio el actor? 9. Las tiendas están abiertas./¿Están abiertas las tiendas? 10. La sala de conferencias es grande./¿Es grande la sala de conferencias?

5 Talking about work and travel • *Ir* and *hacer*

5·1 1. Yo monto a caballo. 2. Ud. trota. 3. Daniela y su hermana nadan. 4. Nosotros patinamos. 5. Roberto monta en bicicleta. 6. Tú caminas. 7. Uds. levantan pesas.

5·2 1. Pablo y yo vamos a la piscina. 2. La familia Soto va al campo. 3. Beatriz va al mar. 4. Yo voy a la cancha de tenis. 5. Tú vas al estadio. 6. Ud. va a la pista. 7. Victoria y Samuel van al bosque nacional.

5·3 1. haces 2. hace 3. hacemos 4. hago 5. hacen 6. hacen 7. hace

5·4 1. Yo voy a llevar mi cartapacio. 2. Ellas van a diseñar un sitio web. 3. Tú vas a sacar a pasear al perro. 4. Nosotros vamos a ir de compras. 5. Ud. va a mirar la televisión. 6. Él va a alquilar una película. 7. Yo voy a hacer la comida. 8. Ud. va a visitar a sus abuelos. 9. Uds. van a preparar unos platos muy ricos. 10. Ella va a ir de vacaciones.

5·5 1. X 2. a 3. a 4. X 5. al 6. X 7. al 8. a 9. X 10. a 11. al 12. a

5·6 1. a / a 2. al 3. a 4. a 5. al 6. a / al 7. a 8. al

5·7 1. Pedro es mi amigo que toca la guitarra. 2. Lorenzo es mi amigo que cocina muy bien. 3. Rebeca y Nora son mis amigas que pintan cuadros. 4. María Teresa es mi amiga que desarrolla software. 5. Manuel y Matilde son mis amigos que trabajan en mi oficina. 6. Ricardo es mi amigo que canta en una banda.

5·8 1. El museo que está abierto los lunes. 2. Los directores que ganan mucho dinero. 3. El hombre de negocios que viaja mucho. 4. El coche que está descompuesto. 5. La cancha de tenis que queda al lado de la piscina. 6. Las blusas que son de algodón. 7. Los estudiantes que hacen deportes.

5·9 1. ¿A quién buscas? 2. No busco a nadie. 3. ¿Esperan a alguien? 4. No, no esperan a nadie. 5. ¿Uds. van a hacer un viaje en el invierno? 6. No, vamos a ir de vacaciones en junio. 7. Javier y

Raquel van al mar pasado mañana.   8. Isabel es mi amiga que diseña sitios web en sus horas libres.
9. ¿Qué vamos a cenar?   10. Vamos a encargar comida china.

6   Talking about what you need and what you know; shopping and cooking • *Tener, saber,* and *conocer*

6·1   1. creo   2. suben   3. rompe   4. vivimos   5. comparte   6. lees   7. resisten   8. mete

6·2   1. Jaime escribe un informe.   2. Tú comes huevos revueltos.   3. Anita abre unos regalos de cumpleaños.   4. Pablo y Miguel discuten el problema.   5. María y yo aprendemos a cocinar. 6. Yo bebo vino.   7. Uds. imprimen sus documentos.   8. Ud. comprende el problema.

6·3   1. quiero   2. comienza   3. duermen   4. prueban   5. piensas   6. vuelvo   7. podemos 8. entiende   9. juegan   10. empezamos

6·4   1. Ud. sigue con su clase a distancia.   2. Juan Diego y Pilar piensan estudiar inglés.   3. Tú quieres dominar el ruso.   4. Esos estudiantes prefieren aprender japonés.   5. Felipe y yo no podemos hablar chino muy bien.   6. Yo comienzo a practicar el alemán.   7. Uds. entienden bien el francés hablado.

6·5   1. sabe   2. conozco   3. sabes   4. conoces   5. sabemos   6. saben   7. sé/conocen   8. sabe 9. conoce   10. conocen/saben

6·6   1. a   2. X   3. que   4. de   5. X   6. a   7. de   8. que   9. X   10. X   11. X   12. a

6·7   1. Espero dominar el español.   2. Empieza a jugar al baloncesto.   3. Prefieren vivir en la costa. 4. ¿No puedes encontrar el plano?   5. Acabamos de volver de la cancha de tenis.   6. Logra tener éxito. 7. Sé leer el alemán muy bien.   8. Quieren asistir a la reunión.   9. Debes contar con nosotros. 10. ¿No tiene que discutir su idea?

6·8   1. Comienza a hacer sol.   2. Va a nevar.   3. Acaba de despejar.   4. Empieza a llover.   5. Va a hacer setenta grados.   6. Comienza a tronar.   7. Va a helar.

6·9   1. Hace seis meses que yo tomo una clase de español.   2. Hace siete años que nosotros vivimos en esta casa.   3. Hace dos horas que Carmen y Alfredo juegan al golf.   4. Hace poco tiempo que Ud. escribe su informe.   5. Hace una semana que tú estás acatarrado.   6. Hace media hora que Beatriz sirve la cena. 7. Hace mucho tiempo que llueve.   8. Hace dos días que nieva.

6·10   1. ¿Sabe cocinar?   2. No, pero quiero aprender a cocinar.   3. Hace mal tiempo. Hace frío y viento. 4. Y comienza a llover.   5. Tengo ganas de ir al mar. ¿Quieres ir conmigo?   6. Acabo de volver del mar. Prefiero ir al campo.   7. Hace quince años que Luis trabaja en este campo.   8. Conoce el mercado muy bien.   9. Piensan tomar una clase de español a distancia.   10. Saben que tienen que practicar mucho para dominar el idioma hablado.   11. Este café sirve los mejores postres de la ciudad.   12. Por eso pido dos. ¡No puedo resistir a la tentación!

6·11   1. treinta y seis   2. setenta y un   3. cien   4. quinientas treinta y una   5. novecientas cuarenta y ocho   6. mil   7. mil cuatrocientas noventa y cinco   8. mil setecientos sesenta y un   9. diez mil ochocientas veintiséis   10. doscientos treinta y cinco mil   11. un millón de   12. setenta y seis millones de

7   Entertaining at home • *Tener*

7·1   1. oyen/oímos   2. vienen/viene   3. tengo/pongo   4. trae/traigo   5. Hace/cae   6. dice/decimos 7. cabemos/quepo   8. hago/ponemos   9. ven/vemos   10. ponen/dice

7·2   1. Paula da consejos. Yo doy consejos también.   2. Tú conoces al gerente. Yo conozco al gerente también. 3. Ellos tienen paciencia. Yo tengo paciencia también.   4. Ud. oye la música. Yo oigo la música también. 5. Uds. caen en la nieve. Yo caigo en la nieve también.   6. Bernardo y Leo traen noticias. Yo traigo noticias también.   7. Felipe traduce el documento. Yo traduzco el documento también.   8. Tú dices que sí. Yo digo que sí también.   9. Todos Uds. van. Yo voy también.   10. Marta sale a las siete. Yo salgo a las siete también.   11. Ud. sabe su dirección. Yo sé su dirección también.

7·3   1. tienen mucha hambre   2. tenemos razón   3. tienen sueño   4. tiene muchos celos   5. tienen miedo   6. tienes mucho calor   7. tengo mucha sed   8. tiene mucha suerte

7·4   1. Sí, las hago.   2. Sí, lo pone.   3. Sí, lo oímos.   4. Sí, la meten.   5. Sí, los veo.   6. Sí, los conoce.   7. Sí, la termino.   8. Sí, las esperan.   9. Sí, lo entendemos.   10. Sí, la sirvo.   11. Sí, los escribo.   12. Sí, las diseña.

7·5   1. Piensan grabarla./La piensan grabar.   2. Acabamos de oírlas./Las acabamos de oír.   3. Raquel quiere verlos./Raquel los quiere ver.   4. ¿Vas a hacerlo?/¿Lo vas a hacer?   5. Debo ponerla./La debo poner.   6. Uds. logran devolverla./Uds. la logran devolver.   7. ¿A qué hora comienzas a servirlo?/¿A qué hora lo comienzas a servir?   8. Prefiero probarlo./Lo prefiero probar.   9. Ud. no trata de entenderlo./Ud. no lo trata de entender.   10. Empezamos a abrirlos./Los empezamos a abrir.   11. Los jugadores pueden usarlas./Los jugadores las pueden usar.   12. ¿Esperas comprarlo?/¿Lo esperas comprar?

7·6   1. no la llevo   2. no los busco   3. no las llamo   4. no la comprendo   5. no lo ayudo   6. no las conozco   7. no lo quiero visitar/no quiero visitarlo   8. no las pienso esperar/no pienso esperarlas

7·7   1. Vamos a comprarlas en la tienda de electrodomésticos.   2. Voy a comprarlos en la juguetería.   3. Vas a comprarlo en la tienda de cómputo.   4. Van a comprarlos en la zapatería.   5. Va a comprarla en la tienda de deportes.   6. Van a comprarla en la pastelería.   7. Va a comprarlo en la tienda por departamentos.   8. Va a comprarlas en la librería.

7·8   1. No, los trae María.   2. No, lo traigo yo.   3. No, los traen Uds.   4. No, la traen Guillermo y Sofía.   5. No, las traes tú.   6. No, la traemos nosotros.

7·9   1. ¿Conoces a esos hombres de negocios?/No, no los conozco pero espero conocerlos.   2. Señorita, ¿puede Ud. ayudarme con la base de datos?/Sí, señora, yo la ayudo ahora mismo.   3. Creo que Sergio y Eva vienen ya./Sí, los veo.   4. ¿Quieres oír este disco compacto?/Acabo de oírlo.   5. Nuestros amigos dicen que la película es excelente./Tienen razón. Yo la acabo de ver.   6. ¿Uds. tienen hambre?/No, no tenemos hambre pero tenemos mucha sed.   7. Va a haber mucha gente en el teatro./Es cierto. Vamos a tener que hacer cola.   8. Antonio toma las fotos hoy, ¿verdad?/No, piensa tomarlas Vicente.   9. Hace frío hoy. Yo tengo mucho frío. ¿Y tú?/La nieve cae pero yo no tengo frío.   10. Pongo la tele. Quiero ver la telenovela./Yo también la quiero ver.

8   Your daily routine • Reflexive verbs

8·1   1. Yo despierto a mis hijos.   2. Arturo y Sofía lavan su carro.   3. Isabel y yo cuidamos al niño.   4. El jefe reúne a los asesores.   5. Tú acercas la computadora.   6. Uds. tranquilizan a estas personas nerviosas.   7. Matilde viste a su hermanita.   8. Ud. alegra a sus invitados.   9. Los chicos bañan a su perro.   10. Yo pruebo unos platos picantes.

8·2   1. Yo me despierto a las siete.   2. Arturo y Sofía se lavan la cara.   3. Isabel y yo nos cuidamos bien.   4. El jefe se reúne con los asesores.   5. Tú te acercas a la computadora.   6. Uds. se tranquilizan fácilmente.   7. Matilde se viste antes de desayunar.   8. Ud. se alegra al ver a sus invitados.   9. Los chicos se bañan al llegar de la cancha.   10. Yo me pruebo unos trajes.

8·3   1. aburre   2. se maquilla   3. enfada   4. te preocupas   5. acuesto   6. se coloca   7. se divierten   8. nos entusiasmamos   9. asustan   10. te pintas   11. llamo   12. exaspera

8·4   1. Julia piensa casarse con Manuel en marzo.   2. Debemos darnos prisa.   3. ¿Necesitas despertarte temprano?   4. Pueden mantenerse en contacto.   5. Yo espero reunirme con los técnicos.   6. ¿Ud. no quiere vestirse todavía?   7. Prefieren sentarse más cerca.   8. Tienes que acordarte de la fecha.   9. Vamos a cortarnos el pelo el viernes.   10. Los invitados empiezan a divertirse.   11. La niñita comienza a reírse.   12. ¿Logras calmar a tus amigos?   13. Dejan de quejarse por cualquier cosa.   14. Acabo de despedirme de ellas.   15. Tratamos de cuidarnos mucho.

8·5   1. Me quiero pasear por el jardín.   2. Alfredo se debe afeitar.   3. Se pueden matricular esta semana.   4. Se van a graduar en mayo.   5. Te acabas de resfriar, ¿no?   6. Nos vamos a arreglar ahora mismo.   7. Alicia se acaba de pintar la cara.   8. Nos podemos instalar en el condominio.   9. ¿No te quieres relajar?   10. Uds. no se deben enojar.

8·6   1. Inés y Roberto se ven todos los días.   2. Felipe y yo nos hablamos por teléfono celular.   3. Carmen y Miguel se quieren mucho.   4. Tú y yo nos mandamos muchos correos electrónicos.   5. Los abogados y los asesores se conocen muy bien.   6. Ester y yo nos damos regalos.   7. Juan Diego y su prometida se besan.   8. Uds. y yo nos comprendemos perfectamente.

8·7   1. hermosamente   2. estupendamente   3. inteligentemente   4. honradamente   5. regularmente   6. alegremente   7. nerviosamente   8. compulsivamente   9. comercialmente   10. tristemente   11. cómodamente   12. fácilmente   13. atentamente   14. arrogantemente   15. asustadamente

1. perfecto   2. general   3. cuidadoso   4. reciente   5. último   6. difícil   7. frecuente   8. rotundo   9. pesado   10. frío   11. normal   12. ruidoso   13. pobre   14. amable   15. tranquilo

8·9   1. Me llamo Gabriela Franco. Al despertarme, me cepillo los dientes, me ducho y me lavo el pelo. Después de vestirme me pinto la cara y me peino. Mi esposo Gerardo se ducha, se afeita y se viste. Gerardo y yo vestimos a nuestros hijos y luego todos tomamos el desayuno (desayunamos). Gerardo y yo llevamos a los niños al colegio y luego nos vamos a la oficina.

2. Me llamo Antonio Lapesa. Acabo de graduarme en la universidad y busco trabajo. Soy contador. Espero colocarme en una empresa importante. También acabo de comprometerme. Mi prometida Pilar, que es diseñadora de sitios web, quiere casarse este año pero yo creo que no debemos apresurarnos. Tenemos que trabajar unos años para poder comprar una casa. No nos preocupamos porque nos queremos, nos comprendemos y siempre nos ayudamos.

3. Me llamo Mateo Vargas. Me acatarro muy frecuentemente. Hace seis semanas que me siento mal. El médico me dice que estoy bien pero que debo cuidarme mejor. Por eso voy a comenzar a hacer ejercicio. Quiero ponerme en forma. Voy a trotar y levantar pesas. También pienso alimentarme (comer) mejor. Voy a dejar de comer comida basura. Y tengo que relajarme más, acostarme más temprano y vivir más tranquilamente. ¡Qué aburrido!

8·10   1. Su cuarto nieto se llama Juan Miguel.   2. Leemos el noveno libro.   3. Escribo el sexto correo electrónico.   4. Siguen el tercer plan.   5. Tomas la quinta clase a distancia.   6. Es la octava semana del semestre.   7. Se reúnen el primer miércoles del mes.   8. Es la primera conferencia del año.   9. Es la tercera vez.   10. Hacen el segundo ejercicio.   11. Es la séptima semana del viaje.   12. Es el décimo año de la empresa.

9   Talking about trips; your likes and dislikes • The preterit

9·1   1. llevó   2. compartimos   3. trabajaron   4. toqué   5. siguieron   6. corriste   7. miramos   8. caíste   9. empecé   10. imprimieron   11. esperaste   12. volvió   13. comprendimos   14. hubo   15. jugué   16. supieron   17. viniste   18. fuimos   19. estuve   20. hizo

9·2   1. ¿Regresaste a Madrid?   2. Leyeron unas revistas.   3. Fue al aeropuerto.   4. Vine en tren.   5. Estuvimos agotados.   6. ¿Uds. hicieron los trámites?   7. Ud. escribió un correo electrónico.   8. Llegué a la puerta de embarque.   9. ¿No pudiste encontrar tu equipaje?   10. Nadie lo creyó.   11. No quisieron quedarse.   12. Fuiste auxiliar de vuelo.   13. Saqué los billetes en línea.   14. Preferimos tomar un vuelo directo.   15. No le dije nada.   16. Tuvieron que irse.   17. Recorrimos el nordeste.   18. Le mostró su pasaporte.   19. Me puse de pie.   20. Te divertiste mucho.

9·3   1. Ya lo pidieron.   2. Ya almorcé.   3. Ya los trajo.   4. Ya las hice.   5. Ya se pusieron de acuerdo.   6. Ya la oímos.   7. Ya los vio.   8. Ya la construyeron.   9. Ya fuimos al zoológico.   10. Ya los analizamos.   11. Ya navegué en la Red.   12. Ya lo sirvió.   13. Ya se vistieron.   14. Ya las desperté.   15. Ya lo comencé.

9·4   1. me desperté / me cepillé / me duché / me vestí / desayuné / me puse / me fui / llegué   2. se levantó / se duchó / se afeitó / se puso / fue / Aparcó / tomó / Llegó / tuvo / pasó / volvió   3. hicimos / conocimos / viajamos / pasamos / tomamos / nos quedamos / llegamos / tuvimos / pudimos   4. cumplió / asistí / comimos / bebimos / se alegró / traje / tuvo / se entusiasmó / fuimos / oímos   5. estudiaron / se graduaron / se colocó / comenzó / se comprometieron / se casaron / compraron / tuvieron / estuvieron

9·5   1. Yo le expliqué mi idea.   2. Ella nos escribió un correo electrónico.   3. Uds. les hicieron una comida muy rica.   4. Tú me dijiste lo que pasó.   5. Nosotros les regalamos libros.   6. Él le mostró su pasaporte.   7. Ellas les leyeron los documentos.   8. Ud. nos devolvió el dinero.   9. Ellos te trajeron el periódico.   10. Ella le pidió un favor.

9·6   1. Ellos le regalaron una raqueta de tenis a su hermana.   2. Daniela les sirvió unas tapas a sus invitados.   3. Ud. les vendió sus libros a otros estudiantes.   4. Yo le hice unas preguntas al asesor financiero.   5. Tú les entregaste el informe a los directores.   6. Uds. le dieron el software a la programadora.   7. Nosotros le pedimos un plato de pescado al cocinero.   8. Ellas les devolvieron el carro a sus padres.   9. Manolo les mostró su nuevo apartamento a sus amigos.   10. Él le dijo la verdad a su abogado.

9·7   1. Me   2. Le   3. le   4. Nos   5. Les   6. Te   7. Les   8. Le   9. Le

1. Nos interesan sus ideas.   2. Le encantaron esos viajes.   3. Les gustaron las obras de teatro.   4. Me hacen falta unas camisas.   5. ¿Te cayeron bien los dentistas?   6. Le faltan unos dólares.   7. Nos quedan unos exámenes.   8. Les sobran unas páginas.

9·9   1. Les va a hacer falta más dinero.   2. Me va a interesar recorrer la ciudad.   3. No nos va a importar lo que dicen.   4. Le van a caer mal estos empleados.   5. ¿Te van a hacer falta dos maletas?   6. No les va a quedar mucho tiempo en el aeropuerto.   7. Me va a convenir hacer los trámites en línea.   8. No le van a gustar los planes.

9·10   1. Llegué a Toledo a las ocho de la mañana y me fui a las diez de la noche.   2. El avión despegó y a los veinte minutos, yo me desabroché el cinturón de seguridad.   3. ¿Te gustó la película?   4. Sí, me encantó.   5. ¿Tuvieron que hacer escala?   6. Sí. Dijeron que fue un vuelo interminable y agotador.   7. ¿Les interesa recorrer el suroeste?   8. Hicimos un viaje allí hace tres años.   9. Los pasajeros le pidieron agua y jugo al auxiliar de vuelo.   10. A ella le cayeron bien pero a él le cayeron mal.   11. Le entregué la tarjeta de embarque.   12. ¿Ud. le trajo el plan de mercadeo al señor Salazar?   13. Sí, le di el plan de mercadeo anteayer.   14. No nos importó para nada.

10 Talking about your childhood • The imperfect

10·1   1. hablaba   2. eran   3. viajábamos   4. iba   5. creías   6. comenzaba   7. escribía   8. veías   9. volvían   10. jugábamos   11. recibían   12. podía   13. pensabas   14. dábamos   15. tenía   16. oía   17. había   18. sabía   19. decían   20. venía

10·2   1. trabajaban   2. recorrían   3. iba   4. nos reuníamos   5. Hacía   6. veías   7. eran   8. prendía   9. contaba   10. servíamos   11. producía   12. interesaban   13. enseñaba   14. daba   15. vestía   16. pensaban   17. quería   18. sabían   19. tomábamos   20. aprovechaba

10·3   1. Yo me reunía con mis amigos todos los viernes.   2. Uds. iban a esquiar todos los inviernos.   3. María Elena almorzaba con nosotros cada semana.   4. Nosotros asistíamos a un concierto todos los meses.   5. ¿Comías granos integrales a menudo?   6. Generalmente Paco no dormía la siesta.   7. Siempre se divertían mucho en tus fiestas.   8. Veía ese programa todas las semanas.   9. Hacía un viaje todos los años.   10. Cada año le daban una beca.

10·4   1. me despertaba / me cepillaba / me duchaba / me vestía / desayunaba / me ponía / me iba / llegaba / tenía / regresaba / comía / me acostaba   2. se levantaban / se duchaba / se afeitaba / se lavaba / se arreglaba / despertaba / preparaba / salía / llevaba / volvía / trabajaba   3. íbamos / quedaba / tomábamos / preferíamos / gustaban / hacía / podíamos / nevaba / esquiábamos / montaba / se llamaba / gustaba / estaban   4. llegaba / eran / soñaban / esperaban / aprendían / trabajaban / era / sabían / vivían / daba   5. eran / Hacía / esperaba / Hacía / llovía / había / despegaban / Había / podían / tenía / esperaba / comía / tomaba / leía / veía / me exasperaba / se casaba / iba

10·5   1. Se lo enseñábamos.   2. Me la dieron.   3. Te los hago.   4. ¿Nos las prestas?   5. Se la entregué.   6. Se lo cuentan.   7. Me los mandaba.   8. Se las trajimos.   9. ¿Te los consigue?   10. Nos las mostraban.

10·6   1. Acaban de traérmela./Me la acaban de traer.   2. Voy a servírselas./Se las voy a servir.   3. Acaba de devolvérnoslos./Nos los acaba de devolver.   4. Vamos a dártelo./Te lo vamos a dar.   5. Acabas de pedírmelas./Me las acabas de pedir.   6. Van a llevárselo./Se lo van a llevar.   7. Acabo de mostrártelos./Te los acabo de mostrar.   8. Van a vendérnosla./Nos la van a vender.   9. Acabas de hacérselos./Se los acabas de hacer.   10. Va a prestármelo./Me lo va a prestar.

10·7   1. Sí, me la puse.   2. Sí, se lo abrocharon.   3. Sí, nos los pintábamos.   4. Sí, me lo corté.   5. Sí, se lo rompió.   6. Sí, se las quita.   7. Sí, nos los cepillábamos.   8. Sí, me lo sequé.   9. Sí, se la maquilló.   10. Sí, se los desabrocharon.

10·8   1. Ya se las puse.   2. Ya se los limpié.   3. Ya se la lavé.   4. Ya se lo quité.   5. Ya se los abroché.   6. Ya se lo corté.   7. Ya se la desabroché.   8. Ya se lo sequé.

10·9   1. Se visita el cafetal.   2. Se sacan fotos.   3. Se cultiva maíz.   4. Se realiza el proyecto.   5. Se hacen los trámites.   6. Se construye un parqueo.   7. Se producen vinos.   8. Se resuelve el problema.   9. Se sirven platos vegetarianos.   10. Se oye música.   11. Se alquilan furgonetas.   12. Se imprimen los informes.

10·10   1. Se llega a la puerta de embarque.   2. Se vive mejor en este país.   3. Se navega en la Red.   4. Se habla por celular.   5. Se trabaja de lunes a jueves.   6. Se sale al jardín.   7. Se abre a las diez de la mañana.   8. Se maneja con cuidado.

10·11   1. Se debe dejar una propina.   2. Se necesita pasar por el control de seguridad.   3. No se puede encontrar un vuelo directo.   4. No se permite fumar.   5. Se necesita apagar el celular.   6. Se puede cambiar el vuelo.   7. Se permite subir a la pirámide.   8. No se debe comer comida basura.

10·12   1. El arroz fue cultivado por el agricultor.   2. Las bebidas fueron servidas por los auxiliares de vuelo.   3. Mil tiendas fueron abiertas por la empresa.   4. La torta de cumpleaños fue hecha por la cocinera.   5. Los contratos fueron escritos por esos abogados.   6. La reunión fue suspendida por la directora.   7. Las fotos fueron tomadas por uno de los turistas.   8. Su problema fue resuelto por unos contadores.   9. Las mesas fueron puestas por la mesera.   10. Los centros comerciales fueron construidos por aquel arquitecto.   11. Mi sitio web fue diseñado por un amigo mío.   12. Nuestra ventana fue rota por el jugador.

10·13   1. fueron pintados   2. fueron entregadas   3. fue vendido   4. fue prendida   5. fueron acostados   6. fue impreso   7. fueron escritos   8. fueron fundadas   9. fueron puestas   10. fue suspendido   11. fueron mandados   12. fue construido

10·14   1. los maletines nuestros   2. la cámara mía   3. el cartapacio suyo   4. las pulseras suyas   5. el equipaje de mano tuyo   6. la flauta suya   7. las tarjetas de embarque suyas   8. el carro suyo   9. los discos compactos míos   10. la pintura nuestra   11. los disquetes suyos   12. el celular suyo

10·15   1. ¿Cuánto tiempo hacía que Uds. vivían en la finca?   2. Hacía quince años que vivíamos allí.   3. Había caballos y vacas en la finca.   4. Yo montaba a caballo todos los días.   5. ¿Cómo eran tus abuelos?   6. Eran muy cariñosos. Nos queríamos mucho.   7. ¿Te mostré las fotos?   8. No, no me las mostraste.   9. Entonces te las voy a mandar/voy a mandártelas hoy.   10. El regalo. ¿Ya se lo dieron a Pablo?   11. Sí, acabamos de dárselo/se lo acabamos de dar.   12. Se producen vinos en España.   13. No se puede cambiar el vuelo.   14. Los billetes fueron reservados en línea.   15. Nuestra casa fue construida por un equipo de arquitectos.

11   Health and accidents • The imperfect and the preterit

11·1   1. conocía, llegaron   2. estábamos, estalló   3. Eran, regresaron   4. tenías, te casaste   5. se durmió, oía   6. picaban, me puse   7. cerré, llovía   8. atrapó, se escapaba   9. retiraba, hubo   10. tenía, se graduó   11. jugaban, comenzó   12. subimos, había   13. buscábamos, vimos   14. tenía, bajó   15. trabajaba, trasladaron   16. fue, dolía   17. empecé, me sentía   18. atendían, llegó   19. se fue, hacía   20. iban, pudieron

11·2   1. Ellos nos dijeron que pensaban mudarse.   2. Jimena les contó que quería estudiar en el extranjero.   3. Nos informaron que el avión aterrizaba.   4. Sus abuelos les escribieron que venían a verlos.   5. Isabel nos dijo que estaba embarazada.   6. Yo les dije que no podía acompañarlos.   7. Le informamos que la cámara costaba trescientos dólares.   8. Antonio me contó que tenía que trabajar en otra sucursal.   9. Sus papás nos contaron que Miguelito era un niño prodigio.   10. Le escribí que a Daniel le dolía la espalda.   11. Me informó que había mucho tráfico en ese barrio.   12. Le escribimos que no sabíamos lo del atraco.

11·3   1. el dedito   2. la ropita   3. la chiquita   4. el jovencito   5. la piernecita   6. cerquita   7. Carlitos   8. el perrito   9. poquito   10. la botellita   11. el pajarito   12. Isabelita   13. el cafecito   14. ahorita   15. la cabecita   16. fresquito   17. la siestecita   18. la vocecita   19. el hermanito   20. el calorcito

11·4   1. d   2. g   3. f   4. b   5. c   6. e   7. a

11·5   1. Ellos nos saludaron cuando subíamos en la escalera mecánica.   2. Laura cambió su estilo de vida porque siempre se sentía cansada.   3. Pablo fue al médico porque le dolía la garganta.   4. Alberto nos dijo que su esposa estaba embarazada.   5. ¿Viste a Jaime? Tiene tantas picaduras de mosquito.   6. Se olvidó de ponerse el repelente contra mosquitos.   7. Me dijeron que un coche atropelló a un peatón en esta esquina.   8. Sí, yo miraba mientras los paramédicos atendían a la víctima.   9. Tomábamos el sol cuando de repente hubo un aguacero.   10. A mi hermanito siempre le duele el estómago / Mi hermanito siempre tiene dolor de estómago porque es comilón.   11. Mateo era gerente de sucursal hasta que lo trasladaron/ fue trasladado.   12. Teresa tenía cuarenta y ocho años cuando se jubiló.

12   At school and the office • Comparatives and superlatives

12·1   1. Yo estoy más entusiasmado que Jaime./Jaime está menos entusiasmado que yo.   2. La chaqueta es más cara que los pantalones./Los pantalones son menos caros que la chaqueta.   3. La profesora de física es más exigente que el profesor de matemáticas./ El profesor de matemáticas es menos exigente que la profesora de física.   4. La novela rusa es más seria que la novela alemana./La novela alemana es menos seria que la novela rusa.   5. Paloma y Gonzalo son más optimistas que Uds./Uds. son menos optimistas que Paloma y Gonzalo.

12·2   1. Pedro es tan ingenuo como tú.   2. El condominio es tan amplio como la casa.   3. Patricia es tan coqueta como su prima.   4. Las composiciones son tan largas como los informes.   5. Su carro japonés es tan caro como nuestro carro estadounidense.   6. Nosotros estamos tan preocupados como Uds.   7. La película es tan aburrida como la novela.   8. Los asesores son tan ambiciosos como el jefe.   9. Yo estoy tan decepcionado como mis compañeros.   10. Marta es tan rara como su cuñada.

12·3   1. Alejandro escucha tan atentamente como Esteban.   2. Sergio trabaja tan cuidadosamente como yo.   3. La familia Suárez vive tan cómodamente como la familia Obregón.   4. Uds. van de compras tan frecuentemente como nosotros.   5. Viviana maneja tan lentamente como tú.   6. Antonio se enoja tan fácilmente como Lucía.   7. Santiago corre tan rápidamente como Roberto.

12·4   1. Yo tomo tantos cursos como tú.   2. El niño tiene tanto sueño como su hermanito.   3. Beatriz asiste a tantos conciertos como María.   4. Mateo come tanta comida basura como sus amigos.   5. Nuestro condominio tiene tantos dormitorios como su apartamento.   6. Inés tiene tanta paciencia como Guillermo.   7. José Luis necesita tantos lápices como Margarita.   8. Nosotros tenemos tanta hambre como Uds.

12·5   1. Raquel es la más considerada.   2. Rodrigo es el más cascarrabias.   3. Laura y Silvia son las más calculadoras.   4. Teresa es la más cortés.   5. Alejandro y Miriam son los más sinceros.   6. Manolo es el más egoísta.   7. David y Miguel son los más encantadores.

12·6   1. facilísimo   2. riquísimos   3. larguísimas   4. dificilísima   5. grandísima   6. interesantísimo   7. simpatiquísimos   8. buenísimo   9. hermosísimos   10. finísima

12·7   1. Prefiero el marrón, pero me gusta el negro también.   2. Prefiero los de química, pero me gustan los de biología también.   3. Prefiero la que tengo ahora, pero me gusta la anterior también.   4. Prefiero los de lana, pero me gustan los de algodón también.   5. Prefiero los de queso, pero me gustan los de carne también.   6. Prefiero la obligatoria, pero me gusta la optativa también.   7. Prefiero los rojos, pero me gustan los azules también.   8. Prefiero la grande, pero me gusta la pequeña también.   9. Prefiero el que queda en la esquina, pero me gusta el que queda a dos cuadras de aquí también.   10. Prefiero los de arte, pero me gustan los de ciencias también.

12·8   1. Mi computadora es más potente que la tuya.   2. Mis profesores son menos estrictos que los suyos.   3. Tu puesto es tan interesante como el mío.   4. Sus cartuchos de tinta cuestan más que los tuyos.   5. Sus cursos son más fáciles que los nuestros.   6. Nuestro apartamento es tan moderno como el suyo.   7. Tu calle es tan tranquila como la suya.   8. Su equipo juega tan bien como el nuestro.   9. Nuestra empresa gana más dinero que la suya.

12·9   1. Me gusta ésta más que aquélla.   2. Me gusta aquél más que éste.   3. Me gustan ésos más que éstos.   4. Me gustan éstas más que ésas.   5. Me gusta aquélla más que ésta.   6. Me gustan éstos más que aquéllos.

12·10   1. No, con él, no.   2. No, para ella, no.   3. No, con ellas, no.   4. No, por él, no.   5. No, para ti, no.   6. No, con ella, no.   7. No, por Uds., no.   8. No, contigo, no.

12·11   1. Anita es más presumida que su hermana.   2. Jorge es menos raro que su hermano.   3. Tú eres tan realista como él.   4. Ellas están tan decepcionadas como yo.   5. Beatriz es la más sensible de la familia.   6. Esa/Aquella película es la mejor de todas.   7. Su computadora es más potente que la nuestra.   8. Esos/Aquellos cartuchos de tinta son tan caros como éstos.   9. Ésta es la ciudad más hermosa del mundo.   10. Esta casa es más amplia que la anterior.   11. Ellos compraron tantos bolígrafos y lápices como yo.   12. Este lavaplatos funciona mejor que aquél.   13. Trabajamos más que nunca.   14. Enrique viaja tan frecuentemente como nosotros.   15. Gané más de doscientos cincuenta mil dólares.

13 Business and the cost of living • The present perfect and the past perfect

13·1   1. he   2. hecho   3. oído   4. ha   5. han   6. dicho   7. has   8. visto   9. han   10. escrito   11. incluido   12. hemos

13·2   1. El equipo ha escrito el plan de negocios.   2. Alejo y yo hemos hecho el presupuesto.   3. Los asesores han recogido los datos.   4. El analista ha analizado los datos.   5. Yo he preparado un informe.   6. Tú has mandado los correos electrónicos.   7. Uds. se han reunido en la sala de conferencias.   8. Ud. ha atendido el teléfono.   9. Leonardo ha diseñado los folletos.

13·3   1. He enviado un email.   2. Él ha muerto de una enfermedad.   3. No te has atrevido a llamar.   4. Ha llovido todo el día.   5. He recogido los datos.   6. Los meseros han puesto las servilletas en la mesa.   7. Ha sido un día estupendo.   8. Los jefes han hecho un plan de negocios.   9. Ha habido poca contaminación del ambiente.   10. Nosotras no se lo hemos dicho.   11. Nadie ha querido pagar los impuestos.   12. Se han incluido los ingresos y los gastos.   13. ¿Te has despedido de tus amigos?   14. Hemos impreso los documentos.   15. Han ido al bautizo.

13·4   1. Nos hemos matriculado ya.   2. Se ha afeitado ya.   3. Se han mudado ya.   4. Me he vestido ya.   5. Me he reunido con ellos ya.   6. Se han casado ya.   7. Se ha peinado ya.   8. Me he duchado ya.

13·5   1. Cuando Fernanda llamó, sus amigas ya habían vuelto del centro comercial.   2. Cuando sonó el teléfono, ellos ya se habían levantado.   3. Cuando despegó el avión, los pasajeros ya se habían abrochado el cinturón de seguridad.   4. Cuando los invitados llegaron para cenar, Paula ya había puesto la mesa.   5. Cuando yo compré los cartuchos de tinta, Ud. ya había impreso el informe.   6. Cuando nosotros vimos a Antonio, su empresa ya lo había trasladado.   7. Cuando Uds. conocieron a Claudia, ella ya se había hecho rica.

13·6   1. alquilado   2. descompuestos   3. descargado   4. despejados   5. abierta   6. guardados   7. entusiasmadas   8. impreso   9. construido   10. recorridas   11. facturado   12. cerrado   13. pagada   14. rotas   15. recibida   16. actualizados

13·7   1. Ellos han vendido su casa./Su casa está vendida.   2. Ella ha apagado las luces./Las luces están apagadas.   3. Tú has servido la cena./La cena está servida.   4. Nosotros hemos abierto las cajas./Las cajas están abiertas.   5. Yo he resuelto esos problemas./Esos problemas están resueltos.   6. Uds. han elaborado el presupuesto./El presupuesto está elaborado.   7. Ud. ha recogido los datos./Los datos están recogidos.   8. Él ha puesto la mesa./La mesa está puesta.   9. Ellas han perdido el dinero./El dinero está perdido.   10. Tú y yo hemos lavado los platos./Los platos están lavados.

13·8   1. ¿Ud. ha elaborado el presupuesto?   2. Sí, he incluido los ingresos y los gastos.   3. ¿Está puesta la mesa?   4. Sí, y la cena está servida.   5. ¡Cómo ha crecido el país!   6. Y la población ha aumentado muchísimo.   7. Nuestro pueblo se ha convertido en una ciudad grande.   8. Hay casi cinco millones de habitantes.   9. Ha sido un día muy difícil.   10. ¿Por qué? ¿Has tenido mucho trabajo?   11. Se han construido muchos rascacielos en los últimos diez años./Muchos rascacielos han sido construidos en los últimos diez años.   12. En efecto. Nuestra ciudad está muy cambiada.   13. Ha habido un accidente de tráfico delante del banco.   15. ¿Alguien ha llamado a la policía?   16. Cuando llegamos, nuestros amigos ya habían almorzado.

14   Giving and following directions • The imperative

14·1   1. Doble a la derecha./No doble a la derecha.   2. Llegue temprano./No llegue temprano.   3. Ande con cuidado./No ande con cuidado.   4. Maneje lentamente./No maneje lentamente.   5. Cruce el puente./No cruce el puente.   6. Siga por el río./No siga por el río.   7. Váyase ahora./No se vaya ahora.   8. Salga con ellos./No salga con ellos.   9. Lea los correos electrónicos./No lea los correos electrónicos.   10. Suba al avión./No suba al avión.   11. Acuéstese a las once./No se acueste a las once.   12. Vístase./No se vista.   13. Juegue al tenis./No juegue al tenis.   14. Analice los datos./No analice los datos.   15. Póngase los lentes de sol./No se ponga los lentes de sol.

14·2   1. Coman mucho./No coman mucho.   2. Elaboren el presupuesto./No elaboren el presupuesto.   3. Añadan la sal./No añadan la sal.   4. Vean el programa./No vean el programa.   5. Almuercen con ellos./No almuercen con ellos.   6. Paséense por el parque./No se paseen por el parque.   7. Hagan cola./No hagan cola.   8. Vengan en taxi./No vengan en taxi.   9. Despídanse de él./No se despidan de él.   10. Siéntense en el comedor./No se sienten en el comedor.   11. Aparquen en este parquímetro./No aparquen en este parquímetro.   12. Naveguen en la Red./No naveguen en la Red.   13. Frían las papas./No frían las papas.   14. Asistan a la conferencia./No asistan a la conferencia.   15. Bajen en la escalera mecánica./No bajen en la escalera mecánica.

14·3   1. Sí, recójalos.   2. Sí, analícenlos.   3. Sí, úselo.   4. No, no lo llame.   5. Sí, asistan a la reunión.   6. Sí, elabórelo.   7. No, no lo hagan.   8. Sí, reúnanse con el jefe.   9. No, no lo escriba.   10. No, no los impriman.   11. Sí, vaya a la sala de conferencias.   12. Sí, síganlos.   13. No, no los envíe.   14. Sí, actualícenlo.   15. No, no lo firme.

14·4   1. Sí, léela.   2. Sí, ponla ahora.   3. Sí, sácalos de la gaveta.   4. Sí, caliéntalo.   5. Sí, bátelos.   6. Sí, añádelo.   7. Sí, échala.   8. Sí, fríelas.   9. Sí, sírvela con las papas.   10. Sí, hazlo ahora mismo.

14·5   1. Tranquilízate.   2. No te pongas nerviosa.   3. Arréglate.   4. Ten paciencia.   5. No seas tonta.
6. Píntate la cara.   7. Vístete.   8. Péinate.   9. Ve a la fiesta sin preocuparte.   10. Diviértete mucho.

14·6   1. Leamos este artículo./No leamos este artículo.   2. Crucemos la calle./No crucemos la calle.
3. Pidamos perdón./No pidamos perdón.   4. Busquemos un atajo./No busquemos un atajo.
5. Hagamos turismo./No hagamos turismo.   6. Vamos al cine./No vayamos al cine.   7. Divirtámonos./
No nos divirtamos.   8. Sentémonos./No nos sentemos.   9. Durmamos la siesta./No durmamos la siesta.
10. Traigamos flores./No traigamos flores.   11. Demos consejos./No demos consejos.
12. Registrémonos./No nos registremos.

14·7   1. Sí, veámosla./ Sí, vamos a verla.   2. Sí, discutámoslas./Sí, vamos a discutirlas.   3. Sí,
descarguémoslos./Sí, vamos a descargarlos.   4. Sí, consigámoslos./Sí, vamos a conseguirlos.   5. Sí,
esperémosla./Sí, vamos a esperarla.   6. Sí, mandémoslos./Sí, vamos a mandarlos.   7. Sí, hagámosla./Sí,
vamos a hacerla.   8. Sí, compartámoslos./Sí, vamos a compartirlos.   9. Sí, comencémoslo./Sí, vamos a
comenzarlo.   10. Sí, pidámoslo./Sí, vamos a pedirlo.   11. Sí, aparquémoslo./Sí, vamos a aparcarlo.
12. Sí, oigámoslo./Sí, vamos a oírlo.

14·8   1. Sí, entréguemelo.   2. Sí, explíquemela.   3. Sí, muéstramelos.   4. Sí, démelo.   5. Sí, pónmelo.
6. Sí, házmela.   7. Sí, tráemelos.

14·9   1. No, no me lo entregue.   2. No, no me la explique.   3. No, no me los muestres.   4. No, no me lo dé.
5. No, no me lo pongas.   6. No, no me la hagas.   7. No, no me los traigas.

14·10   1. Sí, dáselas./Sí, déselas.   2. Sí, escríbeselo./Sí, escríbaselo.   3. Sí, prepáraselos./Sí, prepáreselos.
4. Sí, pídeselo./Sí, pídaselo.   5. Sí, póntelos./Sí, póngaselos.   6. Sí, córtatelo./Sí, córteselo.   7. Sí,
lávasela./Sí, lávesela.   8. Sí, quítatela./Sí, quítesela.

14·11   1. Sí, entreguémoselo./Sí, entréguenselo.   2. Sí, démoselos./Sí, dénselos.   3. Sí, sirvámoselo./Sí,
sírvanselo.   4. Sí, desabrochémonoslo./Sí, desabróchenselo.   5. Sí, ofrezcámoselo./Sí, ofrézcanselo.
6. Sí, mostrémoselas./Sí, muéstrenselas.   7. Sí, devolvámosela./Sí, devuélvansela.   8. Sí, vendámosela./
Sí, véndansela.

14·12   1. Haga el favor de sentarse aquí.   2. Tengan la bondad de llamarme.   3. Hagan el favor de analizar los
datos.   4. Favor de decírmelo.   5. Tenga la bondad de quedarse.   6. Favor de hacérmelo.   7. Hagan
el favor de entregarme los papeles.   8. Tengan la bondad de acercarse al quiosco.

14·13   1. Camine cuatro cuadras y doble a la derecha.   2. No estacione (aparque) en esta calle.   3. Saque la
tarjeta de embarque pero no vaya a la puerta de embarque todavía.   4. Coloquen su equipaje de mano
debajo del asiento.   5. ¿La cámara? Pidámosela. (Vamos a pedírsela.)   6. ¿El teléfono celular? Dámelo.
7. No salgas. Espérame.   8. No vayamos al cine hoy.   9. Veamos (Vamos a ver) la película otro día.
10. Abróchense el cinturón de seguridad.   11. Ten paciencia. No tengas tanta prisa.   12. Añada un
poco de sal a la sopa y caliéntala.

15   Plans for the holidays • The future and the conditional

15·1   1. Él terminará la maestría.   2. Uds. correrán en la pista.   3. Ella recibirá varios paquetes.
4. Cerraré las ventanas.   5. ¿Volverás pasado mañana?   6. Les diré qué pasó.   7. Ellos subirán al
séptimo piso.   8. Jugarán al ajedrez.   9. Serviré aceitunas.   10. Calentará el arroz.
11. Conseguirás los boletos.   12. No vendrán hasta el sábado.   13. Querrán enseñarnos su casa.
14. Te despertarás a las ocho.   15. ¿Uds. se pondrán en contacto?

15·2   1. Asistiré al concierto.   2. Tomaremos una copa.   3. ¿Saldrás con nosotros?   4. No cabrán en el taxi.
5. Habrá un desfile.   6. Te gustará la película.   7. Se irán.   8. No tendremos ganas de ir.   9. Haré
un viaje.   10. ¿Podrás quedarte?   11. Se casarán en julio.   12. Estará de visita.

15·3   1. Viviana querrá ir al centro comercial.   2. Habrá dificultades con el proyecto.   3. Sus colegas sabrán
la hora de la reunión.   4. Será la una.   5. Tu anillo de boda valdrá mucho.   6. Hará mucho frío
mañana.   7. Joaquín estará muy contento con su puesto.   8. Los gemelos tendrán tres años.   9. Nevará
esta semana.   10. La casa costará más de un millón de dólares.

15·4   1. añadiría   2. me ocuparía   3. aprenderían   4. compartiríamos   5. tomarían   6. haríamos
7. saldrías   8. tendría   9. encantaría   10. dirían   11. estarían   12. querría

15·5   1. podrían   2. gustará   3. se mudarían   4. cabremos   5. habría   6. lloverá   7. llamaría   8. querré

15·6   1. ¿Cómo celebrarán el día de la Independencia?   2. Habrá un desfile.   3. Él dice que hará calor y sol.   4. Ella dijo que estaría nublado y llovería.   5. Mis suegros se instalarán en su nueva casa en septiembre.   6. ¿Qué hora será?   7. Serán las nueve.   8. Ellos escribieron que se encargarían del proyecto.   9. ¿Cuántos años tendrán los gemelos?   10. Le tocaría a ella.   11. ¿Te gustaría salir a cenar esta noche?   12. Me encantaría.   13. No puedo encontrar mi tarjeta de crédito. ¿Dónde estará?   14. Si Uds. vuelven al hotel, nosotros iremos también.

16 Talking about relationships; expressing emotions and making judgments • The present subjunctive

16·1   1. lleguen   2. sean   3. nos abrochemos   4. haya   5. apoyes   6. pueda   7. dé   8. haga   9. se ponga   10. compartan   11. empieces   12. almuercen

16·2   1. Es necesario que nos mantengamos en contacto.   2. Es útil que actualice los datos.   3. Urge que vaya al médico.   4. Es mejor que jueguen al tenis por la mañana.   5. Es importante que comas granos integrales.   6. Más vale que vaya en tren.   7. Es preciso que haga los trámites hoy.   8. Hace falta que aprendan las fechas de memoria.   9. Es imprescindible que nos pongamos el repelente contra mosquitos.   10. Es urgente que elaboren el presupuesto hoy.

16·3   1. vuelven   2. haga   3. navegues   4. dicen   5. tenga   6. guste   7. es   8. estás   9. pierda   10. construya

16·4   1. Es verdad que son íntimos amigos.   2. No es cierto que tenga problemas de dinero.   3. Es bueno que se ponga el filtro solar.   4. Es dudoso que sepa dónde están.   5. Es cierto que el sol daña la piel.   6. Estamos seguros que hay una reunión en la tarde.   7. Es una lástima que no se lleven bien.   8. No es verdad que busquen casa en este barrio.

16·5   1. Arturo, yo insisto en que leas este capítulo.   2. Pilar, yo insisto en que saques tu computadora.   3. Gilberto, yo insisto en que dibujes con lápiz.   4. Alonso, yo insisto en que te sientes al lado de Javier.   5. Flor, yo insisto en que tomes apuntes.   6. Marisol, yo insisto en que traigas tu libro de texto.   7. Andrés, yo insisto en que comiences la composición.   8. Silvia, yo insisto en que aprendas las fechas de memoria.   9. Octavio, yo insisto en que te prepares para el examen.   10. Catalina, yo insisto en que hagas la tarea.

16·6   1. Te aconsejo que te cuides mucho.   2. Quiero que salgas con nosotros al cine.   3. Es necesario que te des prisa.   4. Prefiero que oigas esta música.   5. Te pido que apagues la computadora.   6. Te recomiendo que sigas por esta avenida.   7. Es preciso que te pongas los guantes.   8. Me alegro de que vengas a vernos.   9. Es imprescindible que vayas a registrarte.   10. Insisto en que me digas qué pasó.   11. Te exijo que tengas paciencia.   12. Hace falta que te seques el pelo.   13. Dudo que actualices los datos.   14. No creo que me hagas caso.   15. Es importante que te reúnas conmigo lo antes posible.

16·7   1. Sofía quiere casarse con Sergio.   2. Sus padres prefieren que se case con Santiago.   3. Carlitos, yo insisto en que hagas tu tarea ahora.   4. Pero yo quiero salir a jugar al béisbol.   5. Tenemos que prepararnos para la prueba.   6. El maestro nos exige que aprendamos todas las fechas de memoria.   7. Me alegro de poder quedarme con Uds.   8. Nos alegramos de que te quedes con nosotros.   9. Dudo que haya una reunión esta semana.   10. Es importante que los alumnos saquen buenas notas.   11. Es necesario que apoyemos a nuestros amigos.   12. Yo le aconsejo que ahorre más dinero.   13. Es verdad que yo gasto muchísimo.   14. Yo no creo que vengan el sábado.   15. Siento que no nos veamos.

About the authors

Ronni L. Gordon, Ph.D., is a prominent author of foreign-language textbooks, reference books, and materials for multimedia. She is vice president of Mediatheque Publishers Services, a leader in the development of foreign-language instructional materials. She holds a Ph.D. in Spanish language and Spanish and Spanish American literature from Rutgers University and has taught and coordinated Spanish-language programs at Harvard University and Boston University. An education consultant, she has read in foreign languages for the National Endowment for the Humanities, presented at the United States Department of Education, and consulted on states' K–12 academic standards for world languages. She is an associate scholar of a Philadelphia-based think tank and chairman of the board of directors of the Dolce Suono Ensemble.

David M. Stillman, Ph.D., is a well-known writer of foreign-language textbooks, reference books, and materials for multimedia. He is president of Mediatheque Publishers Services, a leader in the development of foreign-language instructional materials. He holds a Ph.D. in Spanish linguistics from the University of Illinois and has taught and coordinated foreign-language programs at Boston University, Harvard, and Cornell. He teaches French, Spanish, Italian, Hebrew, and linguistics at The College of New Jersey where he coordinates an innovative program of student-led conversation practice. He is a frequent presenter at national and regional conventions of language educators, has consulted on states' K–12 academic standards for world languages, and has been appointed to national committees devoted to the improvement of teacher training.

By the same authors

The Ultimate Spanish Review and Practice: Mastering Spanish Grammar for Confident Communication
The Ultimate Spanish Verb Review and Practice: Mastering Verbs and Sentence Building for Confident Communication
The Big Red Book of Spanish Verbs
The Red Pocket Book of Spanish Verbs

The Ultimate French Review and Practice: Mastering French Grammar for Confident Communication
The Ultimate French Verb Review and Practice: Mastering Verbs and Sentence Building for Confident Communication
The Big Blue Book of French Verbs
The Blue Pocket Book of French Verbs